LEADERS

WHO CHANGED HISTORY

LEADERS

WHO CHANGED HISTORY

DK LONDON

SENIOR EDITOR: Chauney Dunford
SENIOR ART EDITORS: Gillian Andrews, Stephen Bere
Mark Cavanagh, Anthony Limerick
LEAD ILLUSTRATOR: Phil Gamble
EDITORS: Jemima Dunne, Joanna Edwards,
Kathryn Hennessy, Victoria
Heyworth-Dunne, Kathryn Hill, Katie
John, Francesco Piscitelli, Helen Ridge
EDITORIAL ASSISTANTS: Daniel Byrne, Michael Clark,
Gwion Wyn Jones
PICTURE RESEARCH: Deepak Negi
JACKET EDITOR: Emma Dawson
SENIOR JACKET DESIGNER: Surabhi Wadhwa
JACKET DESIGN
DEVELOPMENT MANAGER: Sophia MTT
PRODUCER, PRE-PRODUCTION: Jacqueline Street-Elkayam
PRODUCER: Rachel Ng
MANAGING EDITOR: Gareth Jones
SENIOR MANAGING ART EDITOR: Lee Griffiths
ASSOCIATE PUBLISHING DIRECTOR: Liz Wheeler
ART DIRECTOR : Karen Self
DESIGN DIRECTOR: Philip Ormerod
PUBLISHING DIRECTOR: Jonathan Metcalf
CONTRIBUTORS: Alexandra Black, Clive Gifford,
Reg Grant, Anna Samson
CONSULTANTS: Adrian Gilbert, Philip Parker,
Alan Saywood
INDEXER: Helen Peters
PROOF READER: Alexandra Beeden

First published in Great Britain in 2019
by Dorling Kindersley Limited,
80 Strand, London, WC2R 0RL

Copyright © 2019
Dorling Kindersley Limited
A Penguin Random House Company

10 9 8 7 6 5 4 3 2
003-312720-Mar/2019

A CIP catalogue record for this book is
available from the British Library.
ISBN: 978-0-2413-6317-1

Printed and bound in Malaysia

A WORLD OF IDEAS:
SEE ALL THERE IS TO KNOW

www.dk.com

CONTENTS

INTRODUCTION

Throughout history, human societies have been shaped and determined by their leaders. Whether triumphing by conquest or political manoeuvring, or succeeding by self-belief, these figures are the powerful elite that others have sought, or been compelled, to follow.

Leaders take many forms, from monarchs and dictators, social reformers and revolutionaries, to prophets and spiritual guides. Styles of leadership are equally diverse, some achieving and sustaining their authority through fear and brutality, while others inspire loyalty through benevolence, or shared ideals and aspirations. What unites all great leaders, however, is their ability to influence people, whether briefly, such as John F. Kennedy in the US, or throughout their lifetime, such as Eleanor of Aquitaine during her 66-year reign over France and England.

While the legacies of many leaders have faded over time, a notable few have left an indelible mark on the world. The most enduring of these legacies belong to spiritual leaders, such as Muhammad, Moses, and Christ, whose teachings continue to shape the lives of billions of followers around the world, millennia after their own lifetimes. A number of other leaders also live on in spiritual form as cherished national icons, such as Boudicca, Joan of Arc, and Saladin, whose achievements have become legendary. They endure in people's minds as much for the principles they represent as for the historical facts of their stories.

The effect of power

For some leaders, traces of their influence can still be seen in national, geographical, and political boundaries. The vast empires created by Alexander the Great, Suleiman the Magnificent, and Genghis Khan, for example, may have fallen, but the achievements of Qin Shi Huang, Charlemagne, and Otto Von Bismarck endure as modern-day China, France, and Germany. Similarly, through the leadership of George Washington, Mahatma Gandhi, and Kwame Nkrumah, the US, India, and Ghana became new, independent countries.

Another mark of successful leadership is advancement, where courageous rulers have led their society to a brighter future by challenging the current regime. As president, Abraham Lincoln released millions of slaves in the US and turned his country away from slavery, Cuba was freed from capitalist corruption by Fidel

Castro's revolution, while in South Africa, Nelson Mandela overthrew Apartheid, finally granting equality to the country's black majority.

Leaders can be defined neither by gender nor by race. Some of the great leaders have been female, including Sojourner Truth, Susan B. Anthony, and Emmeline Pankhurst, who all worked towards achieving equality for women. As a result of their initiatives, Margaret Thatcher, Benazir Bhutto, and Angela Merkel were able to forge political careers that saw them become the first elected female leaders of the UK, Pakistan, and Germany respectively. The civil rights movement in the US, given voice by Martin Luther King and Malcolm X, successfully campaigned for black equality, and brought the issue to the world stage.

A position of leadership inevitably carries great power, which can be misused and even abused, as witnessed in Adolf Hitler's persecution of the Jews and other minorities during World War II, devastating Europe for generations. Wielding power does not guarantee success, as seen in communist Russia and China, where Joseph Stalin's and Mao Zedong's failed reforms and political ambitions costs the lives of tens of millions of their own people.

However, leaders can and do evolve. In their early lives, entrepreneurs such as John D. Rockefeller, Li Ka-Shing, and Bill Gates led their businesses to global success and earned themselves vast fortunes. Each then used their personal wealth to fund philanthropic projects and, in doing so, improved the lives of those less fortunate, acquiring new supporters around the world.

"The **youth** of **today** are the **leaders** of **tomorrow.**"

Nelson Mandela, 1990

Changing notion of leadership

As societies change, so too does the concept of leadership. However, the one, indisputable uniting quality among all the leaders that appear in this book is ambition – these are people who, even if leadership has been inherited, have chosen to make decisions in order to effect change. They have accepted, welcomed, or fought for their position and they have not been afraid to stand up for what they believe in, whether that be to mankind's advantage or detriment. These are people who lived exceptional lives, many of which still continue to influence lives today.

1

EMPIRES AND RELIGIONS

2000 BCE–1500

Chosen by God to free the Israelites from slavery in Egypt, Moses led them across the desert for 40 years to Canaan, the land that God had promised. As the first prophet to proclaim the coming of the Messiah, and the receiver of the Ten Commandments, Moses is remembered in Jewish tradition as the greatest prophet of the Bible.

MILESTONES

SURVIVES MASSACRE
Discovered and raised by a Pharaoh's daughter, he survives a massacre of newborn Hebrew boys.

FREES HEBREW SLAVE
Murders an Egyptian slavemaster to save a Hebrew slave. Lives as a shepherd for 40 years.

COMMANDED BY GOD
Chosen by God to lead the Israelites from slavery and deliver them to the Promised Land.

SPREADS GOD'S WORD
Receives God's teachings and his commandments, which he compiles to form basis of the Torah.

THE PROMISED LAND
Leads the Jews for 40 years wandering the desert. Dies within sight of the Promised Land.

Born to Hebrew parents (Israelites) in what would become Egypt, Moses lived according to most scholars between 14th–13th centuries BCE. The Israelites had been slaves in Egypt for around 400 years, and worried that they might form alliances with his enemies, the reigning Pharaoh (name unknown) ordered the execution of all newborn males to reduce their population. As a baby, Moses was hidden by his mother, and discovered by the Pharaoh's daughter, who raised him at the royal court.

As an adult, Moses killed an Egyptian slavemaster after he saw him beating a Hebrew slave. Fearing the death penalty, he fled Egypt for the neighbouring area of Midian (believed to be in the Arabian Peninsula).

Power of God
In Midian, Moses spent the next 40 years living as a shepherd, and married a fellow shepherd's daughter, Zipporah. While tending his sheep on Mount Horab, he saw a bush that burned but did not perish in the flames.

Moses was discovered in a reed basket along the banks of the River Nile by the Egyptian Pharaoh's daughter. She adopted him and raised him at the royal court.

"The Lord will fight for you; you need only to be still."

Moses

REMEMBER THE SABBATH

HONOUR YOUR PARENTS

DO

When he investigated, God appeared, and claimed He had chosen Moses for a mission – to free the Israelites from slavery and lead them to the Promised Land (the land that God had pledged to Abraham and his descendants). At first, Moses was afraid, and refused the task, but eventually he placed his faith in God and accepted the mission.

Moses returned to Egypt and demanded that the Pharaoh release his slaves, warning him of God's punishment, but he refused. God inflicted plagues that ravaged Egypt for months, and after the tenth plague, the Pharaoh finally agreed to release the slaves.

Searching for freedom

Moses led the Israelites out of Egypt and into the Arabian desert, and Pharaoh, who regretted his decision to free his workers, sent his chariots to chase them down. When faced with the Red Sea, Moses called upon God, who parted the waves so he and the Israelites could pass, as Pharaoh's chariots were washed away.

Later, God appeared to Moses at Mount Sinai, where He outlined laws that the Israelites must follow in exchange for God's enduring blessing. Moses recorded these as the Ten Commandments, which still form the backbone of Judeo-Christian morality.

According to Jewish tradition, God also dictated further teachings, which Moses compiled in the Torah, the most important text in Judaism. Moses became a channel between God and the Israelites, and his direct communication with God distinguishes him from any other prophet in the Bible.

The Promised Land

As God's messenger, Moses led the loyal Israelites into the desert where they sought to find the Promised Land. There, he sent out 12 chiefs in search of the land for 40 days. When 10 returned despondent at what they had found, the Israelites were punished by God for their lack of faith, and made to wander the desert for a further 40 years, until the generation of doubters had perished. Moses led the Israelites to within sight of the Promised Land, where he handed them over to the care of his assistant, Joshua, and climbed Mount Nebo, where he died, aged 120, having never reached the Promised Land himself.

DO NOT

FOLLOW OTHER GODS

WORSHIP **FALSE** GODS

TAKE GOD'S NAME IN **VAIN**

MURDER

STEAL

COMMIT **ADULTERY**

BEAR **FALSE** WITNESS

COVET

The Ten Commandments, in Judeo-Christian thought, are essential moral teachings. Spread by Moses to the Israelites, they consist of a number of required and forbidden practices.

JUDAISM **GLOBAL FOLLOWERS**

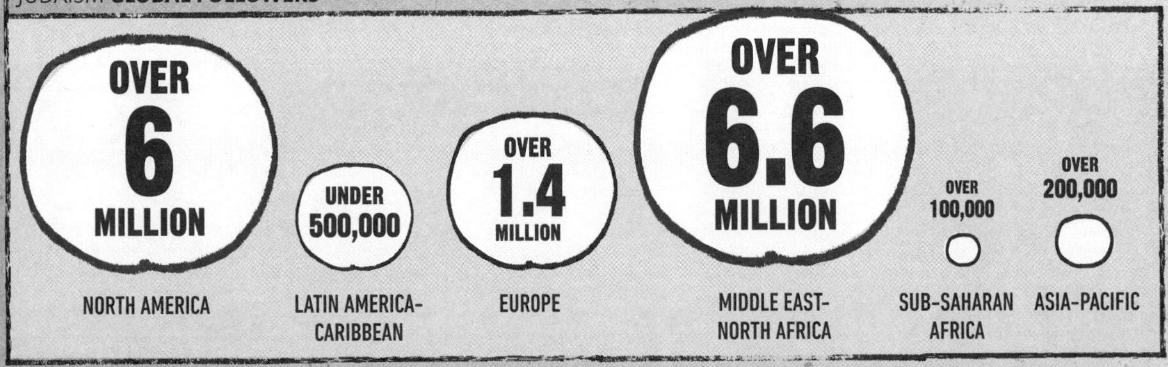

OVER
6
MILLION
NORTH AMERICA

UNDER
500,000
LATIN AMERICA-CARIBBEAN

OVER
1.4
MILLION
EUROPE

OVER
6.6
MILLION
MIDDLE EAST-NORTH AFRICA

OVER
100,000
SUB-SAHARAN AFRICA

OVER
200,000
ASIA-PACIFIC

KEPT FROM REALITY
Spends his life until early adulthood in his father's palace shielded from human suffering.

SHOCKED BY TRUTH
Upon leaving the palace, discovers reality of life. He leaves his family to become a holy man.

SOURCE OF SUFFERING
After meditating, learns that greed, stupidity, and selfishness are causes of human misery.

PATH TO NIRVANA
Develops philosophy of Four Noble Truths and Eightfold Path as a means to reach Nirvana.

SPREADS HIS IDEAS
Aged 35, attracts his first disciples. Founds *Sangha* (monastic order) and sets out *dharma* (teachings).

Better known as the Buddha, Śiddhartha Gautama is revered as the founder of one of the oldest and most widespread of world faiths – Buddhism. An Eastern philosophy and religion, it teaches that life is a process of working towards freedom from suffering.

Śiddhartha (meaning "he who achieves his aim") Gautama was born into the Shakya tribe in Lumbini (modern-day Nepal), in the 6th century BCE. The tribe was poor and isolated, but Śiddhartha's father, Śuddhodana, was the leader, and built a palace where his son, the prince, could live in luxury.

Path to enlightenment
According to Buddhist tradition, Śiddhartha's father ordered the people to hide all signs of human suffering from his son. When Śiddhartha finally ventured out of the palace without his father's knowledge, he was deeply shocked to learn of illness, old age, and death. In response, he left his home, his wife, and his newborn son Rāhula, to seek the truth of human existence.

For a few years, Śiddhartha tried to emulate holy men (such as the hermit saint Alara Kalama), and follow a life of study, prayer, and meditation, but their guidance failed to help him achieve spiritual release. Then, meditating alone under a pipal tree (*Ficus religiosa*), he came to see things as they truly were. When he realized that the causes of suffering are greed, selfishness, and stupidity, and that eliminating these traits would free people from suffering, he reached Nirvana, a state of pure enlightenment, and became the Buddha ("he who is awake").

> "All **conditioned things** are **impermanent** – when one sees this with **wisdom**, one **turns away** from **suffering.**"

The Buddha

Kneeing statues *representing the six devas (spirit beings) offer devotional gifts to the Tian Tan Buddha in Hong Kong, built in 1993.*

563–483 BCE

SIDDHARTHA GAUTAMA

BUDDHA

SELF-MORTIFICATION

DECADENCE

MIDDLE WAY

NIRVANA

Buddha taught his followers eight daily practices to help them find a middle way between self-denial and overindulgence, leading to pure enlightenment.

UNDERSTANDING

CONCENTRATION

INTENTION

MINDFULNESS

RIGHT

SPEECH

EFFORT

ACTION

LIVELIHOOD

During the Buddha's first sermon, he "set in motion the wheel" of his teachings (*dharma*). He spoke of the Four Noble Truths: *dukkha* (the truth of suffering); the arising of *dukkha* (the causes of suffering); the stopping of *dukkha* (the end of suffering); and the path to the stopping of *dukkha* (path to freedom from suffering). He also set out the Eightfold Path – eight practices to be integrated into daily life: right understanding, right intention, right speech, right action, right livelihood, right effort, right mindfulness, and right concentration. By embracing these habitual behaviours, the Buddha taught that each person could achieve a balance between self-mortification and decadence known as the Middle Way.

Teachings and legacy

While some of the Buddha's teachings, such as forbidding the slaughter of living beings, already existed in other schools of thought, his emphasis on equality between human beings and compassion for the poor was a revolutionary concept.

The Buddha spent the rest of his life travelling through India and preaching the *dharma*. However, he did not claim

to be a god or a prophet – only a human being who had reached the highest possible understanding of reality. It is said that when he died he told his disciples not to follow another leader.

After the Buddha's death, his teachings were passed through eastern Asia orally for 400 years before being written down. He also came to be venerated in other religions, such as the Ahmadiyya sect of Islam, while Hindus see him as one of ten incarnations of the god Vishnu.

DALAI **LAMA**

Buddhist monk Tenzin Gyatso is the 14th Dalai Lama, and the spiritual leader of Tibet.

The current lineage of Dalai Lamas began in the 14th century, and is believed to be successive incarnations of religious teachers who return to Earth to guide others. Since the 17th century, these spiritual masters have led the government in Tibet, until the 14th Dalai Lama went into exile in 1959 following a failed uprising against Chinese occupation. He has since become a world figure for his campaign for Tibetan autonomy.

BUDDHISM **GLOBAL FOLLOWERS**

UNDER 500,000
LATIN AMERICA-CARIBBEAN

OVER 3.8 MILLION
NORTH AMERICA

OVER 1.3 MILLION
EUROPE

OVER 500,000
MIDDLE EAST-NORTH AFRICA

UNDER 200,000
SUB-SAHARAN AFRICA

OVER 481 MILLION
ASIA-PACIFIC

ALEXANDER

THE GREAT

Considered by historians to have been one of the greatest commanders of all time, Alexander the Great's tactics influenced military strategists for centuries. Skilful, daring, and ambitious, by the age of 32 he had established an empire that stretched from Greece and Egypt to the Indian subcontinent.

MILESTONES

INSPIRED BY HOMER
Tutored by Aristotle in 343 BCE, and reads Homer's works, *The Iliad* and *The Odyssey*.

BECOMES KING
Succeeds his father and becomes King of Macedonia, 336 BCE. Crushes early dissent.

BUILDS ALEXANDRIA
Founds Greek city named after himself, Alexandria, 331 BCE, as a Hellenistic centre in Egypt.

DEFEATS PERSIA
Takes control of Persian Empire after decisive Battle of Gaugamela, 331 BCE.

Born in Pella, in the ancient Greek kingdom of Macedonia, Alexander was the son of Philip II and his fourth wife, Olympias. In Alexander's early education, he strongly identified with Achilles and Odysseus, the heroes of Homer's epics, *The Iliad* and *The Odyssey*, and from an early age, he sought to emulate their achievements.

When Alexander was just 16 years old, he ruled Macedonia as regent in his father's absence, crushing an uprising in Thrace. Two years later, Alexander led the cavalry charge at the Battle of Chaeronea in 338 BCE, and, according to the Greek-Roman biographer Plutarch, he was the first to force a breach in the enemy line, winning a key victory for his father.

The new king
After Philip II's assassination in 336 BCE, Alexander, aged 19, became king of Macedonia. Immediately, he began quelling rebellions sparked by the death of his father. After killing his main rival, Attalus, Alexander crushed an uprising in the Greek city of Thebes - the first example of his use of ruthless terror to suppress rebellion.

Alexander's first military expedition saw him defeat an uprising by local chiefs in the Danube Valley, north of Macedonia, in 335 BCE. In order to

Alexander's influence helped Hellenism (Greek culture) spread throughout the Ancient World for centuries after his death. The tall stone columns of the Garni Temple in Armenia are typical of Hellenistic architecture.

19

safely cross the river and gain the upper hand, he moved his entire army, with horses and equipment, across the river overnight on rafts made of animal skins stuffed with straw. Alexander's ability to improvise solutions under pressure, based on an astute reading of the landscape and situation, would be demonstrated throughout his career.

Building an empire

With his European lands secure, the 22-year-old Alexander turned his attention east towards Persia, intent on further conquests. Leading a carefully prepared expedition, he crossed the Hellespont, the body of water separating Europe from Asia Minor, into Anatolia.

Alexander's powerful army consisted of 5,000 Macedonian and Thessalonian cavalry, and 40,000 Macedonian and Greek infantry, including Thracian javelin-throwers and Cretan archers. His army's first victory against the Persians came at Granicus (Turkey) in 334 BCE. There, he used tactics gleaned from his father; Philip II had long utilized a phalanx formation – a huge rectangular mass of soldiers armed with shields and pikes. Unlike previous uses of this formation, Alexander's version of the phalanx included skirmishers and cavalry, which reinforced their attack.

The next year, Alexander confronted the Persian king Darius III and his army on the plains of Issus (Turkey). In one of the decisive battles of the ancient world, Alexander defeated the much larger Persian army, but Darius escaped. Alexander then moved on to Egypt, part of the Persian Empire, taking Tyre (Lebanon) and Gaza (Palestine) en route.

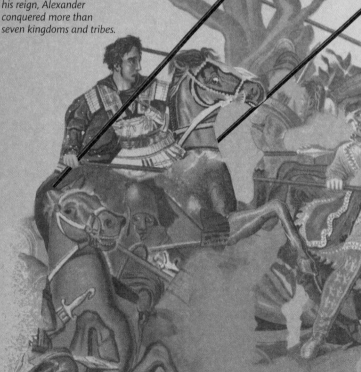

Alexander rode into battle on his horse Bucephalus to fight against the Persian king, Darius, at the Battle of Issus in 331 BCE. During his reign, Alexander conquered more than seven kingdoms and tribes.

PHILIP II OF MACEDON

Philip II (382–336 BCE) was king of Macedon and Alexander's father.

When Philip ascended the throne in 359 BCE he embarked on a long campaign to reform and strengthen the Macedonian army. He brought peace to his country and, following the Battle of Chaeronea in 338 BCE, established dominance over the Greek city states, thereby paving the way for his son's far-reaching conquests. In 336 BCE, Philip was assassinated by his bodyguard while planning an invasion of the Persian Empire.

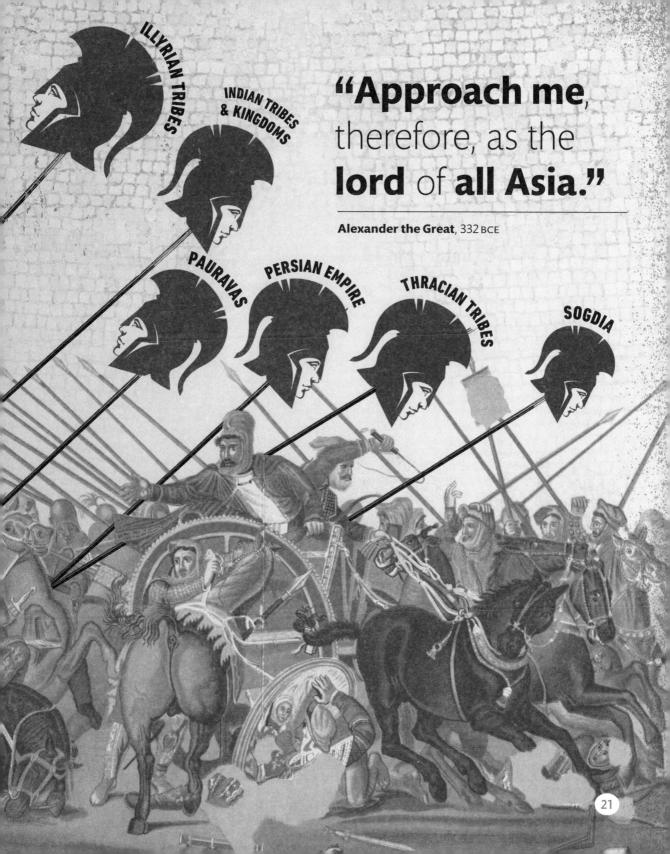

ILLYRIAN TRIBES

INDIAN TRIBES & KINGDOMS

PAURAVAS

PERSIAN EMPIRE

THRACIAN TRIBES

SOGDIA

"Approach me, therefore, as the lord of all Asia."

Alexander the Great, 332 BCE

CONQUERED THE ISLAND CITY OF TYRE IN 332 BCE

DEFEATED A SCYTHIAN ARMY OF 15,000 AT THE BATTLE OF JAXARTES

DESTROYED THE PAURAVA KINGDOM IN 326 BCE DURING THE BATTLE OF HYDASPES

While in Egypt, Alexander used a passage from *The Odyssey* to identify a nearby fishing village as the site on which to build a city. He named it Alexandria, and it went on to become a centre for trade between Europe and the East, and the largest city in the ancient world.

In 331 BCE, Alexander defeated Darius III at Gaugamela (Iraq), although he was once again outnumbered. Shortly after, he captured the administrative capital of Persia: Babylon (Iraq). Darius fled once more, but was later murdered by a small group of conspirators led by his cousin Satrap Bessus. In 330 BCE, Alexander proclaimed himself successor to the Persian throne. The Macedonians believed this would bring an end to his campaigns, but he pressed on, enforcing his claim on all Persian domains, and extending his empire into India.

The turning point

After invading the Punjab, in Northern India, in 326 BCE, Alexander defeated King Porus of the Pauravas at the Battle of the Hydaspes. His army then faced another battle at the River Hyphasis (Beas) in the Himalayas but his men were outnumbered and suffered huge losses. Demoralized and exhausted at the prospect of further military campaigns, Alexander's armies began to mutiny. Heeding his people's needs, Alexander agreed to return home.

Part of Alexander's success in building his empire came from him embracing the customs of the civilizations that he conquered. However, these were not met with such enthusiasm by his Macedonian followers and veterans. Many became jealous as increasing numbers of new Persian followers found favour with Alexander. Discontent was expressed in a series of mutinies that Alexander violently suppressed.

His legacy

When he died of a fever in Babylon on 11 June 323 BCE, Alexander left no heir (his son by his wife Roxana, a Sogdian princess, was born after his death). However, he left a strong legacy as the passage of his army led to unprecedented cultural and religious exchanges between East and West, as well as the expansion of trade routes and the founding of many cities. In antiquity, his fame was unequalled, and he was so revered by his followers that his embalmed body was taken to Egypt where it was displayed for more than 500 years.

"OUR ENEMIES ARE MEDES AND PERSIANS, MEN WHO FOR CENTURIES HAVE LIVED SOFT AND LUXURIOUS LIVES; WE OF MACEDON FOR GENERATIONS PAST HAVE BEEN TRAINED IN THE HARD SCHOOL OF DANGER AND WAR."

Alexander the Great

Addressing troops before the Battle of Issus as quoted in *Anabasis Alexandri* by Arrian of Nicomedia, Book II, 200 CE

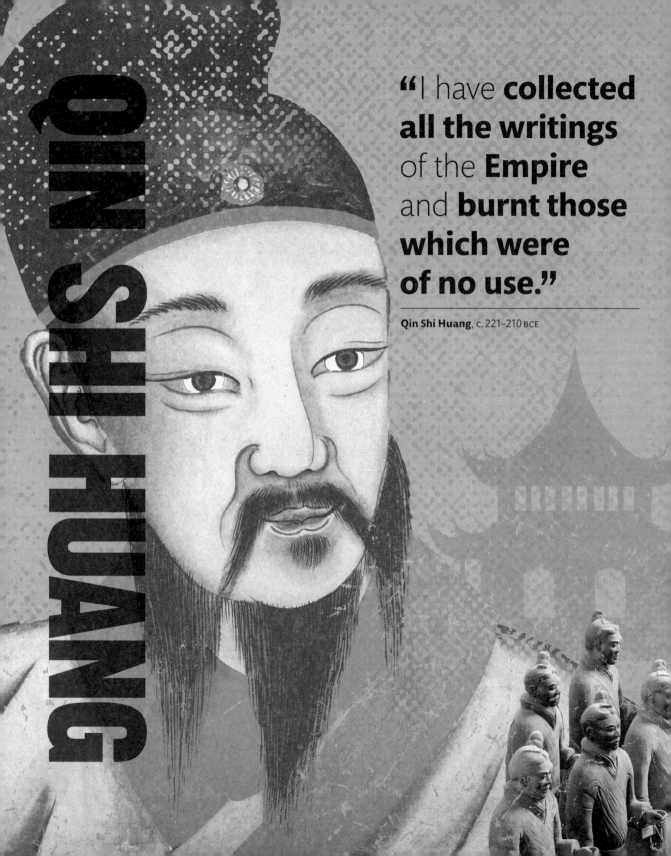

QIN SHI HUANG

"I have **collected all the writings** of the **Empire** and **burnt those** which were of no use."

Qin Shi Huang, c. 221–210 BCE

The self-appointed First Emperor of China, Qin Shi Huang conquered six states and unified them with his own kingdom to create a single nation – China. Stamping his authority upon his country, he introduced laws that are still in place today.

MILESTONES

ASCENDS TO THRONE
Succeeds his father, King Zhuangxiang, and becomes king of Qin state, 246 BCE.

CONQUERS STATES
Leads successful military campaigns against the neighbouring six states during 230–221 BCE.

ESTABLISHES CHINA
Absorbs seven states into a single nation, China, and proclaims himself emperor, 221 BCE.

BUILDS GREAT WALL
Starts construction of first phase of Great Wall of China to prevent invasions, 220 BCE.

Originally named Ying Zheng, the future emperor was born the son of a prince in the state of Qin at a time of conflict between rival Chinese kingdoms, known as the Warring States period (475–221 BCE). Zheng succeeded his father's throne to Qin in 246 BCE, aged just 13, and ruled first with the assistance of his chancellor, Lü Buwei, before taking full control nine years later. As king, Zheng waged war on his neighbouring states and conquered them all between 230–221 BCE, before proclaiming himself Qin Shi Huang, meaning First Emperor of the Qin dynasty.

Establishing China
In order to consolidate his power, Qin and his new chancellor, Li Si, established a system of civil administration across his territory, where positions of power were earned, not inherited. All men were equal under law, but equally powerless and without rights.

Unity and uniformity were guiding principles of Qin's rule, which saw him impose empire-wide laws, and standardize measurements, language, currency, and trade. He also introduced

Qin ordered the creation of 8,000 life-size soldiers made out of terracotta for his tomb. He believed the figures would guard him in the afterlife.

conscription for the poor, and went on to create a powerful army numbering hundreds of thousands, and to establish a labour force that was used to construct new roads, canals, and temples, and start building The Great Wall of China.

Obsession and paranoia

Even as a young king, Qin was obsessed with his own mortality, and ordered the construction of a vast tomb containing life-size terracotta figures designed to protect him in the afterlife. It took 38 years to construct, and required hundreds of thousands of labourers. (It was discovered in 1974.) To avoid assassination attempts – of which three were made during his lifetime – and evil spirits, Qin also built secret tunnels between his palaces.

Determined to secure his legacy, Qin suppressed the histories of previous dynasties and burned the works of scholars that he did not agree with. He also destroyed works that did not suit his aims, including immortality in later life.

In his quest to cheat death, Qin dispatched numerous missions to discover sacred places and people where the elixir of life might be found, and employed scholars to concoct potions that would grant him eternal life. He died, aged 49, believed to be from mercury poisoning, possibly from one of these potions.

LI SI

As chancellor, Li Si (280–208 BCE) was a driving force behind Qin's unification of China and the policies he implemented.

Born in around 280 BCE, Li Si encouraged Qin to invade neighbouring kingdoms in order to unify the country. Throughout Qin's rule, Li Si believed that a diversity of political beliefs would undermine the unity of the single Chinese state, so he ordered harsh treatment for those who held beliefs or expressed views counter to the offical line. After Qin's death, Li Si remained chancellor under his successor Qin Er Shi. In 208 BCE, Li Si was executed after falling out of political favour.

BEGAN BUILDING THE GREAT WALL OF CHINA

HAD **50 CHILDREN** BY NUMEROUS CONCUBINES

ESTABLISHED A **CURRENCY** THAT WAS THE **FORERUNNER OF THE YÜAN**

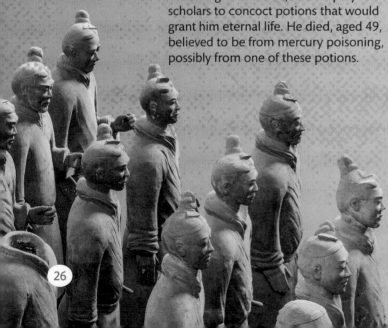

Renowned for her military prowess and shrewd alliances, Queen Cleopatra was the last ruling Pharaoh of Egypt.

Cleopatra ascended the throne of Egypt alongside her younger brother, Ptolemy XIII, following their father's death in 51 BCE. When civil war erupted between the sibling rulers, Cleopatra allied herself with the Roman general Julius Caesar, who was charmed by her beauty and intelligence. Once Ptolemy was defeated, Cleopatra co-ruled first with Ptolemy XIV and then with her son, but she was effectively sole ruler of Egypt.

Following Julius's assassination in 44 BCE, Cleopatra formed a political and romantic relationship with Mark Antony, one of the three administrators who, along with Octavian (see pp.32–35) and (Marcus Aemilius) Lepidus, led Rome. As the Roman leaders vied for power, Octavian declared war on Antony and Cleopatra.

Defeated in battle at Actium in 31 BCE, Cleopatra and Antony fled to Egypt, where besieged and facing capture, and humiliation, they both committed suicide.

MILESTONES

BECOMES QUEEN
After her father Ptolemy XII dies, becomes queen of Egypt, 51 BCE. Rules with brother, Ptolemy XIII.

ALLIES WITH CAESAR
Banished, 49 BCE. Becomes queen again after charming Caesar into defeating Ptolemy XIII in war, 48 BCE.

SOLE RULER
Assassinates co-ruler Ptolemy XIV. Her young son replaces him; Cleopatra now sole ruler, 44 BCE.

PROCLAIMED GODDESS
After successful military campaign, Cleopatra and Mark Antony are lauded as gods, 34 BCE.

Cleopatra Gate, Turkey, where Roman general Mark Antony and Cleopatra struck an alliance in 41 BCE.

CLEOPATRA

JESUS CHRIST

A first-century Jewish preacher, Jesus is the central figure of Christianity and, according to Christian teaching, the Son of God and the long-awaited Messiah prophesied in the Bible's Old Testament. Preaching in Galilee, he amassed a small following that would eventually grow into the world's largest religion.

According to the Gospels, Jesus was born to the Virgin Mary, having been conceived by the power of the Holy Spirit, and born in a stable in Bethlehem, where he was visited by shepherds and Magi. Also known as the Christ or Messiah (meaning "Annointed One"), the story of Jesus is derived from the four Canonical Gospels of the Bible's New Testament: those of Mark, Matthew, Luke, and John. In combination they narrate the birth, life, and death of Jesus of Nazareth, the perceived incarnation of God, and the founder of the Christian faith.

Life and teachings

Jesus was baptized in the River Jordan by John the Baptist, a preacher and prophet, in an act that marked the start of his ministry at around 30 years of age. On emerging from the water, a voice from heaven spoke to Jesus, affirming that he was the Son of God. Jesus then spent 40 days fasting and praying in the desert, while resisting the temptations of Satan. After his final night, Jesus summoned his followers and chose his 12 apostles, or primary disciples. Proclaiming the Kingdom of God, the sovereign rule of God over all creations, and a message of love,

MILESTONES

SAVIOUR IS BORN
Born to the Virgin Mary, his birth, prophesied by Angel Gabriel, was attended by three magi.

THE SON OF GOD
Begins ministry aged 30, after being baptized by John the Baptist. Learns he is the Son of God.

SPREADS GOD'S WORD
Teaches and performs miracles to spread God's word. Acquires hundreds of followers.

CONQUERS DEATH
Betrayed by Judas, then crucified by the Romans. Rises from death – he ascends to heaven.

Jesus had his final communion with his apostles at the Last Supper. The apostle Judas had already accepted 30 pieces of silver to betray Jesus.

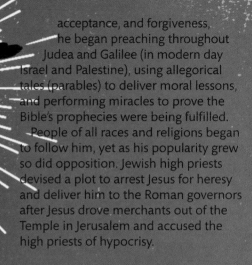

acceptance, and forgiveness, he began preaching throughout Judea and Galilee (in modern day Israel and Palestine), using allegorical tales (parables) to deliver moral lessons, and performing miracles to prove the Bible's prophecies were being fulfilled.

People of all races and religions began to follow him, yet as his popularity grew so did opposition. Jewish high priests devised a plot to arrest Jesus for heresy and deliver him to the Roman governors after Jesus drove merchants out of the Temple in Jerusalem and accused the high priests of hypocrisy.

Death and resurrection

Jesus knew of his prophesied fate to suffer and be killed, and had forewarned his apostles. He also knew the apostle Judas, who had already struck a deal of 30 silver pieces with the Jewish high

REPENTANCE

HOPE

LOVE

SERVITUDE

JUDAISM AT THE TIME OF CHRIST

One of the world's oldest religions, Judaism existed in four main groups with distinct traditions and practises at the time that Jesus was preaching.

The Pharisees considered themselves superior to: Jews who were less observant of the law than them, non-Jews (gentiles), the unclean, and sinners. The Sadducees believed Jewish law should be interpreted exactly as it had been written. The Essenes rejected the Temple of Jerusalem and lived in strict communities. The Zealots, a violent liberation movement, believed social justice could only be achieved by armed revolution.

CHRISTIANITY **GLOBAL FOLLOWERS**

OVER **266** MILLION	OVER **531** MILLION	OVER **558** MILLION	OVER **13** MILLION	OVER **517** MILLION	OVER **287** MILLION
NORTH AMERICA	LATIN AMERICA-CARIBBEAN	EUROPE	MIDDLE EAST-NORTH AFRICA	SUB-SAHARAN AFRICA	ASIA-PACIFIC

priests, would betray him. After Jesus and the apostles' "Last Supper", in which he taught them how to observe the Holy Communion, Jesus was arrested, mocked, beaten, and crucified for claiming to speak with God's authority.

His body was placed in a tomb, which three days later was found empty; he had risen from the dead. Jesus later appeared to his apostles and told them to spread his message to the world, before he ascended to heaven. Although Jesus had a popular following when he died, his church numbered just a few hundred. His teachings were kept alive by his apostles who believed that he had died to save the world from sin. The story of Jesus has endured globally ever since, making him one of the most influential moral teachers of all time.

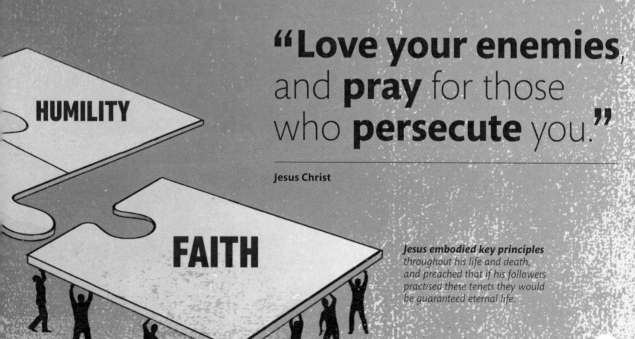

"**Love your enemies**, and **pray** for those who **persecute** you."

Jesus Christ

Jesus embodied key principles throughout his life and death, and preached that if his followers practised these tenets they would be guaranteed eternal life.

A political leader of great cunning, Augustus Caesar transformed ancient Rome from a republic into a hereditary empire and won a series of civil wars, establishing himself as the first Roman emperor. Augustus was also hailed for bringing peace to Rome, and presided over an era of cultural prosperity.

MILESTONES

BECOMES EMPEROR
Enters Roman politics after the assassination of his great-uncle, Julius, 44 BCE, who had named him heir.

POWERFUL ALLIANCE
Establishes a triumvirate with Antony and Lepidus, 43 BCE, legally handing all three shared rule of Rome.

ENDS CIVIL WAR
Decisively destroys forces of Brutus and Cassius at Battle of Philippi, in Macedonia, 42 BCE.

BATTLE OF ACTIUM
Claims victory against combined forces of Antony and Cleopatra at Battle of Actium, 31 BCE.

EMPEROR FOR LIFE
Founds the Principate, 27 BCE, and ascends to position of emperor. Holds power until death.

The future Augustus was born Gaius Octavius Thurinus (Octavian) in Rome in 63 BCE, the great-nephew of Julius Caesar, dictator of the Roman Republic (see p.34). When Caesar was assassinated in 44 BCE, his will revealed Octavian as his adopted son and heir.

The assassination propelled 19-year-old Octavian into the heart of a murderous power struggle. His most dangerous enemy was Mark Antony, who had been Caesar's trusted general, and aspired to inherit the dictator's power. Showing a maturity well beyond his years, Octavian manoeuvred between rival factions, while building up his own army and treasury. After initial skirmishes, Antony and Octavian formed a ruling triumvirate (three-way alliance) with the statesman Lepidus. This deal was sealed by "proscriptions", the legalized murder of thousands of personal and political enemies. The triumvirate then sought retribution on the senators Brutus and Cassius for their roles in the assassination of Julius Caesar, defeating them in battle at Philippi, in Macedonia, in 42 BCE.

Sharing power over Rome

After Philippi, Octavian, Antony, and Lepidus shared the joint rule of Rome's territories. Ruling the republic during such a politically turbulent period was challenging, but Octavian's political skills and ruthlessness proved equal to the task. He guaranteed himself the support of veteran

Roman soldiers, such as those commanded by Augustus Caesar, used the tortoise formation during sieges, in which their tightly packed shields protected against arrows.

AUGUSTUS
CAESAR

The great-uncle of Octavian, Julius Caesar was born into the Roman elite in 100 BCE. His brilliance as a military commander made him one of the leading political figures in the Roman Republic.

Nine years of campaigns against the tribes of Gaul – including raids on Britain – showed his skill as a general and his ruthlessness in crushing revolts. Leading his army into Italy in 49 BCE, Julius launched a civil war against his rival Pompey. Victorious in 45 BCE, he was appointed dictator by the Senate, and embarked on sweeping reforms, including the introduction of the Julian calendar. In 44 BCE he was assassinated by senators who feared that he would turn the republic into a monarchy.

RULED FOR MORE THAN 40 YEARS

DOUBLED THE SIZE OF ROMAN EMPIRE

soldiers by giving them land, and quashed a revolt against his authority with the mass-execution of rebels.

Octavian was equally cunning in family affairs, marrying three times in order to secure allegiances. In 30 BCE, he even divorced his second wife, Scribonia, on the day she gave birth to his only child (Julia), in order to marry Livia Drusilla. Livia was already married to the politician Tiberius Nero, and six months pregnant, but Octavian forced Nero to divorce her.

Struggle for power

Ill feeling between Octavian and Antony mounted as each vied for greater power. This was made worse by Antony's affair with Cleopatra (see p. 27) while he was married to Octavian's sister, Octavia.

In 32 BCE, the hostility between the two turned into civil war. Helped by the general Marcus Vipsanius Agrippa, his childhood friend and a master of war, Octavian's forces surrounded Antony and Cleopatra at Actium in

Greece, in 31 BCE, while Agrippa, leading Octavian's fleet, destroyed Antony's naval force. Facing defeat, he and Cleopatra fled to Egypt, where they both committed suicide in 30 BCE.

Political manoeuvrings

Octavian now faced no further barriers to absolute power. However, he did not want to appear to rule as a totalitarian – becoming the focus of revolts and civil wars like those that had plagued Rome for decades – so he upheld Rome's status as a republic and made a show of returning power to the Senate. In return, in 27 BCE, the Senate granted him the title Augustus, which made him become emperor for life, and the sole ruler of Rome in all but name.

Augustus believed in traditional Roman values, and passed laws rewarding marriage and child-bearing – viewed with irony by Romans aware of his own infidelities.

He also introduced anti-adultery legislation, which he imposed pitilessly, even against his own daughter, Julia, who he had exiled to the island of Pandateria, and never spoke to again.

Augustus was succeeded by his stepson Tiberius in 14 CE, and achieved his aim of founding a new system of hereditary rule in Rome that would last in one form or another until the fall of the Byzantine Empire, in 1453, nearly 1500 years later.

"At the **age of 19**... **I raised an army** by means of which **I restored liberty** to the **republic**, which had **been oppressed."**

Augustus Caesar, C. 14 CE

Augustus remained popular *for much of his reign due to his generosity towards his people. The government-issued grain supply, or cura annonae, flourished under his rule. In 23 BCE, he used his own funds to feed 250,000 citizens.*

Brittonic queen Boudicca earned her place in history by leading a revolt in c. 60 CE against the Roman legions who had invaded Britain 17 years prior.

Boudicca was the wife of Prasutagus, king of the Iceni (a Brittonic tribe), and ruled eastern England following the Roman invasion of Britain in 43 CE. Prasutagus had succeeded in maintaining his tribes' independence, but when he died in c. 60 CE, the Romans saw an opportunity to attack—they flogged Boudicca, raped her daughters, and seized her land.

In retaliation, Boudicca led a revolt, with the support of other Brittonic tribes. She commanded an attack on the major Roman settlement of *Camulodunum* (Colchester), then sacked *Londinium* (London) and *Verulamium* (St. Albans) before the Romans could mount a response. Later that year, the Romans defeated Boudicca, and the uprising collapsed. She died in 61 CE, and Roman rule in Britain was never seriously challenged again.

BOUDICCA

Boudicca commanded 200,000 people in her revolt against the Roman Empire, although historians today agree she would not have led them from a chariot.

"On that field **they must conquer** or **fall.**"

Boudicca, C. 60 CE

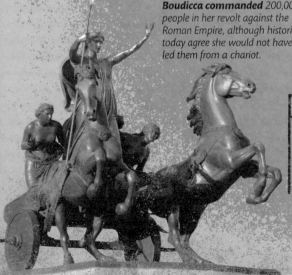

MILESTONES

RAISES REBELLION	**KILLS THOUSANDS**	**ROMANS TRIUMPH**
Takes advantage of the absence of Roman governor Suetonius and initiates rebellion, 60 CE.	Sacks Colchester, London, and St Albans, 60 CE, killing up to 80,000 inhabitants.	Faces defeat at Battle of Watling Street, 60 CE, between modern-day London and Wroxeter.

SEPTIMIA ZENOBIA

Queen of the Palmyrene Empire in Syria, Septimia Zenobia seized Egypt but failed to wrestle control of the eastern Mediterranean from Rome.

Septimia Zenobia married Odaenathus, ruler of Palmyra in Syria, in c. 255 CE, and a few years later, Odaenathus was declared king, and Zenobia queen. In 267 CE, Odaenathus and his eldest son were assassinated, and Zenobia became regent for her son Vaballathus. Exploiting a lack of leadership in the Roman Empire, her armies invaded Egypt, and extended her rule as far north as central Anatolia (Turkey). Meanwhile, her court became a centre of culture, learning, and religious tolerance. To counter her empire-building, Roman Emperor Aurelian swiftly led an army to reimpose his empire's authority on Palmyra. Defeated and captured in 272 CE, she died two years later. Historians are unsure how she died.

MILESTONES

MARRIES KING
Marries Odaenathus, self-styled King of Kings, c. 255 CE, as a teenager.

CREATES KINGDOM
Founds the Palmyrene Empire, 271 CE, after extensive conquests across Egypt and Anatolia.

HUMILIATED IN ROME
Loses the Battle of Immae to Emperor Aurelian, 272 CE, and is paraded through streets of Rome.

Zenobia commanded as many as 70,000 men in battle at the peak of her empire's power.

"Spirit **divinely great**, her **beauty incredible**."

Historia Augusta, c. 4th century

MUHAMMAD

ﷺ

محمد

"**A strong person** is not the person who **throws his adversaries** to the ground. **A strong person** is the person who **contains himself when he is angry.**"

Muhammad

Revered as the Prophet and founder of the Islamic faith, Muhammad was God's final messenger, sent to spread His word. After laying the foundations for an Islamic empire, Muhammad became its political, military, and spiritual leader. He successfully captured Mecca, which Muslims regard as Islam's holiest city.

Muhammad ibn 'Abdallah was born in the city of Mecca (present-day Saudi Arabia) into a branch of the nomadic Quraysh tribe in 570 CE. He was orphaned aged six, and raised by his paternal grandfather, and then his uncle, a camel-train merchant. Young Muhammad accompanied his uncle on trading trips, where he encountered people of many cultures and religions, and gained a reputation for honesty – acquiring the nickname "al-Amin" ("faithful"). He became a business representative for a wealthy widow and camel-train merchant named Khadija, who became his first wife in 595 CE. Together for 24 years, they had several children.

Revelations from Gabriel
In 610 CE, while Muhammad was meditating in a cave on Mount Jabal al-Nour, the angel Jibrail (Gabriel) appeared, granting him the first of many revelations that would eventually make up the Qur'an, Islam's holy book. Muhammad began to talk publicly about the revelations, and slowly gained a following in Mecca. From 613 CE, he claimed the authority of a prophet

Muhammad received God's word via the angel Gabriel. These words form the Qur'an, Islam's sacred text, which is taught in Arab schools such as this one in Algiers.

39

and preached the worship of the one true God, Allah – followers of this new religion, Islam, became known as Muslims.

Islamic city-state

Many tribal leaders saw Muhammad as a threat, as his message condemned their long-standing belief in polytheism (worshipping multiple gods) and idol worship. Hearing of a tribe's plot to assassinate him, in 622 CE (the start of the Islamic calendar), Muhammad and his followers left

PILGRIMAGE

Mecca and travelled north to the city of Yathrib. Here Arab clans accepted Muhammad's status as prophet, and his Muslim community expanded. The city was renamed Medina (meaning "city of the Prophet") and organized into a unified Islamic city-state – the world's first Islamic state.

Muhammad drew up a constitution, which formed the basis of an Islamic political tradition. It addressed the rights and duties of every group within the community, the rule of law, and the moral issue of war. It recognized other religious communities as separate, but agreed reciprocal obligations with them, including the need to unite in battle should the state come under threat. His aims were for internal peace within the Islamic state and a political structure that would help him gather followers

and soldiers to help his conquest of the Arabian Peninsula. Muhammad proved an inspirational leader and, as God's messenger, his word carried unquestioned authority.

Triumphant return to Mecca

Within two years, war erupted between Mecca and Medina. Muhammad's army outmanoeuvred the Meccan tribes, and in 630 CE he successfully captured the city. Most of the population converted to Islam and his position was unassailable.

Muhammad's life as a prophet lasted 22 years. He preached his last sermon on Mount Arafat in March 632 CE, and returned to Medina, where he died. On his death, the Islamic state he founded covered the entire Arabian Peninsula.

FAITH

FASTING

The Five Pillars of Islam are the five duties that every Muslim must perform. One of the Five Pillars is a pilgrimage to the sacred Kaaba in Mecca, which Muslims consider to be the house of God.

PRAYER

A'ISHA

Muhammad's third wife, A'isha bint Abi Bakr (614–78 CE), was the daughter of his loyal supporter Abu Bakr. A child when she married, A'isha became politically active following her husband's death.

A'isha was allegedly around six years old when she was married to the Prophet Muhammad, and although the marriage was politically motivated, A'isha gained Muhammad's deep and lasting affection. A'isha was intelligent, and after the death of Muhammad her political convictions grew. She fiercely opposed the third caliph (leader), Uthman, possibly because of his cruel treatment of Muhammad's companion Ammar ibn Yassir, but she condemned Uthman's eventual assassination. She was defeated in a battle against his successor, Uthman ibn Affan, and returned to Medina to devote herself to Islam.

ALMSGIVING

ISLAM **GLOBAL FOLLOWERS**

OVER 3.5 MILLION	UNDER 1 MILLION	OVER 43 MILLION	OVER 317 MILLION	OVER 248 MILLION	OVER 985 MILLION
NORTH AMERICA	LATIN AMERICA-CARIBBEAN	EUROPE	MIDDLE EAST-NORTH AFRICA	SUB-SAHARAN AFRICA	ASIA-PACIFIC

CHARLEMAGNE

A formidable military leader, Charlemagne established a kingdom during the 8th century that covered much of modern-day Europe. He was an advocate for learning, and his reign heralded a golden age in education and the arts.

MILESTONES

ASSUMES THRONE
Jointly-rules Francia with brother, 768 CE. Aged 23, following brother's death, inherits sole rule.

DEFEATS DESIDERIUS
Successfully besieges Pavia, near Rome, and defeats Lombard king Desiderius, 773–74 CE.

MILITARY DEFEAT
Ambushed by Basque forces on France-Spain border, in his only defeat, 778 CE.

SAXON MASSACRE
Enraged at the killing of some of his nobles in battle, orders the massacre of 4,500 Saxons, 782 CE.

CROWNED EMPEROR
Appointed Holy Roman Emperor by Pope Leo III, 800 CE.

Born in 742 CE, Charlemagne was the eldest son of Pepin III, king of the Franks (Germanic-speaking people who invaded the Roman Empire in the 5th century CE). After jointly inheriting his father's kingdom, Francia, in 768 CE, he became sole ruler three years later following the death of his brother. A devout Christian, he set about spreading Christianity and expanding his kingdom.

Campaign trail
Charlemagne is believed to have carried out 30 military campaigns into surrounding territories during his reign. He prepared carefully for each one, gathering intelligence on a particular region before invading. One of his most successful was in 773–74 CE, in Lombard (now northern Italy). The king of Lombard, Desiderius, had invaded papal territory near Rome, and Pope Hadrian asked Charlemagne to intervene. Charlemagne's decisive military action resulted in the Lombards retreating to Pavia, the Lombard capital, where the Franks laid siege for several months until Desiderius surrendered, securing Charlemagne a lasting papal alliance. However, success was not always guaranteed. In 778 CE, Charlemagne

> ## "The **most famous** and **greatest** of men."
>
> **Einhard**, scholar at Charlemagne's court, c. 815–840

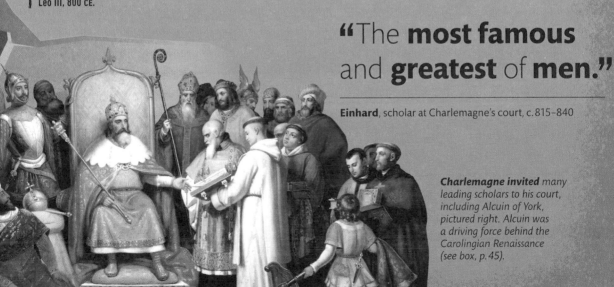

Charlemagne invited many leading scholars to his court, including Alcuin of York, pictured right. Alcuin was a driving force behind the Carolingian Renaissance (see box, p. 45).

> **"The keenest of all kings** to **seek out** and **support wise men** so that they might **philosophize** with all delight.**"**

Walafrid Strabo, writer, referring to Charlemagne, c. 815–849

led an unsuccessful campaign into Basque territory, northern Spain, with the aim of expanding Francia. Forced to retreat across the Pyrenees, his rear guard was ambushed and killed.

Fighting for his faith
Many of Charlemagne's military efforts were directed towards the northeastern frontier of his kingdom in Saxony, where between 770–90 CE, the pagan Saxons repeatedly rose up against his rule.

Charlemagne was determined to stamp out paganism among the Saxons, executing those who refused to convert. In 782 CE, resistance to Frankish rule provoked a massacre at Verden that cost over 4,500 Saxon lives in a single day.

As Charlemagne's dominance across Europe grew, the Catholic church began to regard his support as vital, due to rising tensions between the church and the Byzantine empire. On Christmas Day 800 CE, Charlemagne was crowned

ARTS & MUSIC

LITERACY

EDUCATION

Holy Roman Emperor by Pope Leo III at St Peter's Basilica in Rome. He was the first Western emperor for three centuries, and his lands became known as the Holy Roman Empire.

Cultural legacy

By the time Charlemagne became emperor, his campaigns were reaching an end, and in the years that followed he oversaw a period of growth in culture and education, known as the Carolingian Renaissance period, which lasted into the 10th century.

Although illiterate himself, Charlemagne promoted the learning of grammar and rhetoric, along with art, literature, music, and astronomy, inviting distinguished scholars from the far reaches of his empire to court. He implemented reforms in the language of government and the church, ensuring that the clergy could read

classical Latin. After Charlemagne's death in 814 CE, the Holy Roman Empire would endure for nearly a thousand years, until its dissolution in 1806 by Napoleon Bonaparte (see pp.110–15).

CAROLINGIAN **RENAISSANCE**

The reign of the Carolingians, a family of Frankish aristocrats, marked a brief period of enlightenment during the Dark Ages.

Prior to the reign of the Carolingians (751–987 CE), Europe was in social, political, and economic disarray following the decline of the Roman Empire. During his rule, Pepin III, the first Carolingian king, and a supporter of the Roman church, initiated reforms in writing and education in order to promote Christianity. His legacy was continued by his son, Charlemagne, who brought broader reforms to Pepin's territories, and created a generation of educated churchmen.

FOUGHT IN 18 BATTLES

UNIFIED WESTERN EUROPE

RULED AN EMPIRE OF 1.1 MILLION
SQ KM (430,000 SQ MILES)

POLITICAL UNITY

CHRISTIANITY

Charlemagne unified his newly conquered territories by introducing common political, social, and business reforms, imposing his Christian beliefs, and by promoting the arts.

"PEOPLE ARE CRYING AND WAILING... THE FRANKS, THE ROMANS, ALL CHRISTIANS, ARE STUNG WITH MOURNING AND GREAT WORRY... THE YOUNG AND OLD, GLORIOUS NOBLES, ALL LAMENT THE LOSS OF THEIR CAESAR..."

An anonymous monk
Following the death of Charlemagne, 814 CE

◀ *Charlemagne was crowned* Holy Roman Emperor by Pope Leo III in 800 CE, as depicted in this 1724 fresco by Jacob Carl Stauder.

MILESTONES

WEDDED TO POWER
Inherits duchy of Aquitaine and marries King Louis VII, of France, 1137, keeping control of her lands.

CHAMPIONS SONS
Marries King Henry II of England, 1152, and leads plot with three of her sons against him, 1173.

TAKES CHARGE
Widowed, 1189, rules England while son, king Richard of Lionheart is away on Crusade.

Eleanor married King Louis VII in 1137 (left) who embarked on the Second Crusade in 1147 (right), where he fought for two years.

Queen of France, then queen of England as wife of King Louis VII and then Henry II respectively, Eleanor was one of the most influential political female figures in 12th-century Europe.

Eleanor inherited the duchy of Aquitaine, southwest France, at the age of 15, making her one of the richest women in Europe. Her marriage to King Louis VII of France, in 1137, meant that she was able to keep Aquitaine under her control. Louis coveted Eleanor's wealth and married her with that in mind. In 1152 Louis, frustrated that Eleanor had not produced a male heir, had thier marriage annulled; eight weeks later she married the future King Henry II of England, and they went on to have five sons and three daughters.

In 1173, outraged by her husband's infidelities, and in an effort to advance her sons' political power, Eleanor backed three of them in a rebellion against Henry. When this failed he kept her prisoner for 16 years. After his death in 1189, Eleanor ruled England while her son King Richard the Lionheart was on crusade, then supported her younger son John as successor. She died five years later, aged 81.

ELEANOR
OF AQUITAINE

SALADIN

Sultan of Egypt and Syria, Salah ad-Din Yusuf ibn Ayyub, or Saladin, led his men to victory in the Third Crusade.

Saladin was a Kurdish warrior, born in Tikrit (modern-day Iraq), whose family served the Zengid ruler of Syria. He travelled to Egypt in 1164, where after seven years he ousted the Fatimid rulers and established his own Ayyubid dynasty. Returning to Syria in 1174, it took him eight years to depose the rulers and take control of the country.

In 1187, he crushed the Christian crusaders at the Battle of Hattin and seized the city of Jerusalem, prompting the Third Crusade, in which the forces of Richard I (the Lionheart) of England and Philip II of France fought to reclaim the Holy Land. After his defeat at the Battle of Jaffa in 1192, Saladin retreated to Jerusalem. Exhauted by fighting, he and Richard I signed a truce – Richard I returned to England, leaving Jerusalem to Saladin.

Saladin inspired his men to seize Jerusalem in 1187. While Saladin suffered major defeats during the Third Crusade, his main victory was retaining Jerusalem.

> **"I have won the hearts of men by gentleness."**
>
> **Saladin**, 1193

MILESTONES

FOUNDS DYNASTY	DEFEATS CRUSADERS	RETAINS JERUSALEM
Seizes control of Egypt from Fatimid rulers, 1164, founds Ayyubid dynasty there, 1171.	Defeats Western crusaders at Battle of Hattin, 1187, capturing Jerusalem.	Although defeated by Richard I at Jaffa, 1192, retains Jerusalem following a truce.

"A man of **great ability, eloquence,** and **valour.**"

Marco Polo, about Genghis Khan, c. 1300

Genghis Khan was known to lead his men into battle himself, risking his own life alongside his loyal horde.

GENGHIS KHAN

The founder of the Mongolian Empire, Genghis Khan is one of the greatest conquerors in history. A military genius, he unified the tribes of the Mongolian grasslands, arguably creating the most brutal cavalry force that has ever existed, and established the world's largest unbroken empire.

Temüjin (meaning blacksmith) Borjigin was born into a nomadic tribe in the eastern mountains of the central Asian steppe (a vast grassland region stretching across Mongolia, Manchuria, and North China). His father, Yesügei, the chief of the ruling Borjigin clan, was murdered by a rival group when his son was only nine years old. The clan refused to accept Temüjin as their chief, and cast the family out, leaving them without protection.

The young warrior

As his mother's eldest surviving son, Temüjin took over as head of the family, and quickly learned the resilience needed for its survival, while scraping an existence on foraged food. He gradually built a reputation as a courageous warrior: he escaped from a tribe that had captured him, and he also retrieved horses that had been stolen from a local family. Both incidents helped him gain the loyalty of everyone around him.

Temüjin also recognized the importance of cultivating alliances. At the age of 16 he married Börte, to whom he had been betrothed by his father. Temüjin then made gifts to his father's ally – Toghril, leader of the Keirut people – with Börte's dowry money. When his wife was kidnapped by the rival Merkits (a tribal state in present-day Mongolia) in 1184, in return Toghril

---

MILESTONES

YASSA CODE	**CREATES EMPIRE**	**ESTABLISHES TRADE**
Introduces the Yassa code, 1190, a range of Mongol laws that promote obedience to him and punish wrongdoing.	Successfully unites the tribes of central Asia and renames himself Genghis Khan, 1206. His unified force known as Mongols.	Conquers Khwarezmid Empire (Afghanistan and Iraq), 1225. Brings stability to Silk Road, encouraging trade across empire.

not only supplied Temüjin with an army, but also assisted him in creating an alliance with the leader of the Tangut tribe, Jamuka, who provided Temüjin with an army as well. Reinforced with these allies and armies, Temüjin was successful in attacking and crushing the Merkits, and reclaiming his wife. Although he went on to have many wives, Börte was his only ever empress.

Start of the Mongol Empire
From 1185, Temüjin embarked on several ruthless campaigns that would eventually unite all the nomadic tribes of Mongolia, and create an unstoppable armed force with which he could build his empire. Temüjin's brilliant military campaigns and diplomatic strategy involved executing enemy clan leaders and adopting common people into his army. Although he formed alliances where necessary, he ultimately turned against his allies, including the tribes of Jamuka and Toghril. By 1206, out of tribal warfare and rivalry emerged a united Mongol empire, led by its creator, the newly self-named Genghis Khan ("Universal Leader").

Master conqueror
Once he had established himself as sole ruler, Genghis Khan shifted his focus to civilizations beyond the Mongolian steppe. Over the course of three decades, he pushed the boundaries of his growing empire as far as Beijing in the east and the Caspian Sea in the west, subjugating millions of people, and destroying several ancient cities, including Samarkand, Bukhara, and Nishapur in the process. With a rare and consummate skill, Genghis

HIS MONGOL ARMY COULD TRAVEL **96 KM** (60 MILES) IN ONE DAY

KILLED APPROXIMATELY **40 MILLION PEOPLE** IN HIS CONQUESTS

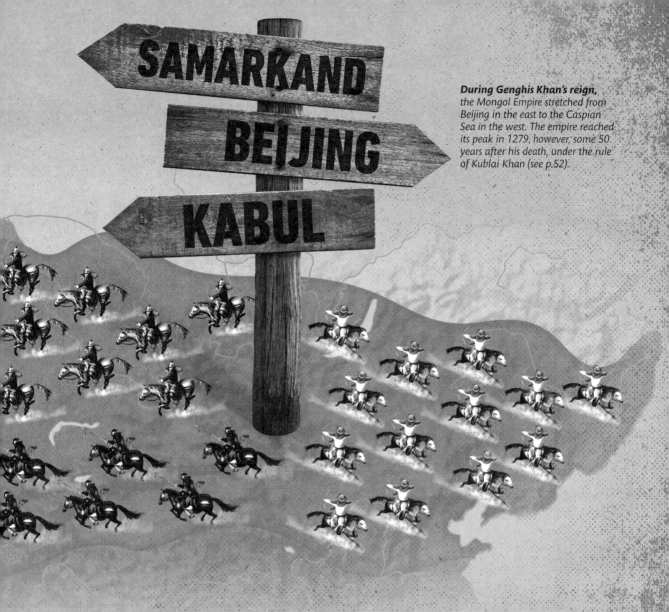

SAMARKAND

BEIJING

KABUL

During Genghis Khan's reign, the Mongol Empire stretched from Beijing in the east to the Caspian Sea in the west. The empire reached its peak in 1279, however, some 50 years after his death, under the rule of Kublai Khan (see p.52).

CONQUERED AN AREA OF
13.5 MILLION SQ KM
(8.4 MILLION SQ MILES)

RULED OVER
50 NATIONS

"**Conquer** your enemies, and **lead long** and **happy lives.**"

Genghis Khan, 1223

Khan commanded expert archers and lancers who, even when not engaged on campaigns, trained constantly. Genghis Khan's forces travelled in hordes where each rider had as many as five horses. By swapping between their mounts, his men could travel vast distances with stealth and accuracy, and at unprecedented speeds – standing armies had little hope of defeating them.

Genghis Khan was also a master of psychological warfare, and in the tradition of nomadic tribes, his conquests were vicious. Anything that was not useful to him or the army, or was a potential threat, would be destroyed. He used spies and propaganda to induce terror into those he intended to conquer, with some cities surrendering before his army had even arrived. Many people even took their own lives preemptively, rather than face being conquered by Genghis Khan.

A lasting legacy

Beyond the battlefields, Genghis Khan proved to be a great and fair ruler. He introduced a series of just laws – the Yassa code – throughout his empire. He encouraged trade, conducted regular censuses, and set up a communication network using a series of messengers who conveyed information across the empire. Moreover, he embraced the cultures of his conquered nations, and allowed some religious freedom within his empire, embracing Confucianism, Buddhism, Nestorian Christianity, Islam, and his own religion: Tengrism.

In 1227, Genghis Khan died while on a military campaign, possibly from a fever. In accordance with his wishes, his body was given a secret burial in the Mongolian steppe. According to legend, in order to preserve the secrecy of his burial, anyone who encountered the funeral procession was killed.

CREATED A **POSTAL SERVICE** THAT USED **50,000 HORSES**

ORDERED THE **CREATION** OF A **NEW WRITING SYSTEM,** BASED ON THE UYGHUR ALPHABET

OUTLAWED THE PRACTICE OF **KIDNAPPING WOMEN**

16 MILLION MEN **ALIVE TODAY** CARRY **HIS DNA**

"I AM THE PUNISHMENT OF GOD... IF YOU HAD NOT COMMITTED GREAT SINS, GOD WOULD NOT HAVE SENT A PUNISHMENT LIKE ME UPON YOU."

Genghis Khan
Quoted in *The History of the World Conquerer*, Ata-Malik Juvayni, Persian historian, c. 1200

A ruthless conqueror from Transoxiana (modern day Uzbekistan), Amir Timur conducted brutal raids across Central Asia, and built a large but short-lived empire that stretched from Turkey to northern India.

Amir Timur was born in Transoxiana, Central Asia, into the Barlas tribe, a Turco-Mongol clan of horsemen, in 1336. He aspired to rebuild Genghis Khan's empire and position himself as its ruler. When Amir Qazaghan, ruler of Transoxiana, was assassinated in 1358, a power stuggle unsued for sovereignty of the territory. Timur formed successive alliances with warlords to defeat competing rivals, who he would later betray - including a descendant of Genghis Khan, and his brother-in-law. By 1370, Timur ruled Transoxiana.

Over the next 30 years, Timur commanded a highly organized army of mounted bowmen in a series of vicious conquests across Western, Southern, and Central Asia. Managing every aspect of his 200,000-strong army, Timur divided each regiment into groups of thousands, hundreds, and tens. His military success lay in the mobility of his army, and his ruthless exploitation of his enemies' weaknesses, massacring thousands and levelling whole cities. Timur also used psychological warfare, building pyramids out of the skulls of his enemies, spreading fear among any that dared to oppose him.

Timur was the last of the nomadic warlords of Central Asia. His dynasty, the Timurids, collapsed after years of infighting among his successors.

Timur led a successful siege on the sea-castle Smyrna (now Izmir, western Turkey), 1402, that was held by the Knights of Rhodes, a prestigious military unit.

"I am **the scourge of God appointed** to **chastise you.**"

Amir Timur, 1401

MILESTONES

TRIBAL LEADER	REGIONAL POWER	DESTROYS RIVAL	CONQUERS INDIA
Becomes head of the Barlas tribe after its leader fled, and forms alliance with Husayn of Balkh, 1358.	Turns on Husayn, leading to Siege of Balkh, 1370. Conquers the city, giving him power over the region.	Defeats Tokhtamysh, a prominent khan of the Blue Horde, at Battle of the Terek River, 1395.	Defeats the Sultan of Delhi, 1398, and absorbs northern India into the Timurid Empire.

AMIR

TIMUR

1336–1405

Encouraged by religious voices, Joan of Arc masterminded a major triumph for the French over the English during the Hundred Years' War when she was just 17 years old. She remains a national icon of France to this day.

Joan was born to a devout Roman Catholic peasant family in a village in the region of Lorraine, France, during what became known as the Hundred Years' War (see p.61). At the age of 13, Joan began to hear voices, which she believed were saints sent from God. They told her that she was destined to go to the French King Charles VI's heir, the Dauphin, to help him defeat the English, and ensure that he was rightfully anointed the king of France. In 1428, aged just 16, Joan made her first attempt to speak with the Dauphin via a local commander, but she was dismissed immediately. Later that year, after her village was attacked by English-supporting Burgundians, the voices started to tell Joan that she must save the French troops besieged by the English in Orléans.

Joan's mission

In 1429, Joan made her second attempt to speak to the Dauphin, travelling to his palace at Chinon through English-occupied territory disguised as a male soldier. After hearing Joan's prophecy, and an investigation of it by a theological council at Poitiers, the Dauphin became convinced, and allowed her to lead a holy war against the English, granting her men, armour, a horse, and her own banner.

Joan's forces reached besieged Orléans on 29 April 1429, where her arrival inspired the French soldiers

Joan rallied her troops in battle using her banner. It pictured angels presenting God with the fleur-de-Lis, a symbol commonly associated with French royalty.

1412–1431

JOAN OF ARC

"I was **13** when I had a **voice from God** for my **help and guidance.**"

Joan of Arc, 1431

already there with renewed religious and patriotic enthusiasm. Roused by Joan's presence, the French troops successfully attacked the English strongholds around Orléans. With the enemy in retreat, the six-month siege was finally lifted.

Fulfilling the prophesies

Following victory at Orléans, Joan began to train her troops, and although she had no formal military training herself, she showed an instinctive grasp of warfare. The Dauphin allowed Joan to merge her army with the Duke John II of Alençon's troops, and was granted joint command of the combined forces. Their aim was to retake Reims, the city where French kings were traditionally crowned.

Fighting their way through the Loire Valley, their troops expelled the English from several towns en route, including Beaugency, Janville, and Meung, and the region surrounding Patay. These victories inspired more people to rise up against the English, and hundreds joined Joan's cause. Towns and cities opened their

gates to her men, and the French people pledged allegiance to the Dauphin, who was crowned Charles VII in July 1429.

With Reims secure and Charles now king, Joan then wanted to retake Paris. In September 1429, French troops made an unsuccessful attack on the English there, which was followed by Joan's capture the following year. Tried for a variety of offences, including heresy and blasphemy by a group of English clerics, and English-supporting French nobles and Burgundians, Joan was burned at the stake in Rouen.

After Joan's death, her mother, Isabelle Romée, successfully petitioned the Pope for a retrial in 1455–56, which reversed the original verdict and declared her innocent. The Roman Catholic church canonized Joan as a saint in 1920.

Joan was burned at the stake on a variety of charges, including dressing as a man, which at the time was seen by many as a transgression of the natural order.

CLAIMED DIVINE REVELATION

HAD BLASPHEMOUS VISIONS

FIRST **RALLIED TROOPS** IN BATTLE AGED **17**

NEVER FOUGHT IN **BATTLE** HERSELF

TRIED FOR **70 CHARGES** (LATER REDUCED TO 12)

DRESSED IN MALE CLOTHING

COMMITTED HERESY

ABANDONED HER PARENTS

"KING OF ENGLAND, AND YOU,
DUKE OF BEDFORD, WHO CALL
YOURSELF REGENT OF THE
KINGDOM OF FRANCE... SETTLE
YOUR DEBT TO THE KING OF
HEAVEN; SURRENDER TO THE
MAIDEN, WHO IS SENT HERE
BY GOD, THE KEYS TO ALL THE
GOOD TOWNS YOU TOOK AND
VIOLATED IN FRANCE."

Joan of Arc
An excerpt from a letter dictated by Joan of Arc to the English forces, 22 March 1429

Joan of Arc depicted on a stained glass window
in St Sulpice Church, Brittany, France. ▶

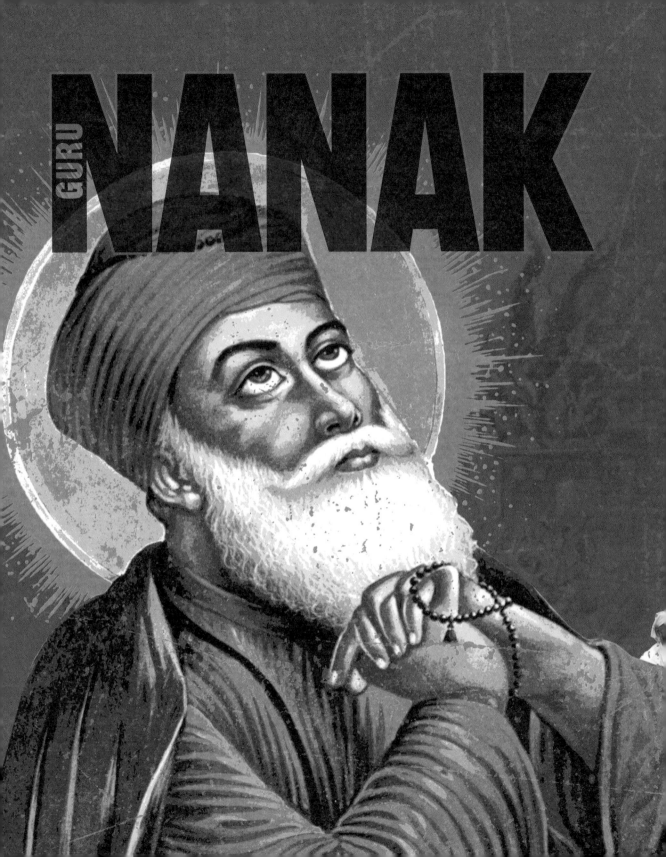

The founder and first guru of Sikhism, Nanak Dev Ji transformed ideas about religion in 16th-century India, teaching that God's presence could be found from within, without ritual or dogma. He preached against caste and gender discrimination, and advocated a selfless, all-encompassing approach to humanity.

Nanak Dev Ji was born on 14 April 1469 in Talwandi (later named Nankana Sahib), a village near Lahore, now in the Pakistan Punjab. His birth date, marked by *Vaishaki* (New Year), is one of the most important events in the Sikh calendar. His family were Hindus, but fascinated by Muslims practising their faith in his community, he studied both Islam and Hinduism.

In his youth, Nanak rebelled against the religious dogma that dominated Indian society, where Hinduism classified people according to their profession, placing them in one of numerous castes and sub-castes. People could not marry across castes, or eat certain foods prepared for them by someone of a lower caste. The only way to achieve a higher social status was to live a virtuous life and be rewarded after death by reincarnation into a different caste. Those outside the caste structure, at the very bottom of society, were known as "untouchables".

Nanak's family were of a high caste, but at the age of 11 he refused the traditional *janeu* (sacred thread) which boys were expected to wear to indicate their caste. Aged 12, he married, then aged 16 followed his father into accountancy and had a family. However, he gradually withdrew from

MILESTONES

DEFIES TRADITION
Rejects caste system and refuses to follow Hindu or Islamic tradition. Seeks a new path by meditation.

DISCOVERS NEW WAY
Receives a vision and learns that men and women are equal, and that the path to God is though devotion.

SPREADS HIS IDEALS
Travels widely, spreading his philosophy on tours across Asia, finding followers and converts.

BECOMES A GURU
Settles in Kartarpur as a peasant farmer, 1521, where, as a guru, he continues to teach.

APPOINTS SUCCESSOR
Nominates Bhai Lehna as his successor, who becomes the second guru of Sikhism, Guru Angad.

The Golden Temple at Amritsar, India, built by the fifth guru, Arjan, in 1601, is the holiest gurdwara (place of worship) for Sikhs.

everyday life, becoming more interested in pursuing spiritual ideals. According to Sikh tradition, Nanak would go to the river before sunrise to bathe, meditate, and sing hymns. On one occasion in 1499, he left his clothes by the side of a stream and disappeared. He returned after three days proclaiming to have seen a vision of God and wanting to spread his message.

Long years of travel

Nanak declared that God existed outside of the confines of religious dogma, and refused to follow Hinduism or Islam.

Instead, he wanted to teach the world about a new democratic, spiritual existence in which there was a universal God above all religions, where men and women were equal, and adopted an ethic of honest work and a selfless devotion to helping those in need.

From 1500 to 1524, Nanak spent his years writing, teaching, and spreading *Sikhi* (his doctrine meaning disciple). He covered an estimated 17,000 miles (28,000 km) on five different tours, known as *Udasis*, that took him across India and as far afield as Sri Lanka, Tibet, Myanmar

The practice of langar, or "free kitchen", first popular with 12th and 13th-century sufis (Islamic mystics), was adopted by Nanak. All visitors to a gurdwara (place of worship) are offered a free meal regardless of their caste, religion, gender, or ethnicity.

(Burma), Turkey, and the Arab countries. His teaching attracted many converts including Muslims and Hindus – among the most devoted was his Muslim travelling companion Bhai Mardana.

Philosophy and final days

Nanak shunned ritual and superstitious practices, which he saw as meaningless, believing that people are responsible for their own actions and can only earn forgiveness by direct meditation with God. Outspoken on equality for women, he contradicted long-held Hindu traditions that forbade women from certain aspects of worship, such as entering a temple. He also formalised the three duties every Sikh must carry out in their daily life: *Naam Japna* (meditate on God's name), *Kirat Karni* (earn an honest living), and *Vand Chhakna* (share one's earnings).

Towards the end of his life, Nanak lived in Kartarpur, a village in central Punjab. It is likely that Nanak had reached *Guru* status (an inspired religious teacher) by this time, and taught and granted blessings to disciples who gathered around him. He died in 1539, aged 70.

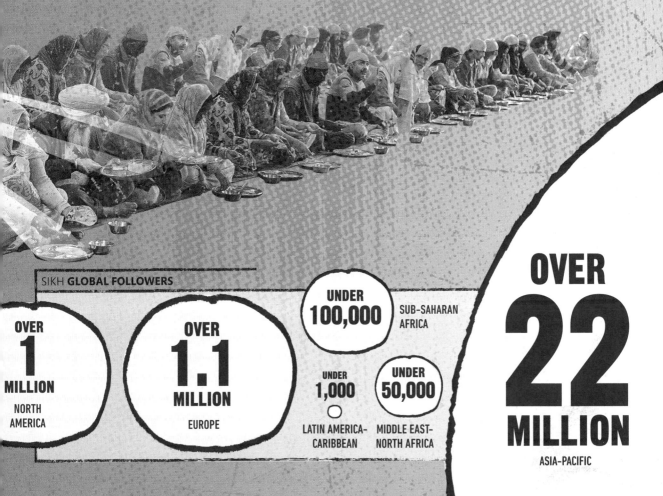

SIKH **GLOBAL FOLLOWERS**

OVER **1 MILLION**
NORTH AMERICA

OVER **1.1 MILLION**
EUROPE

UNDER **100,000**
SUB-SAHARAN AFRICA

UNDER **1,000**
LATIN AMERICA-CARIBBEAN

UNDER **50,000**
MIDDLE EAST-NORTH AFRICA

OVER **22 MILLION**
ASIA-PACIFIC

DIRECTORY

The earliest empires date to around 2300 BCE. Many empires were initially founded by military chiefs, and later maintained by dynastic emperors. The best rulers incorporated the cultures of their conquered people and practised religious tolerance to dispel discontent.

MENES
c.3100 BCE

The legendary first pharaoh of ancient Egypt, Menes is traditionally credited with uniting Upper and Lower Egypt to create a single peaceful and prosperous kingdom, and with establishing the First Dynasty. He is also typically ascribed as the founder of Memphis, the capital of ancient Egypt. However, due to a lack of archaeological evidence to Menes' existence as an individual, many scholars now believe that the name "Menes" is a title used for several early pharaohs, including King Narmer, and that their collective achievements have been attributed to this single identity.

SARGON THE GREAT
c.2334–2284 BCE

In the 23rd century BCE, Sargon of Akkad was said to have risen from humble beginnings to become the founding ruler of the Akkadian Empire. One of the world's first empire builders, he seized the Sumerian (south Iraq) city-states and expanded his territory by conquering southern Mesopotamia, Syria, Anatolia, and Elam (part of modern-day Iran). As such he created the world's first thriving multinational empire, establishing infrastructure, encouraging trade, and even creating the world's first postal system. His 50-year reign is remembered as a golden age of the Akkadian Empire.

HAMMURABI
1810–1750 BCE

The best-known ruler of Babylon's First Dynasty, Hammurabi inherited the throne to become the sixth Babylonian king. He was an accomplished military leader and expanded the kingdom to conquer all of ancient Mesopotamia, uniting it under a single authority. He was known for his public works: constructing canals and irrigation systems, improving food distribution, and building temples. Hammurabi's greatest legacy is his code of law, which established a set punishment for every crime; one of the earliest codes of this type, it set a standard for rulers of later societies to follow.

CYRUS THE GREAT
c.600–530 BCE

Cyrus II of Persia was founder and first king of the Achaemenid Empire, the first Persian empire. His campaigns defeated the most powerful kingdoms of the time – Media, Babylonia, and Lydia – and brought most of the Middle East under Persian control. Yet Cyrus allowed local administrations to persist and accepted the cultures and religions of those he conquered. In doing so he earned respect and loyalty, and became known as the "Father" of his people.

CONFUCIUS
551–479 BCE

The Chinese philosopher Confucius (Kongfuzi) set out a series of moral and ethical teachings that have greatly influenced Chinese culture to this day. He saw himself as the voice of an ancient moral tradition that promoted virtuous living, the respect of elders, and family loyalty, and emphasized the importance of teachers and leaders as role models for society. His teachings are contained within the *Analects* – a collection of his thinking, compiled by his disciples, and which includes, most famously, the quote: "What you do not wish for yourself, do not do to others".

ASHOKA
c.300–238 BCE

The third and last emperor of India's Mauryan Empire, Ashoka expanded the empire to cover almost all of the Indian subcontinent, from modern-day Afghanistan to Bangladesh. Initially a harsh ruler of his own people and conqueror of other territories – notably a state called Kalinga – he later converted to Buddhism and proclaimed remorse for the suffering he had inflicted. From that point Ashoka renounced war. In further edicts, he called for social compassion and religious freedom. He also turned the tradition of Buddhism into a state ideology and is largely responsible for its status as a world religion today.

SPARTACUS
c.111–71 BCE

While little is known conclusively about the life of Spartacus, historical records agree that he was a famous former gladiator who led the most successful slave rebellion in ancient Roman history. Formerly from Thrace, a region northwest of Macedonia, Spartacus was enslaved by the Romans and was then trained as a gladiator in Capua. Along with 70 others, he escaped from a gladiatorial training camp and spent two years trying to avoid recapture while raiding towns for supplies. Spartacus proved himself a master military tactician, leading two successful victories over the Romans.

ATTILA THE HUN
406–53 CE

One of the most feared and brilliant military leaders in history, Attila ruled the Huns, an ancient nomadic people, and headed an empire including other nomadic tribes. A charismatic leader and skilled horseman, Attila forged his Hunnic Empire in less than 10 years. He led his vast armies in a series of campaigns against the Eastern and Western Roman Empires, to conquer an area reaching from Central Asia to Gaul (modern-day France). He died on his wedding night, choking on his own nosebleed while in a drunk stupor. Within 15 years of his death, Attila's empire had crumbled.

JUSTINIAN I
c. 482–565 CE

Flavius Justinius, also known as Justinian the Great, was emperor of the Byzantine Empire (the Eastern Roman Empire). During his 40-year reign he fought the Persians in the Caucasus and re-took North Africa from the Vandals, and Italy and Sicily from the Goths. He also launched an empire-wide initiative to build forts, bridges, churches (notably the church of Hagia Sophia in Constantinople), monasteries, and reservoirs. His greatest achievement was the codification of all Roman laws; known as the *Codex Justinianus*, these legal reforms laid the foundations of Byzantine law for over 900 years.

SUNDIATA KEITA
c. 1217–55

Information about Sundiata Keita, the founder of the Mali Empire in western Africa, is sourced from oral history. Born into the Keita clan in the kingdom of Kangaba, Sundiata survived the massacre of his family and became head of his clan. The ruling Ghanaian Empire was in decline and Sundiata increased his power by invading other states. When he destroyed the capital of Ghana, the former empire crumbled and Sundiata founded his own Mali Empire. He established Niani as his capital city, which became a centre for trade in West Africa.

ISABELLA I
1451–1504

Isabella I of Spain united two Spanish kingdoms by becoming Queen of Castile in 1474 and of Aragon in 1479; ruling both kingdoms with her husband Ferdinand II of Aragon. A staunch Catholic, Isabella established the Inquisition, a judicial institution intended to identify heretics. Among her greatest achievements was the capture of Granada – completing the Christian reconquest of Spain – and her sponsorship of Christopher Columbus's voyage to the Americas, which led to the founding of the Spanish Empire.

BABUR
1483–1530

A direct descendent of both Genghis Khan (pp.50–55) and Amir Timur (pp.56–57), Babur was the founding emperor of the Mughal Empire. Babur was born into the Turkish-influenced Barlas tribe, in central Asia. His first achievement, at 15 years old, was to briefly reclaim the empire's capital of Samarkand. He seized Kabul in 1504 and then Delhi in 1526, winning control of northern India. He is considered one of the Mughal dynasty's greatest emperors; in addition to his political and military achievements, he was also a gifted orator, poet, and writer.

MARTIN LUTHER
1483–1546

The German theologian Martin Luther was a pivotal figure in the development of Christianity and civilization in Europe. Having been ordained in 1507, he became disillusioned by the corruption in the Roman Catholic Church, and published several works rejecting its teachings. Luther was excommunicated, but his writings triggered the Protestant Reformation, resulting in the division of Western Christianity into different denominations. He also published a translation of the Bible's New Testament in the German vernacular, which helped the development and spread of a standardized German language.

2

CONQUEST AND LIBERTY

1500–1820

CORTES

HERNÁN

Courageous, daring, and ruthless, Hernán Cortés was a Spanish explorer and soldier who was responsible for conquering the vast Aztec Empire – in open defiance of the wishes of his superiors. The success of his expeditions opened the gold-rich region to Spain and other European powers, who went on to plunder it mercilessly.

Born in Medellín, south-western Spain into a family of lesser nobility, Hernán Cortés was ambitious from a young age. Aged only 19, he sought his fortune in the Americas, where Spain had recently established its first colonies, and sailed to Hispaniola, in the Caribbean Sea. In 1511, Cortés joined Diego Velázquez de Cuéllar, an aide of the governor of Hispaniola, on an expedition to conquer Cuba. Velázquez, now Governor of New Spain (Spain's colonies in North and Central America), was so impressed with Cortés' abilities that he appointed Cortés as his secretary; Cortés also served as mayor of Santiago, Cuba, and worked in Cuba's civil government, acquiring political power and influence in the thriving colony.

In 1518, Cortés persuaded Velázquez to make him commander of an expedition to Mexico. However, Velázquez, doubtless aware of Cortés' ambitious nature, restricted the scope of the expedition to exploration and trade. When Velázquez became aware of Cortés' intentions to personally profit from the enterprise, he cancelled the mission at the last minute. In an act of open mutiny, Cortés

Upon arriving in Mexico, Cortés had his ships scuttled to ensure that his men could not desert him. This tactic ensured the loyalty of his soldiers to their mission.

"What **men in all the world** have shown such **daring?**"

Bernal Díaz del Castillo, soldier under Hernán Cortés' leadership, 1568

MILESTONES

SEEKS FORTUNE	MEETS VELÁZQUEZ	DEFEATS THE AZTECS	FINAL CONQUEST
Sails to Santo Domingo, the capital of Hispaniola, 1504. Works nearby as a notary for several years.	Befriends Diego Velázquez and aids his conquest of Cuba, 1511. Becomes Velázquez's secretary.	Sails for Mexico, defying Velázquez's orders, 1519. Within just two years, wipes out the Aztec Empire, 1521.	Conquers the Baja California Peninsula, in northwestern Mexico, during his final expedition, 1536.

nevertheless set sail for Mexico, landing in the southeast state of Tabasco in March 1519. There, he fought and overcame local groups, including the Totonacs and the Tlaxcalans, and eventually challenged the Aztec ruler, Montezuma II. Montezuma accepted the Spanish peacefully and, as they advanced inland, he ordered the people of Cholula – a small town outside the Aztec capital of Tenochtitlán – to welcome them. However, Cortés, suspecting a trap, destroyed the town and massacred its entire population.

Tenochtitlán falls

In November 1519, Montezuma invited Cortés and his men into Tenochtitlán, in a bid to identify their weaknesses and later crush them. After hearing that several Spaniards had been killed on the coast by Aztecs, Cortés took Montezuma hostage in his own palace. Meanwhile, Velázquez had sent an expedition of 1,100 Spanish soldiers to Mexico to arrest Cortés, who left Tenochtitlán to defeat them. Upon his return, Cortés discovered that his deputy governor, Pedro de Alvarado, had ordered an unprovoked massacre of Aztecs. Montezuma had been killed, by the Spanish or by his own people (according to differing accounts), and Tenochtitlán had fallen into disarray. Cortés and his men fled the city, before returning in 1521 to lay siege to it for three months. Weakened by hunger, lack of fresh water, and diseases brought by the European invaders, such as smallpox, the Aztecs were unable to defend their capital. Cortés renamed Tenochtitlán as Mexico City and plundered the fallen empire for Spain.

Cortés ruled Mexico from 1521 to 1524 and was made governor of "New Spain" (Spain's conquered territory in the Americas). He continued to conduct expeditions before returning to Spain for the final time in 1541. When he died in 1547 in Seville, he was planning another voyage to the New World.

"We Spaniards know a sickness of the heart that only gold can cure."

Hernán Cortés, c. 1521

Cortés and his forces were comprehensive in their destruction of the Aztec Empire through their superior weaponry and sophisticated military strategies. They also inadvertently spread diseases that the Aztecs had no resistance to, which killed thousands.

400,000 AZTECS LIVED IN TENOCHTITLÁN ON THE EVE OF HIS CONQUEST

FIRST SAILED TO MEXICO WITH 11 SHIPS, 508 SOLDIERS, AND 16 HORSES

OVER HALF THE POPULATION DIED IN THE SIEGE OF THE CITY

MONTEZUMA II

Born in 1466, Montezuma II served as a captain under his uncle Ahuitzotl before succeeding him in 1502 and becoming emperor.

Montezuma controlled the Aztec Empire when it was at its greatest extent, stretching as far as modern-day Honduras and Nicaragua. He first met with Cortés on 8 November 1519, on the causeway leading into Tenochtitlán, where he showered Cortés with gifts before inviting him into the city. Montezuma was regarded as a traitor due to his affiliation with his Spanish captors, and was taken hostage by the Spanish and forced to placate the growing unrest of his people. It is believed that he was eventually killed in 1521, either by rioting Aztecs or by the Spanish.

Known in the West as "the Magnificent" and in the Muslim world as "the Lawgiver", Sultan Suleiman I was the greatest ruler of the Ottoman Empire, governing lands across Europe, Asia, and Africa. A patron of the arts who displayed religious tolerance, Suleiman was nonetheless merciless to his rivals and also to his own sons.

MILESTONES

COMES TO POWER
Becomes sultan of the Ottoman Empire at age 25, 1520, succeeding his father Selim I.

WAR WITH EUROPE
From the 1520s, embarks on war with Christian Europe that continues for most of his reign.

AGREES TO PEACE
Signs Treaty of Constantinople, 1533, briefly halting his war against Christian Europe.

CONQUERS BAGHDAD
From the 1530s, wages war with the Safavid Empire in Persia. Gains control of Baghdad.

SIGNS PEACE TREATY
Signs Peace of Amasya, 1555, securing a truce with the Safavid Empire that lasts 20 years.

Born in around 1494, Suleiman came from a line of Ottoman conquerors. His great-grandfather Mehmed II had captured the great city of Constantinople from the Christians in 1453, and his father, Selim I, expanded the empire enormously, adding Egypt and the holy city of Mecca to the Ottoman domains in 1516–17.

Suleiman spoke several languages fluently and was an acclaimed poet, as well as a competent goldsmith. Under his rule, the Ottoman Empire enjoyed a golden age in culture and administration. He founded schools and embellished his capital with magnificent mosques. Unlike former Ottoman Sultans, he allowed Christians and Jews to practise their faith. The sultan also issued a new legal code that would last for three centuries, which reformed taxation, education, land ownership, and criminal law.

War and conquest
Since Mehmed II's capture of Constantinople, Ottoman sultans had claimed imperial authority over all other rulers. Suleiman spent most of his reign at war with Christian Europe, asserting this claim to Ottoman dominance by expanding his territory and the scope of Islam. Starting with the conquests

Suleiman commissioned grand architect Mimar Sinan to build the Süleymaniye Mosque, an architectural landmark of modern-day Istanbul, in 1550.

"**In this world** a **spell of health** is the **best state.**"

Suleiman the Magnificent

1494–1566

SULEIMAN

THE MAGNIFICENT

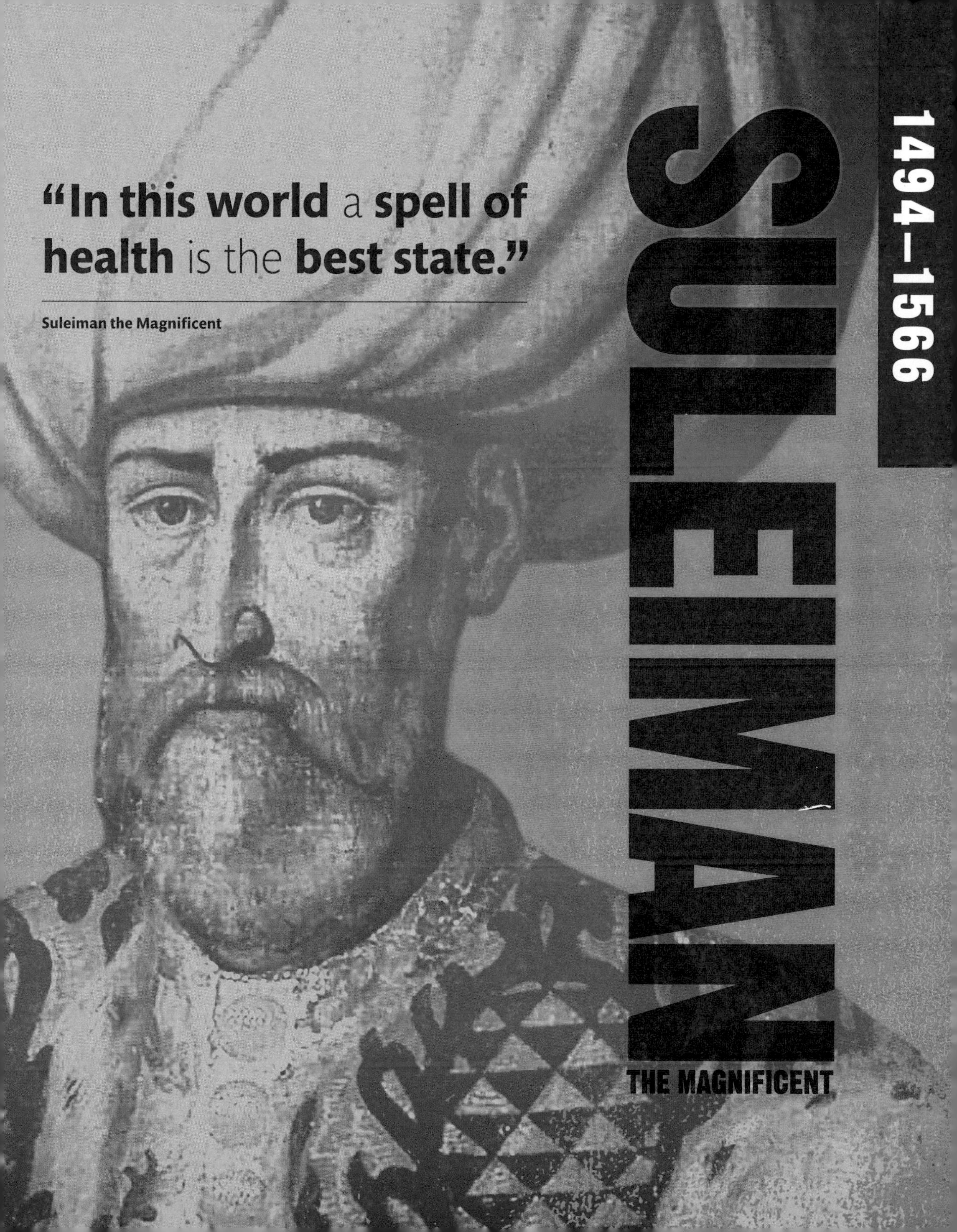

of Belgrade (Serbia) and Rhodes (Greece) in 1521–22, and most famously crushing the Hungarian forces at the Battle of Mohács in 1526, he led a great army that combined gunpowder weapons with the fighting skills of Asia's nomadic horsemen. At sea, his vast naval fleet dominated the Mediterranean, and reached as far as Yemen, India, and Indonesia.

In 1529, Suleiman unsuccessfully tried to capture Vienna, heart of the Habsburg-ruled Holy Roman Empire – a second attack on Austria in 1532 also failed. Over the next decade he fought repeatedly with the Habsburgs when invading Hungary and Moldavia, while also waging war with the Safavid rulers of Persia. Suleiman eventually gained control of Baghdad and part of the Persian Gulf coast, while Persia remained under Safavid rule.

Power struggles and death
In contrast to his military successes, Suleiman's personal life was tumultuous. Ibrahim Pasha, his grand vizier (prime minister) had been a friend since his youth; but in 1536, Suleiman, fearful of his vizier's growing influence, ordered him to be executed.

Mustafa, Suleiman's son by his wife Gülbehar, was deemed the most suited successor to the sultan by the 1550s.

Suleiman's other wife, Hürrem, persuaded him that Mustafa was plotting to oust him. In 1553, Suleiman had Mustafa executed, triggering a power struggle between Hürrem's sons Bayezid and Selim. Bayezid was also killed on his father's orders, leaving Selim as the sole heir.

The last years of Suleiman's life were darkened by failure in war. In 1565 his forces failed to drive the Knights of St John out of their stronghold on Malta. The following year, while on campaign in Hungary, Suleiman died in his tent aged 72.

Suleiman's reign oversaw the golden age of the Ottoman Empire, which was marked by territorial expansion, an economic boom, and a flourishing culture.

GOLDEN AGE

TAX REFORM   **JUST LAWS**

BECAME SULTAN AT THE AGE OF 25

EXECUTED 2 OF HIS SONS

RULED AS SULTAN FOR 46 YEARS

"The **sultan of sultans**, the sovereign of sovereigns... the shadow of god upon Earth."

Suleiman the Magnificent, 1536

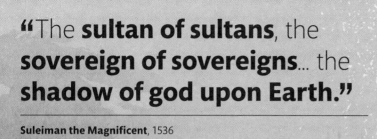

MIHRIMAH **SULTAN**

Born in 1522, Mihrimah was the daughter of Suleiman the Magnificent and his wife Hürrem.

Mihrimah exercised significant influence over political decision-making and diplomacy. She married Rüstem Pasha, grand vizier for much of Suleiman's reign, becoming Suleiman's most trusted female adviser after Hürrem's death in 1558. During the subsequent reign of his brother, Selim II, she held sway in the Topkapi Palace as a patron of the arts and chief of the imperial harem. She died in 1578.

SPREAD OF ISLAM

SUCCESSFUL CONQUESTS

Elizabeth I, Queen of England and Ireland, was the second daughter of King Henry VIII, and the last Tudor monarch. During her reign she led England to victory over the Spanish Armada, began to formalize the separation of the Church of England from the church in Rome, and paved the way for a "Golden Age" in English art and literature.

MILESTONES

ACCUSED OF TREASON
Held captive in the Tower of London on grounds that she has taken part in a Protestant coup, 1554.

SUCCEEDS MARY
After Mary's death, becomes queen, 1558. Crowned at Westminster Abbey.

ACT OF SUPREMACY
Puts forward Act of Supremacy, placing the monarchy over the Church of England, 1559.

SPANISH ARMADA
Leads country against unsuccessful invasion by Philip II and his Spanish Armada, 1588.

Born at Greenwich Palace, London, 7 September 1533, Elizabeth was the first child of Henry VIII and Anne Boleyn, his second wife. When Elizabeth was just two-and-a-half years old, her mother was accused of adultery and treason, and subsequently executed. Elizabeth was declared illegitimate, and denied the right to accession. Following Henry VIII's death in 1547, Elizabeth's nine-year-old half-brother, Edward, was crowned King, and she joined the household of Henry VIII's sixth wife, Catherine Parr. During his brief reign, the Protestant Edward made lasting contributions to the English Reformation that Elizabeth would eventually further. Upon Edward's death in 1553, Elizabeth's Catholic elder, half-sister, Mary, became queen.

The road to monarchy

Soon after taking the throne, Mary had Elizabeth imprisoned in the Tower of London, suspecting her involvement in the Wyatt rebellion, a Protestant coup which took its name from one of its leaders, Thomas Wyatt. Mary's reign was largely characterised by brutality and religious persecution. A fiercely devout Catholic, she had hundreds of Protestants burned at the stake for heresy. In 1558, following Mary's death, the Protestant Elizabeth came to the throne, and many hoped she would represent a step away from Mary's ideals. While she re-established the

Elizabeth was held in the Tower of London for two months on suspicion of treason. No evidence could be found by interrogators, however, and she was released.

ELIZABETH I

1533–1603

"I am **already bound** unto a husband... **the kingdom of England.**"

Queen Elizabeth I, 1599

Protestant religion, she also made attendance at Catholic Mass punishable by fine, and made the saying of Mass punishable by death, although this sentence was very rarely carried out. To Elizabeth, there was little benefit in persecuting Catholics, so long as they obeyed her laws.

Married to her country

Elizabeth's advisers urged her to marry to ensure a successor to the throne, and in the interests of foreign diplomacy – Parliament even threatened to withhold money in a bid to force her hand. However, Elizabeth believed that if she married, she would have to cede some of her power to her consort; hence, she became known as the Virgin Queen.

Elizabeth received proposals from many European leaders, including Philip II of Spain, but she rebuffed them all.

Diplomatic prowess

Politically, Elizabeth demonstrated shrewd understanding. In speeches to Parliament, she often used a "language of love" to appeal to her audience's sympathies and make the rulership of a female monarch seem more palatable.

In military affairs, she also showed considerable strength. In 1588, in one of the most well known sagas in English history, Philip II of Spain launched an Armada of ships to invade England and topple Elizabeth. Its resounding failure, and her patriotic defiance, created a surge of support for Elizabeth's reign.

The arts also flourished under Elizabeth's patronage, and her name has since become synonymous with an era of unrivalled creativity in English literature.

In her final years, Elizabeth became increasingly isolated. Upon her death, aged 69, the English crown went to James VI of Scotland.

HENRY VIII

King Henry VIII (1491–1547) was Elizabeth I's father and founder of the Church of England.

Henry VIII was intelligent and cultured, but frivolous with the Crown's money. Widely known as the king who married six times in order to father a male successor, he is also known for establishing the Church of England, in part so that he could have his first marriage, to Catherine of Aragon, annulled. Henry VIII was the first monarch in England to deny papal authority, instead claiming the divine right of kings.

EXECUTED 750 CATHOLIC REBELS WHO PLOTTED TO DEPOSE HER IN 1569

REIGNED FOR 44 YEARS AND 127 DAYS

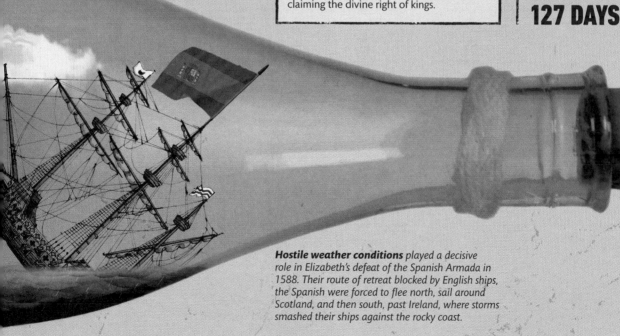

Hostile weather conditions played a decisive role in Elizabeth's defeat of the Spanish Armada in 1588. Their route of retreat blocked by English ships, the Spanish were forced to flee north, sail around Scotland, and then south, past Ireland, where storms smashed their ships against the rocky coast.

"I KNOW I HAVE THE BODY OF A WEAK, FEEBLE WOMAN; BUT I HAVE THE HEART AND STOMACH OF A KING, AND OF A KING OF ENGLAND TOO, AND THINK FOUL SCORN THAT PARMA OR SPAIN, OR ANY PRINCE OF EUROPE, SHOULD DARE TO INVADE THE BORDERS OF MY REALM."

Queen Elizabeth I

Excerpt from a speech to troops at Tilbury in anticipation of the Spanish Armada, 9 August 1588

◄ *Elizabeth addresses her troops* in an engraving from a book by Theophilus Camden, 1832.

TOKUGAWA

EYASU

One of the most influential figures in Japanese history, Tokugawa Ieyasu was a warlord and politician who unified Japan and maintained undisputed control of the country. He founded the Tokugawa shogunate, which brought an end to clan warfare in Japan, and heralded over two centuries of peace and unity.

Originally named Matsudaira Takechiyo, Ieyasu was born into the Matsudaira clan at Okazaki castle, in Mikawa, 1542, during the Sengoku Period (1467–1600), a time of conflict between rival Japanese clans. As the son of a *daimyō* (warlord), Ieyasu was seen as a prize hostage, which saw him abducted first aged five by the Oda clan, led by Oda Nobuhide, and then handed over, aged nine, as a hostage to the Imagawa clan, under Imagawa Yoshimoto.

Aged 13, and with his father now dead, Ieyasu was allowed to return to Mikawa by Yoshimoto, under orders to fight for him against the Oda clan. However, when Yoshimoto was defeated by the new Oda leader, Nobunaga, in 1560, Ieyasu seized his ancestral home, and pledged allegiance to the Oda. In 1566, he took the name Tokugawa Ieyasu, linking himself to a distantly related Tokugawa clan that had previously ruled Japan.

Rise to power

Ieyasu led many military victories for the Oda clan against enemy clans, such as the Battle of Anegawa (1570) and the Battle of Nagashino (1575). In 1579, when Nobunaga accused Ieyasu's wife and eldest son of

"Patience is the source of eternal peace; treat anger as an enemy."

Tokugawa Ieyasu, 1604

MILESTONES

ASSUMES POWER
Forced to fight for a rival clan, he seizes his family lands in 1560, when the clan leader is defeated.

BUILDS CLAN ALLIANCE
Allies himself with the Oda clan and fights alongside them until its leader, Nobunaga, dies in 1582.

FOUNDS A KINGDOM
Consolidates his territories in Japan while new Oda leader, Hideyoshi, tries to invade Korea, 1592–98.

DEFEATS RIVALS
When Hideyoshi dies, he defeats clans loyal to his young son in 1600, at Battle of Sekigahara.

JAPAN IS UNITED
Appointed shogun in 1603, he becomes sole ruler of Japan, before handing power to son.

"Harm will **befall** one who **knows only success** and has **never** experienced **failure."**

Tokugawa Ieyasu, 1604

*Ieyasu's **hard-line reforms** to Japan's political structures and international trade laid the stable foundations of the Tokugawa shogunate, lasting 265 years.*

ISOLATIONISM

CHRISTIANITY OUTLAWED

FOREIGN TRADE MONOPOLIZED

STRICT SOCIAL CLASS HIERARCHY

conspiring against Oda clan interests, Ieyasu displayed ruthless dedication to their cause by having his wife killed, and forcing his son to commit suicide.

Nobunaga died and was succeeded in 1582 by one of his captains, Toyotomi Hideyoshi (see box). Ieyasu challenged his rule two years later, but was defeated.

In 1590, Ieyasu and Hideyoshi became cautious allies to fight the opposing Hojo clan. After their victory, Hideyoshi ordered Ieyasu to vacate his homelands and relocate to new provinces. While Hideyoshi led two failed invasions of Korea, Ieyasu began to consolidate forces and administrative bases in his newfound provinces in Japan, centred around Edo (present day Tokyo).

When Hideyoshi died in 1598, his son, Toyotomi Hideyori, was too young to rule, so Ieyasu joined a council of regents that ruled in his name. Eventually, vying for control of Japan at the Battle of Sekigahara in 1600, Ieyasu led a coalition of eastern clans to defeat opposing western clans loyal to Toyotomi Hideyori. Victorious, Ieyasu was appointed shogun in 1603 and became sole ruler of Japan. His shogunate would be the last in Japanese history.

The final shogunate

Ieyasu passed the title of shogun on to his son just two years later, but continued to run the country. He established peace and stability by banning Christian missionaries and restricting European trade with Japan, both of which he regarded with contempt as disruptive influences.

In the winter of 1614–15, Ieyasu, perceiving those loyal to Hideyori as the last major threat to his hold on power, besieged Hideyori and his supporters in Osaka Castle. The siege was split into two campaigns, lasting until the following summer: in June 1615, the castle fell, and Ieyasu had Hideyori and all of his surviving relatives killed. The next year, returning to his home at Sumpu, Ieyasu fell ill and died. Japan then remained at peace under the Tokugawa dynasty's rule for over two and a half centuries.

CLAIMED TO HAVE FOUGHT IN

90

BATTLES

LED

94,000 TROOPS IN THE SIEGE OF OSAKA

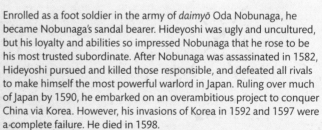

TOYOTOMI **HIDEYOSHI**

Known as the "Napoleon of Japan", Hideyoshi was born into a poor peasant family in 1536. Along with Ieyasu, he was a captain of the Oda clan, and later became a *daimyō* (warlord).

Enrolled as a foot soldier in the army of *daimyō* Oda Nobunaga, he became Nobunaga's sandal bearer. Hideyoshi was ugly and uncultured, but his loyalty and abilities so impressed Nobunaga that he rose to be his most trusted subordinate. After Nobunaga was assassinated in 1582, Hideyoshi pursued and killed those responsible, and defeated all rivals to make himself the most powerful warlord in Japan. Ruling over much of Japan by 1590, he embarked on an overambitious project to conquer China via Korea. However, his invasions of Korea in 1592 and 1597 were a complete failure. He died in 1598.

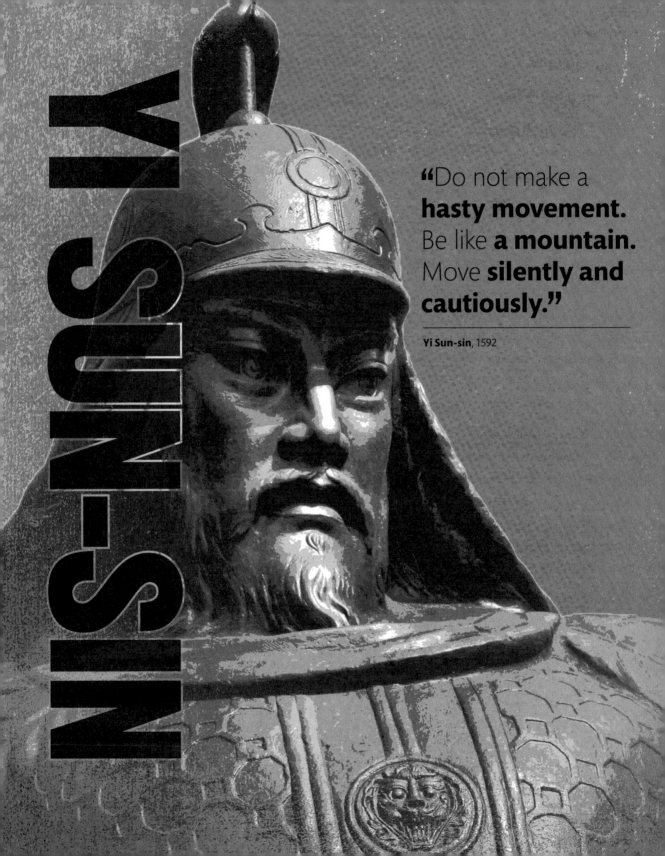

YI SUN-SIN

"Do not make a **hasty movement.** Be like **a mountain.** Move **silently and cautiously.**"

Yi Sun-sin, 1592

Admiral Yi Sun-sin was the hero of Korea's resistance to Japanese invasions in the late 16th century. Seen as one of the best naval commanders in history, he continues to be revered by Korean people today.

MILESTONES

FALSELY ACCUSED
Becomes a junior officer aged 32 but is demoted after false accusations of desertion.

COMMANDS FLEET
Appointed commander of Left Jeolla Naval District in 1591, he strengthens his fleet.

DEFEATS JAPANESE
Wins 15 battles against Japanese, 1592–94, ending their first invasion without losing a single Korean ship.

UNLIKELY VICTORY
Resumes command, 1597, and defeats Japanese at Battle of Myeongnyang with a fleet of only 13 ships.

FINAL CAMPAIGN
Finally defeats Japan, 1598, but is fatally wounded during battle.

Yi was born in Seoul on 28 April 1545 but grew up in the town of Asan. His family were aristocrats of the Deoksu Yi clan, who were out of favour with the Korean royal court. This may account for Yi's initial slow progress in his military career; he did not achieve junior officer rank until he was 32.

Fighting incursions by Manchurian Jurchen horsemen, Yi distinguished himself with his intelligence and bravery. Lacking wealth or political influence, however, he had little defence against the jealousy that was rife under the Korean monarchy. In the mid-1580s, he was falsely accused of desertion and reduced to the rank of a common soldier. However, his disgrace was brief – after progressing through a number of senior army positions, he was appointed commander of a fleet in southwest Korea in 1591.

Naval commander
With Korea facing seaborne invasion by the Japanese, Yi analyzed the situation and made a tactical battle plan, despite having no prior naval training. As the Japanese had more ships and soldiers than Korea, Yi predicted they would try to win by boarding and overpowering Korean vessels. Korea's advantage over Japan lay in it's ability to build

Yi updated the design of the 200-year-old kobukson (turtle ship), covering its deck with iron plates and spikes, and placing a cannon that could fire through the dragon's-head prow.

91

DESTROYED
30
JAPANESE
SHIPS
AT MYEONGYANG
WITHOUT LOSING A
SINGLE SHIP OF HIS OWN

UNDEFEATED IN ALL 23 OF HIS NAVAL ENGAGEMENTS

cannons, so Yi ordered the construction of many *panokseon* (cannon-armed warships) for his fleet. He also developed an improved armoured warship, the *kobukson* ("turtle ship") that would be secure against Japanese attack.

In April 1592, the Japanese invaded at Busan on Korea's south coast. Yi inflicted serious losses on the enemy ships. At the Battle of Sacheon in July his *panokseon* proved a huge success. Yi was shot in the shoulder, but he survived, and a flotilla of Japanese ships was destroyed. Later that year, in the Battle of Hansan Island, Yi won a resounding victory over the

Japanese, enveloping their fleet in a U-shaped "crane's wing" formation and devastating it by cannon fire. Out of 73 enemy ships, only 14 escaped. The Japanese abandoned their invasion, and the Korean government gave Yi total command of its navy.

Final stand

However, gratitude did not last, and enemies at King Seonjo's court, including a Japanese spy, conspired to have Yi dismissed in 1597. He was arrested and tortured, then reduced again to the rank of a common soldier. Later that year, the

133 WARSHIPS 200 SUPPORT SHIPS

RETREATED AFTER 30 WARSHIPS DESTROYED

HALF OF JAPANESE FORCES WOUNDED OR KILLED

Japanese invaded again, and in the ensuing battle Yi's successor Admiral Won died. Most of Korea's fleet was destroyed and the king had no choice but to recall Yi to command. Despite having only 13 warships, Yi defeated 133 Japanese ships in the Battle of Myeongnyang.

The Japanese invasion was forced to retreat; Yi routed them at the Battle of Noryang, 1598, but was shot and killed. On his orders, his death was hidden until the battle was over, to protect morale. Yi was not mourned at court, but his achievements were recognized later, with shrines built in his honour.

SEONJO OF JOSEON

Seonjo was the king of Korea during the Japanese invasions. Born in 1552, he succeeded to the throne at the age of 16.

The early years of his reign brought much-needed reforms. He is credited with reviving Confucian scholarship, fighting corruption, and improving the welfare of the people. Conservative advisors convinced him to reduce Korea's military, which left Korea unprepared to resist the Japanese invasions. By the time the Japanese were defeated in 1598 his son, Crown Prince Gwanghaegun was exercising power. Seonjo died in 1608.

KOREAN SHIPS OUTNUMBERED 10:1

Admiral Yi relied on his knowledge of local tide currents and lured the Japanese fleet into a trap during the Battle of Myeongnyang in 1597. The Japanese were first carried by strong tides into the firing line of his panokseon's cannons and then swept away in disarray.

"The battle is at its height... **Beat the war drums. Do not announce** my **death.**"

Yi Sun-sin, 1598

"I am the state."

Louis XIV, 1655

LOUIS XIV

One of the longest-serving European monarchs, and the most powerful of the French kings, Louis XIV came to the throne aged four and reigned for 72 years and 110 days. Known as the Sun King, Louis saw himself as the embodiment of state. His court was a centre of luxury and his reign was marked by costly wars.

MILESTONES

ASSUMES POWER
After becoming king aged four, starts to rule France with absolute power in 1661, aged 23.

STRATEGIC MARRIAGE
Marries Spanish princess Marie Thérèse to secure peace between France and Spain, 1660.

SQUANDERS WEALTH
Starts work improving Versailles, 1661, where he lavishes vast amounts of money over 50 years.

IMPROVES FINANCES
France almost bankrupt. Instigates tax and trade reforms during 1660s to bolster state finances.

EXPENSIVE WARS
Leads France in three costly wars with its neighbours (1672–1714) but gains little from them.

Louis XIV was born on 5 September 1638 into one of the most powerful dynasties in Europe, the Bourbons. After Louis's father, Louis XIII, died in 1643, his mother, Anne of Austria, ruled as sole regent on Louis's behalf, and governed France in conjunction with chief minister, Cardinal Mazarin.

After Mazarin's death in 1661, the 23-year-old Louis refused to appoint a prime minister, and began his personal reign, believing that he had a divine right and a God-given duty to rule France with absolute authority. In this break with convention, Louis established a system of monarchical rule that lasted until the French Revolution in 1789.

The extravagant king
In the late 1660s, Louis became increasingly devoted to the project of reconstructing his father's hunting lodge at Versailles, extending it into a conspicuously magnificent royal palace, which glorified him as the Sun King. Likening himself to the Greek deity Apollo, god of the sun, light, and knowledge, Louis emphasized his power and influence. A fervent patron of the arts, he left Paris for Versailles, which became a focus

Jean-Baptiste Colbert ran the state's financial affairs for Louis XIV. His economic reforms were undermined by Louis's costly wars.

for writers, artists, and musicians. Crucially, Louis permanently moved his court and the seat of government to Versailles, a decision that further alienated him from his people.

The Dynastic Wars

Seeking to make territorial gains, Louis waged a series of costly wars, known as the Dynastic Wars, as they involved some of the older noble families of Europe. In 1667, he initiated an unsuccessful attack on the Spanish Netherlands, although conquered territory along France's frontiers in a more successful second invasion five years later.

In 1685, Louis, a Roman Catholic, revoked the Edict of Nantes – legislation that had been introduced in 1598 to end the French Wars of Religion (1562–98), as it reinstated the civil rights of French Protestants. By revoking the act, Louis made Protestantism illegal, and forced Huguenots (French Protestants) to either convert or flee the country.

The revocation of the edict was also a factor in the formation of a "Grand Alliance" of Protestant powers – a European coalition of the Holy Roman Empire, including Holland, Austria, and Spain – that fought France from 1688–97 in a stalemated conflict, known as the War of the Grand Alliance.

Louis's final campaign was the War of the Spanish Succession (1701–14), in which France fought to secure the claim of Louis's grandson, the Duc d'Anjou, to

"It is **legal** because **I wish it.**"

Louis XIV, 1655

the Spanish throne. The 1713 Peace of Utrecht crowned the Duc as Philip V of Spain, but divided the Spanish Empire with few gains for France.

Legacy of the Sun King

Louis's reign enabled a golden age of the arts in France, brought industry under state control and boosted trade, and established France as the leading power in Europe. Yet the final years of his rule were also clouded by bereavement, military defeat, and a country-wide collapse in the French economy. By the end of his reign, Louis had created a pattern of absolute rule that would endure in France until the revolution (see p.108–09) in 1789. The Sun King died in 1715, aged 76.

Louis XIV was a patron of the arts, but caused religious disunity, and his extensive war campaigns undermined the French economy.

EDICT OF NANTES

WILLIAM OF **ORANGE**

Sovereign Prince of Orange and stadtholder of the Dutch Republic, William (1650–1702) was crowned king of England, Scotland, and Ireland in 1689, ruling jointly with his wife, Mary.

The Protestant son of Prince William II of Orange, and Mary, eldest daughter of Charles I of England, William was appointed stadtholder, or "king" of the Dutch Republic in 1672. Uniting the Netherlands with Spain in the Grand Alliance, he led his army against the invading French Catholic forces under Louis XIV. In 1677, William married his first cousin Mary, daughter of the Catholic James II of England. When James was deposed in 1688, William and Mary were made joint sovereigns the following year, restoring Protestantism to England, and securing greater powers for Parliament. Until his death William continued to lead European forces against French expansionism, mostly by championing the Grand Alliance.

SPENT **54 YEARS** REBUILDING **VERSAILLES**

COMMISSIONED **OVER 300** PAINTINGS AND STATUES OF HIMSELF

TRIPLED STATE DEBT BETWEEN **1645** AND **1715**

FREDERICK THE GREAT

Known as "Frederick the Great", Frederick II of Prussia established the state as a major European power. Although he had a reputation as a military genius, he lost as many battles as he won. His reign increased the militarism of the Prussian state, which was later glorified by Hitler.

Frederick was drawn to music and poetry, and was homosexual, all of which appalled his father, King Frederick William I, who often had him flogged. Aged 18, Frederick tried to flee to Britain with a friend, but his father had him arrested and forced him to witness his friend's execution.

After ascending the throne in 1740, Frederick introduced significant administrative reforms, built palaces, and was a patron of art and literature – but he devoted most of his energy to expanding his territory.

Military prowess

Within weeks of his succession, Frederick invaded Silesia (central Europe), triggering two wars with Austria (1740–42; 1744–45). In 1756, his troops then overran Saxony (north Germany), resulting in the Seven Years' War (1756–1763). When allied with Britain, he battled against the combined forces of Austria, Russia, and France, retaining Silesia in the process.

Frederick earnt widespread admiration for his set-piece (planned) battles, in which he often personally led his troops to victory. However, he also suffered serious defeats, notably at Kunersdorf in 1759.

Away from the battlefield, Frederick transformed Prussia, improving its agriculture and industry, and promoting education and the arts. In old age, he grew increasingly solitary, and died in 1786.

MILESTONES

PLANS FOR PRUSSIA
Succeeds father, 1740, seeking to unite his scattered kingdom in a single boundary.

SEIZES TERRITORY
Embarks on a series of wars with several neighbouring countries, seizing territory, 1740–72.

EUROPEAN POWER
Doubles size of Prussia's army by 1870, making the state one of the most powerful in Europe.

"Do you think **I take any pleasure** in... **causing death** in people unknown to me?"

Frederick the Great, 1749

Frederick defeated a French army twice the size of his own at the Battle of Rossback in 1757. His Prussian forces inflicted 7,000 casualties on the enemy within two hours, losing only 550 men.

99

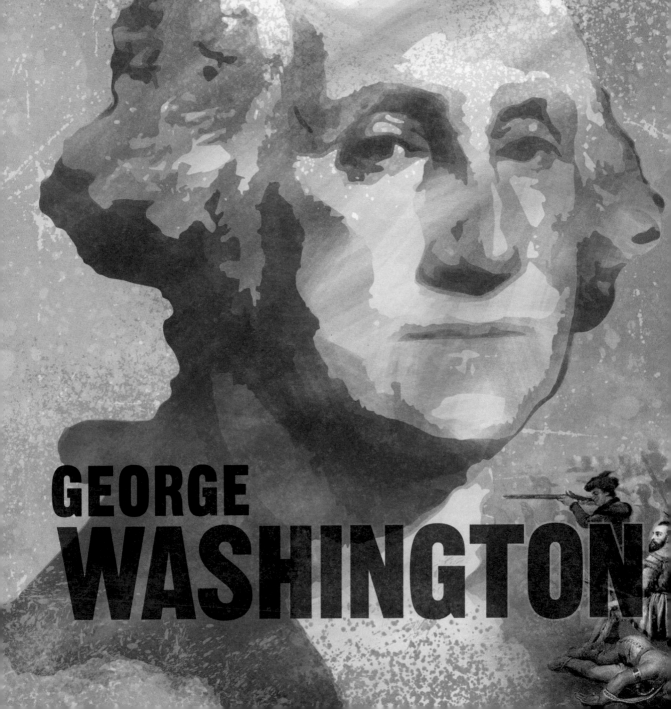

GEORGE
WASHINGTON

A soldier and statesman, George Washington is regarded as the "Father of America". He commanded the Continental Army during the American War of Independence and became the first US president.

George Washington was born in Virginia on 22 February 1732, to a wealthy landed family descended from English colonists. At the time, Virginia was one of the 13 colonies in North America ruled by the British Empire. When Washington was three years old, the family moved to a 2,500-acre plantation called Epsewasson, later renamed Mount Vernon by his brother. Washington inherited the plantation, and in 1759 he married Martha Custis, a widowed plantation owner with two children.

Washington's father died when George was only 11, and he was kept at home instead of following his brothers to school in Britain. He studied mathematics and began a career as a surveyor at the age of 16. His older brother Lawrence served in the Virginian militia, and after his death in 1752 the 20-year-old Washington decided to join the army.

Successful military career

Washington rose quickly through the ranks, and by February 1753, had been promoted to major at the age of just 21. He then became British military ambassador to the French officials, who were seeking to colonize what would become Ohio. By 1754 he was Lieutenant Colonel in the newly formed Virginia Regiment. The British and French fought over their American colonies in what became the French and Indian War (1754–63),

MILESTONES

JOINS MILITARY
Begins military career and enlists in the Virginian militia to honour his late brother, 1752.

FRENCH AND INDIAN WAR
Rallies troops during chaos of the Battle of Monongahela, 1755. Secures victory.

FIGHTS FOR FREEDOM
Chosen to lead the battle for American independence from the British Empire, 1775.

SIEGE OF YORKTOWN
Leads Continental Army to defeat the British at the Siege of Yorktown, 1781.

ELECTED PRESIDENT
Sworn in as the first president of the United States, 1789. Serves two terms.

During the French and Indian War (1754–63) *Washington (right) fought with the British against the French in a war over their expanding colonies.*

101

"FREEDOM OF SPEECH"

"GENERAL WELFARE"

"COMMON DEFENCE"

"WE THE PEOPLE"

"ESTABLISH JUSTICE"

"TRIAL BY JURY"

the North American setting for the global Seven Years' War (1756–63). Washington volunteered to fight with the British against the French. After success in the first battle, he was welcomed home and hailed as a hero by his fellow Virginians. A second battle, however, ended with Washington's only military surrender.

Meanwhile, many in the American colonies wanted independence from the British Empire that governed them.

This movement led to the American Revolution (see box) and in 1776 to the Declaration of Independence.

Leading a revolution

Determined to serve, Washington was unanimously elected leader of the military campaign for independence. In the initial battles, his troops scrutinized his leadership and doubted his abilities, but in 1776 he rallied them with a speech that changed their minds – "your country is at stake, your wives, your houses, and all that you hold dear" – and led his men to a decisive victory at the Battle of Princeton.

Washington showed ingenuity and bravery. His troops were inoculated against smallpox, and he enlisted a network of spies who supplied intelligence on British troops. He stood with his men

---

THE **AMERICAN REVOLUTION**

From 1765, colonists started to campaign for self-governance. After generations of being governed from overseas, they had grown tired of paying high taxes and prices to the British Empire. The American War of Independence against the British began in 1775.

In June 1775, Washington was elected Commander-in-chief of the Continental Army (the military force of the colonies) and he led the military campaign against the British forces between 1775–1781. On 4 July 1776, delegates from each of the 13 colonies signed the Declaration of Independence, which outlined a political philosophy that later became the basis for the US government.

THE CONSTITUTION

"**No man** ever lived more **deservedly beloved** and **respected.**"

First Lady Abigail Adams after Washington's death, 1799.

Washington authorized and *enacted the US Constitution in 1789. It is the oldest written constitution still in use today and has been amended 27 times as the US has developed.*

UNANIMOUSLY ELECTED
US PRESIDENT WITH
69 VOTES FROM
10 STATES

VETOED JUST 2 BILLS
DURING HIS PRESIDENCY

GAVE THE SHORTEST
INAUGURAL ADDRESS EVER AT
135 WORDS

SET THE PRECEDENT OF SERVING A
MAXIMUM
OF TWO TERMS
AS PRESIDENT

fearlessly, and was once seen observing a British unit using a telescope on a hilltop while under heavy fire for 10 minutes.

Washington's victory at the Siege of Yorktown, 1781, marked the end of hostilities, and in 1783 the British Empire recognized independence.

Birth of a country

In 1783, the US was born. However, the newly independent states struggled to govern themselves. Initially, Washington resisted all requests to attend meetings to decide on the constitution, but he finally relented. He and various statesmen drew up the constitution and he was unanimously elected the first US president in February 1789.

Washington's legacy

As president, Washington demonstrated humility. He refused grandiose titles that the delegates wanted to attach to the office and insisted on being referred to simply as "Mr. President". He recognized the need for a strong federal government, but knew he could not govern effectively by himself, so he recruited trusted advisers. He travelled to each state to learn about the people's lives and to understand how to govern them. He also worked with Alexander Hamilton, a fellow Founding Father, and formulated how the government would function. Power was spread as evenly as possible between the people, states, the nation, and Congress (the national legislative body).

Factions within the fledging government urged the reluctant Washington to stand for a second term, and he was re-elected along with his Vice President John Adams on 13 February 1793. Slavery remained an issue throughout his presidencies, and he often spoke about a desire to end it.

Washington retired in 1797, and returned to his beloved Mount Vernon. He firmly refused all requests to return to government. He died on 14 December 1799 and was buried on his plantation.

Olaudah Equiano was a slave who bought his freedom through intelligent trading and careful saving. He challenged the slave trade by exposing its horrors in his extensive writing.

MILESTONES

BUYS FREEDOM
Purchases freedom from his last master, Robert King, and is released from slavery, 1766.

OPPOSES SLAVERY
Joins abolitionist group Sons of Africa. Campaigns in London, 1786.

WRITES AUTOBIOGRAPHY
The Interesting Narrative of the Life of Olaudah Equiano, published 1789, is the first exposé of the slave trade.

Known as Gustavas Vassa in his lifetime, Equiano was kidnapped from West Africa at the age of about 10. As a slave, he had several owners in Britain and America. The last – an American Quaker – let him purchase his freedom in 1766. He spent 20 years as a seafarer, merchant, and explorer before settling in Britain in the 1780s. His brutally honest accounts of his experiences as a slave and his tireless campaigning in the abolitionist movement aided the passing of the Abolition of the Slave Trade Act in 1807. He died in London on 31 March 1797.

OLAUDAH EQUIANO

MILESTONES

JOINS THE BAR
Becomes criminal judge in Arras, France, 1782; soon resigns due to early opposition to death penalty.

ENTERS POLITICS
Becomes the fifth of eight deputies for the Third Estate, aged 30, initiating his political career.

PROMOTES LIBERTY
Joins National Assembly, which issues "Declaration of Rights of Man and the Citizen", 1789.

OVERTHROWS KING
Secures enough votes from the National Convention to execute King Louis XVI, January 1793.

REIGN OF TERROR
Oversees the issuing of almost 17,000 death sentences, 1793–94, before he is executed.

A leading lawyer and politician, Maximilien Robespierre was one of the most influential figures of the French Revolution (1789–99). A member of the revolutionary National Assembly, he came to lead a government that was as tyrannical as the monarchy it had replaced.

Maximilien Robespierre was born on 6 May 1758 in Arras, in the province of Artois, northeastern France. In October 1769 he received a scholarship to study in Paris, where he studied until he was 23 and trained as a lawyer, like both his father and grandfather before him, and developed a passionate interest in the history of Rome and the Swiss philosopher Jean-Jacques Rousseau.

After his studies, Robespierre returned to Arras and was called to the bar in 1782. He became a criminal judge but soon resigned due to his opposition to capital punishment. A man of principles, instead Robespierre took on cases to defend poor clients, and campaigned for universal male suffrage, price controls on food, and the abolition of slavery in the French colonies. He also disapproved of the aristocracy and argued that France's Estates-General political structure did not represent the people (see p.108).

The French Revolution

In 1788, King Louis XVI announced elections for the Estates-General. Robespierre responded by calling for political reform. Although he was only 30 years old and lacking patronage, he was elected deputy of the Third Estate of Artois (see p.108), which represented 98 per cent of the French population – the poor commoners.

Robespierre brought terror and death to supposed counter-revolutionaries, before he was himself captured and executed.

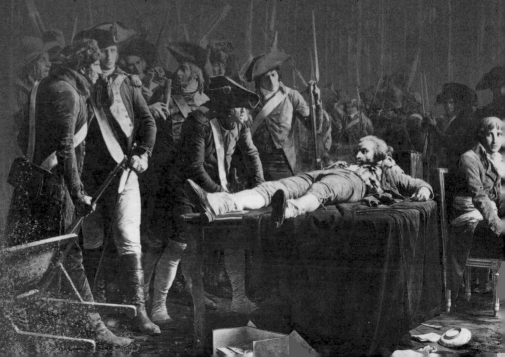

"Any institution that **does not suppose the people good**, and **the magistrate corruptible, is evil.**"

Maximilien Robespierre, 1789

MAXIMILIEN
ROBESPIERRE

1758–1794

REVERENCE DECLINED

The Age of Enlightenment during the 18th century undermined the perceived sanctity of monarchies throughout Europe. Ideas of universal equality spread.

BANKRUPT STATE

Following two costly wars, and heavy expenditure by previous kings, France, under Louis XIV (1638–1715), became bankrupt.

NATIONWIDE HUNGER

While the elite lived in luxury, most French citizens faced daily hunger. Poor harvests in 1788 led to widespread riots.

On 13 June 1789, the Third Estate broke away from the Estates-General and declared their own National Assembly. The king ordered the Assembly's meeting place to be closed, but the people of Paris, who were angry about food shortages and high taxes, rose up in revolt. On 14 July they stormed the Bastille prison, which stood as a symbol of the monarchy's despotism. By the end of July the revolution had spread across France, and the Assembly had effective control.

With Robespierre at the forefront, the revolutionaries abolished the ruling classes and crushed the power of the Catholic church. They published the "Declaration of the Rights of Man and the Citizen", a constitution to underpin their new government. The constitution urged self-government by the people and democracy; it declared that all men and women are born equal; and

stated that kings and nobles had no inherent right to rule over those of common birth.

By 1792, Robespierre was a leading figure in a political group called the Jacobin Club. When the National Assembly moved its headquarters from Versailles to Paris, Robespierre and the Jacobin Club began to recruit wealthier,

A **DIVIDED** SOCIETY

In pre-revolutionary France, society was split into three classes, or "Estates". The First and the Second Estates were the clergy and the nobility; the Third Estate – the majority – were the commoners.

The First and Second Estates were extremely wealthy but paid almost no taxes; the Third Estate, however, was subject to full taxation. Each Estate had representatives in the government assembly, or Estates-General. The disparity of wealth, plus food shortages after the poor 1788 harvest, led to riots. During the French Revolution, the common people created their own government.

LIGHTING THE FUSE

To restore his finances, Louis XVI increased taxes on the poor in 1789. Riots ensued, which led to the French Revolution spearheaded by Robespierre.

"It is **with regret** that I pronounce the fatal truth: **Louis must die,** so that **the country may live."**

Maximilien Robespierre, 1792

educated Parisians to their cause. In September, France was declared a republic, and in December, the king was tried for treason. Robespierre claimed that the king's existence was a threat to freedom and national peace. Despite once objecting to capital punishment, he argued for the execution of King Louis, but he asked for the king's wife, Marie Antoinette, and their son to be spared. Louis was executed on 21 January 1793.

The Reign of Terror
The new parliament, led by Robespierre, now governed France, establishing a new army and bringing stability to the economy. Robespierre, however, then instated what became known as the "the Terror". Around 40,000 "enemies of the Revolution" across France were executed by guillotine. Eventually Robespierre's rivals, wary of his insatiable tyranny, arrested and executed him in 1794.

Robespierre coined the phrase "Liberté, Égalité, Fraternité" (Liberty, Equality, Brotherhood) in a speech on 5 December 1790.

NAPOLEON BONAPARTE

With his political brilliance and military prowess, Napoleon Bonaparte elevated himself to the position of French emperor. He was victorious in 54 conflicts over 22 years – no other leader fought and won so many battles in such a short time.

The future emperor of France was born "Napoleone di Buonaparte" in Ajaccio, on the island of Corsica. Napoleon's parents were poor Corsican noblemen of Italian origin, and while he learnt French as a child, he never lost his native accent. He was sent to military school in Brienne-le-Château, France, aged 10, then attended the Royal Military School in Paris, where he completed a two-year course in just 12 months. At 16 he was commissioned as a sub-lieutenant in the artillery in 1785. After achieving the rank of captain in 1792, he returned to Corsica.

The following year, during the French Revolution, Napoleon and his family were forced to leave nationalist-leaning Corsica because of their pro-French views. Back in France, Napoleon seized every opportunity to fight for Robespierre's revolutionary government (see pp.106–109) and

> "I am **only at the beginning** of the course **I must run**... and **I cannot give it up.**"

Napoleon Bonaparte, 1788

MILESTONES

LEADS ARMY
Rapidly ascends the military ranks and takes command of the Army of Italy, 1796.

MILITARY CONQUESTS
Defeats Austria, Piedmont (northern Italy), and the Papal Army using expert military tactics, 1796–97.

ABSOLUTE POWER
Founds the Consulate, ending the French Revolution, 1799. Then becomes Emperor, 1804.

NAPOLEONIC CODE
Issues the Napoleonic Code, 1804, a highly influential collection of national laws.

FINAL DEFEAT
Leads 72,000 men to defeat at Waterloo, Belgium, against allied European forces, 1815.

Napoleon captured many Russian officers during the Battle of Austerlitz in 1805, which is widely considered to be one of his greatest victories.

RAISED AN ARMY OF 1.5 MILLION SOLDIERS

WON AT LEAST 48 BATTLES OUT OF 60

crush royalist uprisings. In the same year he returned to the mainland, Napoleon was promoted to brigadier general aged 24. He survived the government's downfall in 1794, and its political successors, the Directory, gave him command of the Army of Italy (an army stationed at the French-Italian border) in 1796. Napoleon led his forces to spectacular victories over Austria and Piedmont (northern Italy) and defeated the Papal Army, which made him a French hero. In 1798, he invaded Egypt to further French interests in the Middle East, and established trade links with India to compete with those of Britain.

Reshaping France

Napoleon was inspired by a sense of destiny and he desired supreme power. In 1799, he overthrew the Directory in a coup and set up a new government, the Consulate, with himself as First Consul. He then went on to crown himself emperor in 1804.

As head of state, Napoleon rewrote the French Constitution to include the Napoleonic Code, which forbade privilege based on class, allowed religious freedom, and stated that government jobs must be given to the best-qualified people.

The Napoleonic Wars

Napoleon spent almost all of his years in power at war with other European countries and coalitions. By 1806 he had integrated what is now Belgium, the Netherlands, northern Italy, and western Germany under his rule by 1806. The one nation he failed to overcome was the UK, which along with its allies, defeated him in 1805 at the Battle of Trafalgar. In retaliation, he attempted to cripple

"You **write to me** that it is **impossible. That word** is **not French.**"

Napoleon Bonaparte, 1813

Napoleon's Grande Armée achieved a series of victories between 1805 and 1815, giving him control over large areas of Europe.

the UK's economy by barring French-controlled areas from trading with it, but this was also unsuccessful.

The end of the empire

Napoleon's campaigns against Prussia, Austria, and Russia ended in defeat in 1813. Forced to abdicate in 1814, he was exiled to the Mediterranean island of Elba, but escaped a year later. After returning to France, he was defeated once more by a coalition of forces at the Battle of Waterloo in 1815. Napoleon was then imprisoned on the Atlantic island of St Helena, where he died in 1821.

EMPRESS **JOSEPHINE**

Napoleon's first consort, Marie Josèphe Rose Tascher de la Pagerie, was born in Martinique to a wealthy Creole family.

During the French Revolution, her first husband, Alexandre de Beauharnais, was guillotined and she was imprisoned for three months because of her aristocratic connections. Released in 1794, she met Napoleon a year later. Josephine was six years older than him. They had a passionate affair – many love letters were exchanged – and then a civil marriage. However, his family disapproved of her as she was an older woman who already had children. The marriage was finally annulled in 1810, as the couple were unable to have children of their own.

"IF THE ART OF WAR WERE NOTHING BUT THE ART OF AVOIDING RISKS, GLORY WOULD BECOME THE PREY OF MEDIOCRE MINDS... I HAVE MADE ALL THE CALCULATIONS, FATE WILL DO THE REST."

Napoleon Bonaparte
Excerpt from a speech made at the 1813 campaign, in which he led France against an alliance of European leaders

Napoleon crossed the Alps with his army in 1800, as depicted in this artistic rendition by French painter Jacques-Louis David, which was commissioned by Napoleon himself a year later. ▶

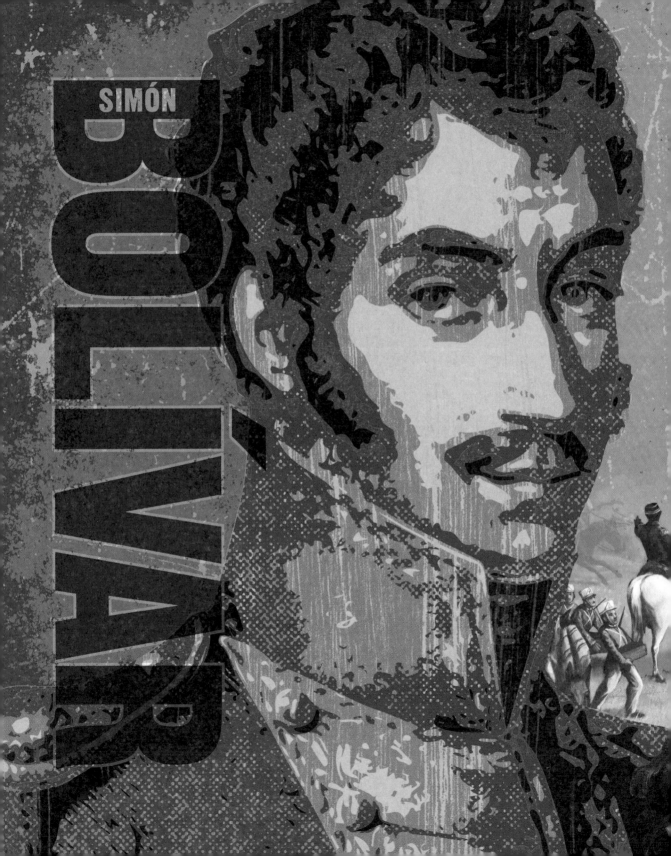

Known as "The Liberator", Simón Bolívar was the driving force behind the South American colonies' struggle for independence from Spain in the 19th century. An inspirational leader, he steered his army to remarkable feats of endurance and military victories, but failed in his dream to unite the freed colonies into one country.

Baptized Simón José Antonio de la Santísima Trinidad Bolivar y Palacios Ponte y Blanco, Bolívar was born in Caracas, Venezuela, on July 24 1783. His family, wealthy, landed Creoles (whites born in the Americas) - had settled in Venezuela in the 16th century. When he was 14 years old, Bolívar entered a military academy and, in 1799, was sent to Europe to complete his education. Bolívar married in Madrid in 1802 and took his wife back to Venezuela, but she died within a year, and he returned to Europe.

Bolívar returned to Venezuela in 1807, inspired by radical European ideas of national liberation. The same year, war broke out between Spain and Napoleon, and settlers in Venezuela took advantage of the turmoil to seize independence from Spanish rule. In 1810, the Spanish governor was expelled, and a junta (military government) was established, which sent Bolívar to Britain seeking political recognition. There, he recruited Francisco de Miranda, who had previously fought for Venezuelan independence in 1808, and persuaded him to return to the country. In 1811, Miranda declared the first Venezuelan Republic, supported by Bolívar. However, as their forces lost territory to Spanish royalists, the republic collapsed the following year - Miranda was captured and Bolívar fled.

Simón Bolívar (centre) led his patriotic army to victory against the Spanish at the Battle of Ibara, Ecuador, on 17 July 1823.

MILESTONES

FINDS INSPIRATION
Inspired by revolutionary ideals in Europe in the 1800s, determines to liberate South America.

SUPPORTS UPRISING
Fights under Francisco de Miranda, leading to the First Venezuelan Republic, 1811.

FLEES TERRITORY
Returns to Venezuela, 1813, but is defeated by Spanish royalists again; flees to Haiti, 1815.

DEFEATS SPAIN
Leeds surprise attack on Spanish at Boyacá, 1819, then takes Bogotá. Triumphs over Spanish.

AMASSES CONTROL
Becomes president of Venezuela, New Granada, Panama, Ecuador, and Peru by 1825.

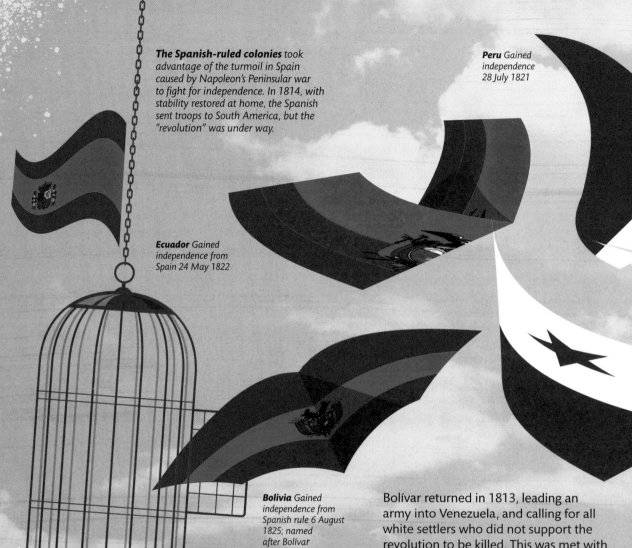

The Spanish-ruled colonies took advantage of the turmoil in Spain caused by Napoleon's Peninsular war to fight for independence. In 1814, with stability restored at home, the Spanish sent troops to South America, but the "revolution" was under way.

Peru Gained independence 28 July 1821

Ecuador Gained independence from Spain 24 May 1822

Bolivia Gained independence from Spanish rule 6 August 1825; named after Bolívar

Bolívar returned in 1813, leading an army into Venezuela, and calling for all white settlers who did not support the revolution to be killed. This was met with further unrest, Venezuela was pitched into civil war, and he was forced to flee to Jamaica. Bolívar finally returned to Venezuela in 1817 to try to liberate his country of birth, with assistance from the small republic of Haiti.

Ultimate liberation project
By 1819, Bolívar had assembled an army and led it from Venezuela, across mountains and swamps, to victory over the Spanish at Boyacá, New Granada

"To **practise justice** is to **practise liberty.**"

Simón Bolívar, 1819

Venezuela *Declared independence 5 July 1811; Spanish rule ended 1821*

Colombia *Spanish rule ended 17 December 1819*

Panama *Spanish rule ended 28 November 1821*

JOSÉ DE **SAN MARTIN**

San Martín (1778–1850), an Argentine solider, led the revolutions against Spanish rule in Argentina, Chile, and Peru.

Raised in Spain, he returned to Argentina in 1812 to support the colonial independence struggle. He subsequently defeated the Spanish royalists at the battles of Chacabuco and Maipú in 1817, gaining independence for Chile. He then seized control of Peru, the last Spanish stronghold, in 1821 and a year later handed it to Bolívar. He then retired from public life and died in France.

(now Colombia), and on to occupy its capital, Bogotá, ending Spanish rule. Further victory at Carabobo in 1821 then finally won him control of Venezuela.

Bolívar wanted to unite Hispanic South America. By 1825, he was simultaneously president of Venezuela, New Granada, Panama, Ecuador, and Peru. Although in favour of democracy, he behaved like a dictator, and his dominance was contested by power-hungry rivals. As opposition towards him increased, Bolívar, who had always experienced violent mood swings, sunk into a deep depression when civil war broke out in New Granada, and resigned. Bolívar was preparing for self-imposed exile in Europe when he died from tuberculosis.

ROAD TO **REVOLUTION**

SPANISH RULE
Discovered 1498 by Columbus, colonization of Venezuela by Spain began, 1522.

VENEZUELA GROWS
Venezuela became major exporter of cocoa to Europe and the US, 1700s.

RESENTMENT BUILT
Spain angered cocoa growers in Venezuela by imposing unfair trading rules, 1740.

BIRTH OF A REBEL
Born in Venezuela, 1750, Miranda travelled to Spain and became an army captain, 1773.

FIGHT FOR FREEDOM
Political turmoil in Spain undermined its control over its colonies. Bolívar seized chance to revolt.

SPAIN CONQUERED
Napoleon Bonaparte of France invaded Spain, 1808, installing his brother Joseph as king.

FIRST UPRISING
Miranda raised private army in US and led unsuccessful uprising in Venezuela, 1804.

REVENGE PLANNED
Embittered by his treatment in Spain, Miranda plotted to end colonial rule, 1780s.

A national heroine, and often called "Brazil's Joan of Arc", Maria Quitéria de Jesus defied the male dominance of the military to fight for Brazilian independence.

MILESTONES

JOINS THE FIGHT
Volunteers to fight in the Brazilian War of Independence, 1822.

RAPID CAREER RISE
Promoted to cadet July 1823, then becomes a lieutenant a month later.

PRAISED BY ROYALTY
Emperor Pedro I awards her Knight of the Imperial Order of the Star of the South, 1823.

RETURNS HOME
She returns to Bahia, 1824, with a letter from Pedro I asking her father to forgive her for disobeying him.

Quitéria enlisted to fight wearing her brother-in-law's clothing. As a soldier in battle, she wore a male uniform, too.

Maria Quitéria de Jesus was born in Bahia, Brazil on 27 July 1792. Her mother died when she was only 10, and she was raised mostly by her farmer father, Gonçalo Alves de Almeida, from whom she learnt horse-riding, hunting, and how to handle weapons.

Brazil was under Portuguese rule, when Quitéria, aged 28, learned that pro-independence supporters were recruiting. Posing as a man, she enlisted against her father's wishes, and joined the Brazilian War of Independence (1822–24). Brave and tactical, she led many successful battles against larger forces, and in just a year, was promoted from volunteer to cadet, then lieutenant. Such was her renown within the army that even after her father revealed her true identity, she was allowed to continue fighting, and to create and lead an all-female contingent.

In later life, Quitéria became blind, and died in poverty in 1853. The story of her military success sparked the women's rights movement in Brazil many years later.

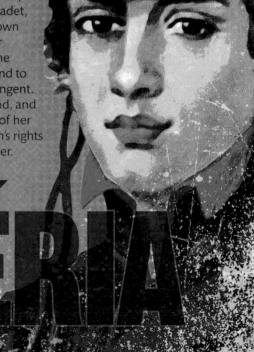

MARIA QUITÉRIA

DIRECTORY

The period from 1500 to 1800 saw the rise of colonial conquerors, political reformers, and revolutionaries who toppled monarchs. In Europe, an age of liberalism was born, creating forward-thinking individuals and nations. Most leaders were men, but powerful women emerged.

CATHERINE DE' MEDICI
1519–89

This Italian-born noblewoman was queen consort to Henry II of France and mother of three more French kings. Following Henry's death, she became the power behind the throne for her son Francis II until he died, then ruled as regent for the young Charles IX; and on Charles's death she then became adviser to her next son, Henry III. Her sons' reigns spanned the French Wars of Religion between the Roman Catholics and the Protestant Huguenots, during which Catherine ran the monarchy and the state. She is also remembered as a patron of the arts, which she used to help maintain the monarchy's power.

IVAN THE TERRIBLE
1530–84

Ivan IV of Russia, or "Ivan the Terrible", was grand prince of Moscow until 1547, when he became the first ruler to be crowned tsar of all Russians. His army captured several Khanates around the Black Sea and conquered Siberia, thus transforming Russia into an empire. He established a centralized government with a new legal code. A patron of the arts and the church, he commissioned the building of St Basil's Cathedral in Moscow. In a darker period of Ivan's reign, he became paranoid of betrayal and brutally terrorized the aristocracy.

MAURICE OF NASSAU
1567–1625

The son of the Prince of Orange, Maurice of Nassau was *stadtholder* (principal official) of all but one of the provinces in the Dutch Republic. As a brilliant military strategist, Maurice organized and led the Dutch rebellion against Spanish rule. He restructured the Dutch army, improving provisions and pay, and trained a united force that drove the Spaniards from the northern provinces and also consolidated the republic's borders, although the south remained under Spanish control. He is considered a pioneer of modern warfare and a great general of his time.

SHAH JAHAN
1592–1666

The fifth Mughal emperor, Shah Jahan, was a skilled military commander who expanded the Mughal empire. Highly educated, he was a Muslim leader who showed tolerance towards his Hindu subjects. Jahan's greatest legacy is his patronage of Mughal architecture, including his commission of the Taj Mahal. Although his military and artistic exploits almost bankrupted the Mughal Empire, his reign is considered its golden age.

GUSTAVUS ADOLPHUS
1594–1632

Gustav II Adolf (Gustavus Adolphus) became king of Sweden aged only 16. Still in his youth, he faced wars with Russia, Denmark, and Poland. He skilfully brought these conflicts to an end and blocked Russia's attempt to gain influence in the Baltic Sea. He also introduced governmental reforms that centralized Sweden's administration, established Stockholm as its capital city, and boosted the economy. His brilliant military tactics led Sweden to victory in many conflicts including the Thirty Years' War and played a crucial role in maintaining the balance of power in Europe.

OLIVER CROMWELL
1599–1658

The chief architect behind the English Civil War and the execution of Charles I, Oliver Cromwell remains one of the most divisive figures in British history. Cromwell was a Puritan who opposed the king on religious grounds and demanded power for parliament, then led the Parliamentarians into battle against the Royalists. In 1649, he defeated the Royalists and founded a new republic, the Commonwealth. Fearing the Irish Confederate Catholics for their Royalist alliance, Cromwell also led an invasion into Ireland that was marked by brutal massacres. The monarchy was restored shortly after Cromwell's death, but as ruler he boosted Britain's prestige in Europe and laid the foundations for modern constitutional government.

JOHN CHURCHILL
1650–1722

The first Duke of Marlborough, and an ancestor of Sir Winston Churchill (pp.196-201), General John Churchill was a statesman as well as a soldier. A commander-in-chief under the Catholic king James II, he switched allegiance to the Protestant William III, and became leader of the Allied armies in the War of the Spanish Succession. Marlborough led the British army to victory against Louis XIV of France, thwarting French dominance in Europe, and establishing Britain as a leading power. His various military victories were unprecedented; until the rise of Napoleon, he was the foremost soldier in Europe.

PETER THE GREAT
1672–1725

Peter I is remembered for his sweeping reforms, which turned Russia into a major European power. As well as expanding the Tsardom's territory to the Crimea, Peter modernized the government, strengthened the navy, encouraged the development of science, technology, and commerce, and founded Russia's first newspaper. To gain political and practical knowledge, he also toured Western Europe, even working as a shipbuilder in the British Navy's Royal Dockyard.

His reforms were based on the principles of the Enlightenment and Westernized Russian society. He also moved Russia's capital to St Petersburg, and dubbed it a "window to Europe".

NADER SHAH
1688–1747

From lowly beginnings as a bandit in the Turkish Afshah tribe, Nader Shah rose in power to found the Afsharid dynasty, which ruled Iran for 60 years. Having provided military support to the Safavid shahs of Iran, Nader then seized power from them and proclaimed himself ruler of Iran in 1736. A skilled military leader, he created a vast empire stretching from the Caucasus to the Indus Valley and the shores of Arabia. While he was one of the most powerful Iranian rulers of all time, Nader was cruel and tyrannical, and was eventually assassinated by his own people.

MARIE ANTOINETTE
1755–93

The last queen of France before the French Revolution, Austrian-born Marie Antoinette headed the Crown's resistance against the revolutionaries. Her daring styles dictated the dress code for French society and made her the most fashionable woman in Europe. Yet her extravagance at a time when France's economy was failing and its people starving brought her public condemnation. In 1789, the Revolution began in Paris, Marie-Antoinette attempted to crush it with foreign mercenaries, Parisians fought back and stormed the Bastille, marking the end of an oppressive regime. Marie Antoinette attended her execution in another new outfit - her audacity symbolizing her betrayal of the people.

CATHERINE THE GREAT
1729–96

German-born Catherine II usurped her husband from the throne to assume control of the Russian Empire. She greatly expanded Russian territory, annexing Crimea and Poland. She also tried to modernize the government's values and to reform serfdom, but with only limited success. An intelligent ruler, Catherine promoted Russian culture, invested in building new towns, and boosted trade. She also founded schools and established St Petersburg as a centre of culture. Her reign, spanning three decades, was heralded as a golden age for Russia.

HORATIO NELSON
1758–1805

A British naval commander, Admiral Nelson was the master tactician and strategist behind several key naval victories during the Napoleonic Wars. Renowned for his innovative methods, his care for his men, and his bravery, Nelson saw action in the Indian Ocean and against the American colonists in the Caribbean. He achieved his greatest victories, however, in his destruction of Napoleon's fleet at the Nile, thwarting the French invasion of Egypt, and his victory over the French and Spanish fleets at Trafalgar, which saved Britain from invasion. His death at the Battle of Trafalgar has cemented Nelson as one of Britain's great national heroes.

KING KAMEHAMEHA
1758–1819

Hawaiian ruler Kamehameha, founder of the Kamehameha dynasty, captured the throne from his cousin, Kīwala'ō. He then conquered all but two of the

Hawaiian Islands, the final two ceding to him after peaceful negotiations, to become the uncontested ruler of all the Hawaiian Islands. During his reign he provided administration to each island, outlawed the traditional practice of human sacrifice, and boosted the economy. He also established strong trade ties with Europe and the US, helping preserve Hawaii's independence.

WILLIAM WILBERFORCE
1759–1833

British politician William Wilberforce won renown as a tireless campaigner for the abolition of the slave trade in the British colonies. He became an evangelical Christian in 1785, which stoked his desire to improve society. He lobbied parliament and raised awareness of African people's human rights until the slave trade was abolished in 1807; he then campaigned for full emancipation. In 1833 the Slavery Abolition Act was passed, ending slavery in the British Empire; Wilberforce died just three days later.

TECUMSEH
1768–1813

Chief Tecumseh of the North American, indigenous Shawnee tribe was the leader of a resistance movement that campaigned against the settlement of white Americans in Ohio in the early 1800s. A gifted speaker, Tecumseh united many tribes in a confederacy in a plan to establish an independent Indian state. Having led them in an unsuccessful war against the US, he then formed an alliance with the British fighting the Americans in the War of 1812, but he was killed. Without his clear-sighted and skilled leadership, the intertribal alliance broke down and many tribes were driven from their lands.

ARTHUR WELLESLEY
1769–1852

The man who became the first Duke of Wellington was born Arthur Wellesley, an Irish aristocrat. Joining the army in 1787, he rose quickly through the ranks, seeing action in Flanders and India. He became a commanding officer during the Napoleonic Wars; with unsurpassed leadership skills, he achieved a series of victories before he defeated Napoleon at the Battle of Waterloo in 1815. Having already entered Parliament in 1806, Wellesley was elected twice as prime minister. As a politician he was unpopular and divisive, yet he has a lasting legacy as the hero of Waterloo.

JUANA AZURDUY DE PADILLA
1780–1862

Female freedom fighter Juana Azurduy de Padilla was a leading figure in the early 19th-century battle for South American independence from Spanish rule. A guerrilla leader in the Bolivian War of Independence, she fought in 23 battles between 1811 and 1817, even during pregnancy, disguising herself in male uniform and commanding armies of up to 6,000 men. Her crowning achievement in driving the Spanish from modern-day Bolivia was largely forgotten during her lifetime, and she died in obscurity and poverty. More recently, however, her contribution has been recognized and she is now a national hero of Bolivia and Argentina.

WINFIELD SCOTT
1786–1866

One of the most eminent American military figures of the 19th century, Winfield Scott spent 53 years in active service and held the rank of general during three wars. In recognition of his exemplary record and military success, he was promoted to lieutenant general in 1855. At the outbreak of the American Civil War, Scott was military adviser to Abraham Lincoln, proposing one of the battle plans used by the Union to defeat the Confederate Army. He also stood for election as US President in 1852; although he lost, he remained a popular figure.

SAM HOUSTON
1793–1863

Leader of the US settlers in Texas, which was then a Mexican territory, Sam Houston commanded the Texan army in a stunning victory over the Mexican government, securing Texan independence. He became the first president of the Republic of Texas and oversaw Texas' unification with the United States. A controversial figure, he had a strong rapport with the Cherokee people and was against the expansion of slavery. In the American Civil War, he refused to support the Confederacy and the secession of Texas from the Union, and was deposed.

NAT TURNER
1800–31

A fiercely defiant slave from Virginia, Nat Turner led around 75 slaves in a rebellion against white plantation owners in 1831. In just two days the rebels slaughtered 60 white people, including children, while plundering weapons and horses. The uprising was crushed by militia, and up to 200 slaves were killed. As a result of the rebellion, laws against slaves were toughened, and the emancipation movement in the region was abandoned. Turner was criticized for his violent methods, yet became a symbol of black resistance.

3

NATIONHOOD AND INDUSTRY

1820–1920

GIUSEPPE

GARIBALDI

The idealistic freedom fighter Giuseppe Garibaldi was a key figure in the Risorgimento, which sought to free many Italian states from Austrian and French rule, and unify all of them under the banner of the Kingdom of Italy.

MILESTONES

FIRST CONFLICT
Makes his name as a revolutionary in Brazil during failed Ragamuffin War, 1836–40.

CIVIL WAR FIGHTER
Leads the Italian Legion, an army of red-shirted emigrants, in civil war in Uruguay, 1843.

FIGHTS FOR ITALY
Returns to Italy, 1848, to join unsuccessful uprising against Austrian rule. He flees abroad.

TAKES COMMAND
Successfully leads a force on behalf of King Emmanuel II against Austrian rule, 1855.

UNITES HIS COUNTRY
Returns southern Italy to Emmanuel, who is crowned king of a united Italy, 1861.

Giuseppe Garibaldi was born Joseph-Marie Garibaldi into a seafaring family in Nice in 1807. Nice was then under French rule but, during his childhood, it reverted to being part of the Kingdom of Sardinia, one of a number of states into which Italy was then divided.

In the early 1830s, Garibaldi, a fierce nationalist, joined the revolutionary Young Italy movement, founded by Giuseppe Mazzini (see p.129). Inspired by Mazzini's vision of a unified Italy under a republican government, he took part in a failed uprising against the French Empire in Genoa in 1834. He fled to France and then to South America, where he took part in civil conflicts in Brazil and Uruguay, and proved himself to be a skilled guerrilla leader.

Hero of two worlds
Nationalist and republican revolutions broke out across Europe in 1848 and Garibaldi sailed home to join the struggles. His time as a freedom fighter in South America had won him renown among radicals. Assembling a body

Garibaldi claimed victory at the battle of Calatafimi, on 15 May 1860. As his forces came under pressure, he spoke the famous words, "Here, we either make Italy or we die."

"I offer only **hunger, thirst, forced marches, battles** and **death**. Anyone who loves his country, **follow me.**"

Giuseppe Garibaldi, 1849

of volunteer fighters, he joined Mazzini in Milan, where a popular uprising had driven out the city's Austrian rulers. When the tide of war in northern Italy turned decisively in favour of the Austrian Empire, and against the nationalists, Garibaldi and his forces headed south to Rome in spring 1849. On his arrival, the Pope, threatened by liberal forces, fled the city, and a Roman Republic was declared. France sent an army to restore papal authority – and, although Garibaldi led a spirited defence of the city, after two months the Republic was forced to surrender and Garibaldi to retreat.

Garibaldi fled to South America again in 1854, and bought half of the island of Caprera in 1855, where he worked as a farmer and fisherman. Living this simple life enhanced his image as a man of the people. Seeing the usefulness of Garibaldi's popularity, in April 1859 the Sardinian king Victor Emmanuel II invited Garibaldi to command a force of volunteer troops fighting Austria for control of northern Italy in the Second Italian War of Independence.

Attack on Sicily

When the war was over, in July 1859, Victor Emmanuel II controlled most of the north, but the south remained in the hands of the Spanish Bourbons (the Spanish royal house). With the support of the king's chief minister, Camillo Cavour, Garibaldi invaded Sicily in 1860. Against vastly superior numbers, he seized control from the Bourbons, then crossed to mainland Italy, occupying Naples by September. Bourbon troops tried to block any further advance northwards but were defeated by the king's army at the river Volturno. Accepting royal authority, Garibaldi handed over his southern conquests, and Emmanuel became king of Italy in 1861.

Final years

Garibaldi's fame had spread far internationally. He was widely regarded as an inspiring and honourable leader. Visiting Britain in 1864, he received a hero's welcome. Although he was an elected member of the Italian parliament, in his later years Garibaldi continued to live simply on his island in Italy, rarely involving himself in politics. Confined to his bed by arthritis, he died in 1882.

SPENT **14 YEARS** FIGHTING **GUERRILLA WARS** IN **SOUTH AMERICA**

INVADED **SICILY** WITH **1000 VOLUNTEERS IN 1860**

OFFERED A POST IN THE **UNION ARMY** TO FIGHT IN THE **US CIVIL WAR** BY ABRAHAM **LINCOLN**

GIUSEPPE **MAZZINI**

Born in 1805, the political activist Mazzini was a key figure in the drive for Italian unification.

In 1831, he founded the Young Italy movement, which aimed to create a united Italian republic through revolution. After a failed uprising in 1834, he fled to the UK, returning in 1848 to lead short-lived republican governments in Milan and Rome. In 1849, after the fall of the Roman Republic, he returned to exile. His opposition to monarchy left him sidelined when the king of Sardinia unified Italy in 1861. He died in 1872.

The unification of Italy was first muted in the 15th century. However, it was another 300 years before Garibaldi would help unify the many Italian states.

Largely unknown during his lifetime, but now lauded as a visionary, Karl Marx was a philosopher, economist, socialist, and political theorist. Considered to be the founding father of social science, his works have inspired revolutions around the world, with Marxism becoming the official ideology of states, such as China, and the former Soviet Union.

Marx published The Communist Manifesto *in 1848. Here, he views the printed sheets with Friedrich Engels at his shoulder.*

Karl Marx was born in Trier, in the Kingdom of Prussia (now northern Germany) on 5 May 1818 to devoutly Jewish parents; in adolescence, he became a firm atheist. His father was a successful lawyer and, in 1836, Marx enrolled to study law at the Friedrich Wilhelm University, Berlin, although he immersed himself in philosophy and radical politics, which he was more interested in.

From student to journalist
When Marx moved to Berlin to study, he was finally able to mix with like-minded intellectuals, and joined a left-wing group called The Young Hegelians Doctors' Club. Marx turned to journalism and moved to Cologne in 1842, where he began writing about socialism for the political newspaper *Rheinische Zeitung*. However, when the conservative Prussian government called for the paper to be banned, he left Prussia to live in Paris, where he fostered a friendship with the wealthy socialist Friedrich Engels (see p.133). The two became lifelong friends. While in Paris, in 1847, Marx and Engels joined a secret society called the League of the Just (later renamed the Communist League), which aimed to create an egalitarian society by overthrowing the government.

1818–1883

KARL
MARX

REGAL POWER

From the early Middle Ages to the 18th century, most of Europe was ruled by monarchies and society was divided by class and wealth.

GREATER DIVISION

The Industrial Revolution (1760–1820) saw the rise of capitalism, and a greater inequality between the rich and the poor.

UNITED VOICES

Inequality led to the French Revolution (1789–99). Marx's writings helped to spread revolutionary ideas throughout Europe in the 19th century.

POWER SHIFT

In 1848, multiple revolutions swept Europe, as different groups demanded greater control in over 50 countries.

Marx's socialist writings, such as The German Ideology, The Communist Manifesto, *and* Das Kapital *have been adopted by movements throughout the world.*

After being expelled from Paris for his radical views, Marx returned to Brussels, where he and Engels co-authored *The Communist Manifesto* (1848).

Marx and Capitalism

In his manifesto, Marx exposed the class struggle that he saw existing in capitalist societies, and called on workers to unite and overthrow the system. Marx believed it flawed that the ruling class (bourgeoisie) held all the power, leaving the working class (proletariat) to be no more than cogs in a machine. This uneven balance, Marx reasoned, would drive the working classes to depose "the system", leaving

"The **history of all**... society is the history of **class struggle.**"

Karl Marx, 1848

dissolved during the 1850s and, in October 1864, he joined the International Working Men's Association in an attempt to coordinate assorted left-wing groups. He collated his ideas in his major work *Das Kapital*, which fundamentally challenged the way society is organized. The first volume was published in 1867, and he spent the rest of his life working on two further volumes.

While Marx's predictions for a worldwide revolution did not happen, his views triggered many political movements, and today left-wing political parties throughout the world continue to adopt Marxism as an ideology.

communism to replace it. Marx argued that such change could only be reached through a process of violent revolution.

The following year, expelled from Belgium, Marx moved to London, where he spent the rest of his life in exile. At the time, the UK was more liberal than the rest of Europe, and Marx could express his views without fear of reprimand or punishment. The Communist League

FRIEDRICH **ENGELS**

Engels (1820–95), a philosopher born in Barmen, Prussia, now Germany, was the eldest son of a wealthy cotton family with mills in the UK.

Although their paths had crossed previously, it was after meeting in Paris in 1844 that Engels and Marx began writing socialist works together. Their first collaboration, published in 1845, *The Condition of the Working Class in England*, was followed by a collection of manuscripts – *The German Ideology* (*Die Deutsche Ideologie*) – written in 1846, but not published until 1932. Engels joined Marx in London in 1849 and supported him financially for the rest of his life. Engels devoted his final years to editing the last two volumes of *Das Kapital*.

"IN A HIGHER PHASE OF COMMUNIST SOCIETY... ONLY THEN CAN THE NARROW HORIZON OF BOURGEOIS RIGHT BE FULLY LEFT BEHIND AND SOCIETY INSCRIBE ON ITS BANNERS: FROM EACH ACCORDING TO HIS ABILITY, TO EACH ACCORDING TO HIS NEEDS."

Karl Marx
Critique of the Gotha Program, a document based on a letter written by Marx, 1875

Karl Marx addressed left-wing political groups and trade unions at the Hague Congress in Holland, 1872. ▶

Born into slavery, human rights activist Sojourner Truth became one of the most influential African-American women of the 19th century. Famed for her heartfelt and impromptu speeches, she actively campaigned for many causes, including prison reform, property rights for all, and universal suffrage.

MILESTONES

CHILD SLAVE
Passes, as a slave, between three owners over four years, from the ages of 9–13.

SAVES HER SON
Escaping from slavery, 1826, wins custody of her son, Peter, two years later, after he was illegally sold.

DEMANDS EQUALITY
Delivers "Ain't I a woman" speech on racial inequality to the Women's Convention in Akron, Ohio, 1851.

CIVIL WAR LEADERS
Meets US president Abraham Lincoln while working to help African-American troops, 1864.

ENDURING ACTIVISM
Meets US president Ulysses S. Grant to secure land grants from government for former slaves, 1870.

Isabella (Belle) Baumfree was born into slavery in 1797 in Swartekill, a Dutch settlement in New York State. Aged 13, she was sold to her fourth owner, John Dumont, in 1810, who allowed her to marry a slave known as Thomas, and they had five children.

In 1826, Dumont reneged on a promise to grant Belle her freedom, and although it meant leaving her family behind, she fled with her baby daughter Sophia, and was granted emancipation in 1827. While in the care of an abolitionist family, the Van Wageners, Belle learned that Dumont had illegally sold her five-year-old son Peter. With the family's help, she took legal action to recover Peter, and she won back custody of him in 1828.

Belle moved to New York City, where after claiming to have heard divine voices, she renamed herself Sojourner Truth on 1 June 1843. She left her job as a housekeeper, and over the coming years, she spoke to hundreds of audiences across the country, campaigning for the abolition of slavery and for women's rights. During the US Civil War (1861–65), Truth helped to support African-American troops and sought to improve conditions for freed slaves. She continued speaking and campaigning well into old age.

"And **ain't I a woman!** Look at me! Look at **my arm.**"

Sojourner Truth, 1851

Truth funded the Underground Railroad, the secret network of trails through the northern US states to Canada that escaped slaves were guided along, using money she earned from her lectures and book sales.

1797–1883

SOJOURNER **TRUTH**

ABRAHAM LINCOLN

Known as "The Great Emancipator", Abraham Lincoln was the 16th president of the United States. His opposition to the expansion of slavery was one of the catalysts for the American Civil War, but his strong leadership during the conflict prevented the country from becoming permanently divided.

Abraham Lincoln was born in a log cabin near Hodgenville, Kentucky into a poor family of farmers on 12 February 1809. After his mother died when he was nine, he was raised by his stepmother. He had little formal schooling but, determined to better himself and escape from poverty, he studied on his own while earning a living through hard manual labour.

Lincoln and his family moved to Macon County, Illinois, when he was 21, and by the time he was 30, he was a self-taught lawyer and a member of the liberal Whig Party, with a seat in the Illinois House of Representatives. Lincoln now moved in higher social circles, although many still frowned upon his backwards manners.

Following his election to the US Congress in 1846, Lincoln's first foray into national politics was a failure, largely due to his opposition to the ongoing Mexican-American War, which the majority of the public were in favour of. Returning to Illinois, Lincoln focused on progressing his legal career and making money for his self-advancement.

MILESTONES

ELECTED TO CONGRESS
Becomes a member of US Congress, 1846, but faces criticism for opposing the Mexican-American War.

BECOMES PRESIDENT
Runs for Senate seat in Illinois, 1858. Loses, but is elected president two years later.

OUTBREAK OF WAR
Delivers speech calling for national unity, 1861, but secession continues, and the Civil War begins.

FREES SLAVES
Issues Emancipation Proclamation, 1863, declaring all slaves in the US to be free.

DEFEATS SOUTH
Civil War victory, 9 April 1865. Assassinated by a Confederate sympathizer on 14 April 1865.

Lincoln's rejection of the expansion of slavery was the primary trigger for the American Civil War. Union troops are shown here in Fredericksburg, Virginia, 1864.

HIS EMANCIPATION PROCLAMATION FREED 3.5 MILLION SLAVES IN 1863

Lincoln's call for the abolition of slavery in 1863 almost caused the US to permanently split in two. The southern states that supported slavery seceded from the north and were independently governed for four years until their defeat in the American Civil War.

HAND-WROTE FIVE VERSIONS OF THE 272-WORD-LONG GETTYSBURG ADDRESS

Lincoln's belief that slavery was wrong was cultivated at an early age as his family regularly attended anti-slavery Baptist churches. He was convinced that his ability to rise from humble beginnings to the White House showed that a free man could make anything of himself and that slavery denied an individual the chance to better himself. It was the issue of slavery in the Kansas-Nebraska Act of 1854 that brought him

WAS THE FIRST US PRESIDENT TO HAVE A BEARD

"Government of the people, by the people, for the people, shall not perish from the Earth."

Abraham Lincoln, 1863

back into politics. The act, which founded Kansas and Nebraska, offered residents a vote on whether to legalize slavery within the two new states. Lincoln, who wanted slavery abolished at a national level, left the ailing Whig party and joined the newly formed Republican party, which opposed the westward extension of slavery.

In 1858, he ran for a senate seat in Illinois against the Democrat candidate Stephen A. Douglas (see above).

STEPHEN A. **DOUGLAS**

A skilful Democrat from Illinois, Stephen Douglas (1813–61) was the author of the Kansas-Nebraska Act. He argued that the people of each state should be able to vote on state law regarding slavery.

In 1858, Douglas and Lincoln ran against each other for the Senate, and took part in a series of seven debates. Lincoln stated that slavery was immoral and should not be allowed to become more widespread, but accepted that it would continue in the south, where it was protected by the Constitution. Douglas won the seat in the Senate, but the conflict over slavery split the Democratic Party. In 1860, he ran against Lincoln for the presidency as a Democrat but lost. When the Civil War erupted, he denounced secession and rallied supporters for the Union cause, but died of typhoid fever a few weeks later.

Lincoln lost the election but only two years later he won the presidential nomination for the Republicans and went on to be elected president. To many southern politicians, Lincoln's opposition to the extension of slavery was unacceptable, and in 1860, South Carolina seceded from the US. Within three months, Mississippi, Florida, Alabama, Georgia, Louisiana, and Texas followed suit. Lincoln then denied them the right to secede, claiming that they were destroying the US without just cause. They, in turn, united to form the Confederate States of America; the states that did not secede became known as the Union.

Outbreak of war
As president, Lincoln delivered a carefully prepared inaugural address on 4 March 1861, which was aimed at stopping

> **"A house divided** against itself, **cannot stand.** I believe this **government cannot endure** permanently, **half slave** and **half free."**

Abraham Lincoln, 1858

other southern states from joining the secessionists. However, six weeks later, war broke out when Union forces at Fort Sumter in South Carolina refused to heed Confederate demands to evacuate, and Confederate General P. G. T. Beauregard attacked – the first military engagement of the American Civil War.

Lincoln's role as a wartime president was precarious. The political elite hated him, factions on both wings of his party opposed him, and he had almost no military experience. Nevertheless, he was determined to succeed, and came to show an intuitive understanding of the principles of war. In 1862 he issued the Emancipation Proclamation, which came into effect on 1 January 1863, declaring all slaves in Confederate states free. His Gettysburg Address in November that year redefined the Civil War as not only a struggle to preserve the Union but also as a moral battle against slavery.

In March 1864, Lincoln appointed General Ulysses S. Grant commander of the Union army. A man with an implaccable will to match Lincoln's own, Grant led the Union army to victory.

Lincoln's final months

Abraham Lincoln stood for re-election in 1864, but the high number of casualties from the war threatened his success. However, with the Union forces capture of Atlanta, Georgia, and, in September, with the support of a coalition of Republicans and War Democrats, Lincoln won the election with an even greater majority.

The Civil War ended a few months later, following General Lee's surrender on 9 April 1865, but Lincoln never lived to see America reunited. On 14 April 1865 he was assassinated at Ford's Theatre in Washington, D.C. by John Wilkes Booth, a Confederate sympathizer.

RE-ELECTED TO SERVE A SECOND TERM WITH 55% OF THE VOTE

$100,000- REWARD OFFERED TO CATCH HIS ASSASSIN IN 1865

AFTER HIS DEATH, HIS FUNERAL TRAIN PASSED THROUGH 180 CITIES

MILESTONES

POLITICAL REFORM
Delivers first speech at the Rochester Daughters of Temperance, 1848. Elected its president, 1849.

ANTI-SLAVERY ACTIVISM
Plays a major part in organizing an anti-slavery convention in Rochester, New York, 1851.

EQUALITY CAMPAIGNS
Co-founds the American Equal Rights Association with Elizabeth Cady Stanton, 1866.

SUFFRAGE LEADER
Fights for women's rights as president of the National American Woman Suffrage Association, 1892.

An abolitionist, a fighter for educational reform, and a tireless women's rights campaigner, Susan Brownell Anthony's pioneering activism was central to securing the vote for women in the US.

Born into a family of politically active Quakers in Massachusetts, in 1845 Anthony's family moved to a farm in Rochester, New York, which became a regular meeting place for anti-slavery activists.

After several years teaching, Anthony returned to her family home in 1848 and threw herself into political reform. When denied the right to speak at a temperance rally, she set up The Women's New York State Temperance Society.

In 1851 Anthony was introduced to fellow reformer Elizabeth Cady Stanton and together they campaigned on many issues. Anthony joined the Women's Rights Movement in 1852, and in 1856 became a principal organizer for the American Anti-Slavery Society. Her ceaseless work paved the way for the 19th Amendment to the US Constitution of 1920, which gave the right to vote to all American women over the age of 21. It became known as the Susan B. Anthony Amendment.

SUSAN B. ANTHONY

Anthony's name was written on street cars during the suffrage parade of 1913 in Washington, D.C.

OTTO VON
BISMARCK

The architect of the modern German nation, Otto von Bismarck was a Prussian statesman central to European politics during the second half of the 19th century. Through a combination of diplomacy, political manoeuvring, and military power, he united more than 20 German states to create the German Empire.

MILESTONES

ENTERS POLITICS
Embarks on a career in politics, 1851; appointed Prussia's ambassador to the German Federal *Diet*.

PLAN FOR PRUSSIA
Becomes prime minster, 1862, with an agenda to unite Germany under Prussia dominance.

FORMS ALLIANCE
Conquers territory from Denmark and Austria, and creates the North German Federation, 1867.

UNITES GERMANY
Instigates the Franco-Prussian war, 1870, to compel German unification – he succeeds, 1871.

Otto Eduard Leopold, Prince of Bismarck and Duke of Lauenburg, was born into an aristocratic "Junker" family in Schönhausen, in the Prussian state of Saxony, on 1 April 1815. Junkers were the land-owning elite, who owned large estates near the major towns and cities of Prussia.

After studying law at the University of Göttingen, Bismarck entered the Prussian civil service, and he spent time in the army as an officer in the reserves. Following the death of his mother in 1839, he returned to the family estates to help his father, where he remained for several years.

The path to power
Bismarck began his political career in 1847 in the newly-formed Prussian legislature. Two years later, he was elected to the Prussian Chamber of Deputies and moved to Berlin, where he became known as an ultra-conservative, reactionary politician. He firmly believed in the monarch's divine right to rule, and that the established social and political order should be defended, but he opposed the liberal revolution that was

The Franco-Prussian War (1870) served to unite southern German states with Bismarck's North German Confederation.

sweeping through Europe at the time. To Bismarck's mind, the aims of the liberal revolution were the preserve of the educated and propertied middle class, motivated by their self-interest, and were not shared by the majority of Prussians, who were peasants and artisans loyal to the monarchy.

In 1851, the Prussian king, Frederick Wilhelm IV, appointed Bismarck as the state's representative to the Federal *Diet* (Assembly) in Frankfurt. Bismarck then served as Prussian ambassador to both Russia and France, coming to know the details of French, British, Russian, and Austrian foreign policy.

Road to unification

Under Frederick's successor, Wilhelm I (see box), Bismarck was made prime minister in 1862. However, following his time in Frankfurt, his views on nationalism had broadened, and he now aspired to unite the German states into a single empire, albeit with Prussia at its core.

In 1864, Bismarck sent the Prussian army to annex the provinces of Schleswig and Holstein from Denmark. He then provoked Austria and its allies into a war in 1866, winning further territory, which he consolidated as the North German Confederation in 1867. To encourage the reluctant southern German states to unite with him, Bismarck initiated hostilities with France, which led to the Franco-Prussian War in 1870. After victory, and with all states united, the German Empire was founded in 1871, with Wilhelm I of Prussia as *kaiser* (emperor) and Bismarck as chancellor.

The new nation

With his country united, Bismarck now sought peace not further territory, and strove to build cordial relationships with other European powers. The one exception was France, which he isolated for demanding the return of territories seized during the Franco-Prussian War.

In Germany, Bismarck promoted industry, introduced health insurance and pensions, and improved the rights for workers. However, ever the conservative, when the liberal Wilhelm II succeeded the throne in 1888, the two men clashed. After the 1890 elections, Bismarck resigned, aged 75, feeling he had lost his country to enemies of the empire. He retired to his estate, where he spent his final years.

"A conquering army on the border will not be stopped by eloquence."

Otto von Bismarck, 1867

In the early 19th century, the region that is now Germany was ruled by a loose confederation of states, with Prussia being by far the largest. Bismarck unified these states into one empire.

WILHELM I

The first emperor of Germany, Wilhelm Friedrich Ludwig, was the second son of Frederick William III, and not originally expected to reign.

Wilhelm had a distinguished military career and became a spokesman for the Prussian forces. He considered it within his rights as monarch to increase the size of the military and the years of military service, but the liberal legislature did not approve these reforms, so Wilhelm installed Bismarck as prime minister in 1862 to assist him. Although both men were conservatives, Wilhelm had concerns about some of Bismarck's policies, such as his battle against Catholicism. As the Prussian king he was initially reluctant to accept his title as *kaiser* of the German Empire.

UNITED 25 STATES TO FORM GERMAN EMPIRE

CREATED THE FIRST MODERN WELFARE STATE

LONGEST SERVING CHANCELLOR OF GERMANY; 19 YEARS

TASUNKA WITKO

CRAZY HORSE

One of the most famous North-American indigenous chiefs, Tasuŋka Witko, or "Crazy Horse", had trance-like visions which foretold that he would be a successful warrior. He resisted US government forces on Lakota lands from 1860 to 1877, which made him a lasting icon of defiance in American history.

MILESTONES

PROPHETIC TRANCES
Has visions aged 15, 1854. Sees a warrior struck by lightning, who says he would not be hurt in battle.

SUCCESSFUL AMBUSH
Lures US troops into an ambush and massacres them outside Fort Phil Kearny, Wyoming, 1866.

LEADS ALLIANCE
Commands several tribes during the Great Sioux War, 1876–77; famously wins Battle of Rosebud, 1876.

ADMITS DEFEAT
Surrenders to the US Army at Camp Robinson, Nebraska, in May 1877. Dies four months later.

Born in the Black Hills, now the border between South Dakota and Wyoming, Crazy Horse was a member of the Oglala sub-tribe of the Lakota, and the son of a healer. His mother died when he was four years old. From an early age, Crazy Horse showed promise as a fierce warrior and often fought rival tribes.

During the mid-1860s, however, he fought alongside fellow Oglala chief, Red Cloud, against the US Army, which had invaded their lands. Even after Red Cloud brokered a peace deal in 1868, Crazy Horse continued to resist, leading several tribes to fight against US intrusion during the Great Sioux War (1876–77).

In 1876, Crazy Horse fought in the Battle of Little Bighorn, killing General George Custer and annihilating the US 7th Cavalry. The army's counter-attack forced Crazy Horse to become a fugitive. Pursued by US troops for months, he finally surrendered to protect his people. Four months later, during a struggle against US troops, he was bayoneted and died.

"Today is a good day to die."

Crazy Horse

Crazy Horse led, along with fellow chief Sitting Bull, up to 2,000 warriors to victory against 600 US troops at the Battle of Little Bighorn in 1876.

JOHN D. **ROCKEFELLER**

From humble farming origins, John D. Rockefeller went on to lay the foundations for modern American capitalism, becoming one of the richest men of all time in the process. His control of the US oil industry was so tight and all-consuming that it prompted the world's first anti-monopoly laws.

Born in Upstate New York in 1853, John Davison Rockefeller moved with his family to Cleveland, Ohio, where his journey to incredible wealth began. His father, a travelling salesman, passed on his entrepreneurial spirit, while his mother, a devout Christian, taught him thriftiness.

Unable to afford a college education, Rockefeller learned book-keeping and the basics of commerce at business school, before beginning work aged 16. When he was refused a pay rise after three years with his first wholesale employer, he quit and went into business with Maurice Clark, selling produce to the government during the American Civil War (1861–65).

The oil business

In 1863, Rockefeller and Clark, looking for further investment opportunities, partnered with the inventor Samuel Andrews to buy oil refineries. Recognizing the decline of the whale oil industry, Rockefeller anticipated the recently discovered oil fields in Pennsylvania to be commercially

Rockefeller's company Standard Oil controlled 90 per cent of US pipelines and refineries by 1880. He had begun employing scientists to refine his product for maximum efficiency.

MILESTONES

STANDARD OIL
Founds oil business with Samuel Andrews, 1863. Establishes Standard Oil seven years later.

OIL MONOPOLY
Uses his shrewd business acumen to acquire 90 per cent of US oil refineries by 1880.

COMPANY TORN APART
Dissolves Standard Oil into 34 separate companies, by order of the US Supreme Court, 1911.

FOUNDS CHARITY
Establishes philanthropic foundation, 1913, along with his son, John D. Rockefeller Jr.

lucrative. His refineries were economically efficient – they sold the by-products of their oil such as petroleum jelly and tar, unlike his competitors, who discarded 40 per cent of the oil product. Rockefeller's company soon prospered and he began persuading other oil refining companies to either merge with his company or allow themselves to be bought out. This led to the creation of a single entity, the Standard Oil Company, in 1870. The company went on acquiring competitors until it controlled around 90 per cent of oil refineries in the US. Rockefeller drove competitors out of business by undercutting them until they were forced to sell up.

Standard Oil became the first monopoly in modern business history. In the face of growing public concern about the conglomerate's economic power, the US Supreme Court brought an action against it in 1911 under the 1890 Sherman Antitrust Act, breaking Standard Oil into 34 smaller companies.

Philanthropic work

Rockefeller was not only a ruthless businessman but also a generous philanthropist. Between 1890 and 1916, he founded the University of Chicago, the Rockefeller Institute for Medical Research, and the schools of public health at Johns Hopkins and Harvard universities. He is best known for establishing the Rockefeller Foundation in 1913. The foundation developed a cure for yellow fever in 1937, the year he died, and continues to fund improvements in health and education and to raise living standards in the US and overseas to this day.

ANDREW **CARNEGIE**

A contemporary of Rockefeller's, Andrew Carnegie built the US steel industry and became another of the US's richest individuals.

Born in Scotland in 1835, Carnegie emigrated to Pittsburgh, US, at the age of 13. There, he started Carnegie Steel in 1892, replacing wooden bridges with iron ones. He amassed a fortune of $250 million, most of which he gave away, building more than 2,500 public libraries, Carnegie-Mellon University in Pittsburgh, and Carnegie Hall in New York.

Rockefeller's monopolization of the US industry earned him unrivalled wealth. However, he never lost his sense of Christian duty, and donated substantial amounts of money to charity throughout his life.

CHURCH

EDUCATION

OIL PRODUCTION

INDUSTRY

WEALTH PEAKED IN 1913, EQUIVALENT TO **$400 BILLION** TODAY

GAVE AWAY **$530** MILLION TO CHARITY BETWEEN **1855** AND **1934**

"I believe the **power** of **making money** is a **gift from God.**"

John D. Rockefeller, 1932

Widely regarded as the "Father of Indian Industry", Jamsetji Tata laid the foundations for what would become the country's biggest conglomerate: the Tata Group.

Descended from a long line of Parsi Zoroastrian priests in Gujarat, India, Jamsetji Tata initially worked with his father, who had broken from family tradition by starting a business in Bombay (now Mumbai), trading in goods including cotton, opium, and tea. Having joined his father's business straight from school, after nine years working for him he launched his own company in 1868, trading in cotton, pearls, and opium. Tata travelled to Britain, and while there he saw huge potential in textiles, which Britain dominated at the time. For the next 12 years he successfully embarked upon cotton manufacturing. In 1880, Tata set his sights on building a world-class steel plant, a hydroelectric plant, and an institute for scientific education and research in India, but by the time of his death in 1904, these plans had yet to come to fruition. However, Tata had created the basis for what his successors would develop into the Tata group, a global enterprise headquartered in India with over 100 companies across six continents.

Tata created plans for the Taj Mahal Palace hotel in 1898, and it opened its doors to guests in 1903. The hotel is an architectural marvel and has 550 extravagant rooms and suites.

JAMSETJI **TATA**

MILESTONES

WELL EDUCATED
Graduates from the prestigious Elphinstone College in Bombay (now Mumbai), 1958.

ESTABLISHES MILL
Founds a cotton mill in Nagpur, 1874. Names it "Empress Mills" after Queen Victoria, 1877.

FUNDS STUDENTS
Establishes JN Tata Endowment in 1892, to provide scholarships for deserving students to go abroad for higher studies.

DESIGNS NEW CITY
Conceives plan, 1902, to build a city, Jamshedpur, around his steel plant, with high-quality housing.

BUILDS LUXURY HOTEL
Completes luxurious Taj Mahal Palace Hotel, Bombay, 1903. First building in the city lit with electricity.

SWAMI VIVEKANANDA

A philosopher and spiritual leader, Swami Vivekananda brought Hinduism to global attention and awakened Indian nationalism.

Born into a wealthy Bengali family in Kolkata, Narendranath Datta changed his name to Vivekananda, meaning "the joy of discernment", after becoming a Hindu monk in 1886. Vivekananda modernized Hinduism by stripping away complex traditions, and focusing on two basic tenets: that all religions are equal and that God is inside everyone. Vivekananda preached this message to a global audience at the World Parliament of Religions in Chicago, US, in 1893. He soon became a popular teacher on Hinduism, lecturing all around the world, and teaching meditation and yoga as a way of connecting with God. His words have inspired leaders such as Mohandas Gandhi (see pp.188–92) and Barack Obama (see pp.302–05). In India, he is revered for uniting Indians with his calls to end poverty, the caste system, and colonial rule.

Vivekananda's birth was celebrated on its 150th anniversary at the World Youth Festival, Kolkata, in 2013.

MILESTONES

MEETS RAMAKRISHNA
Meets Hindu mystic Ramakrishna, 1881, becoming an avid follower and devotee.

REINVENTS HINDUISM
Develops simplified version of Hinduism, focused on self-help practices, 1884.

SPREADS MESSAGE
Promotes his vision of Hinduism on pilgrimages across India, made on foot, 1888–93.

GLOBAL AUDIENCE
Introduces Hinduism to the West at conference in New York, 1893. Becomes globally respected.

155

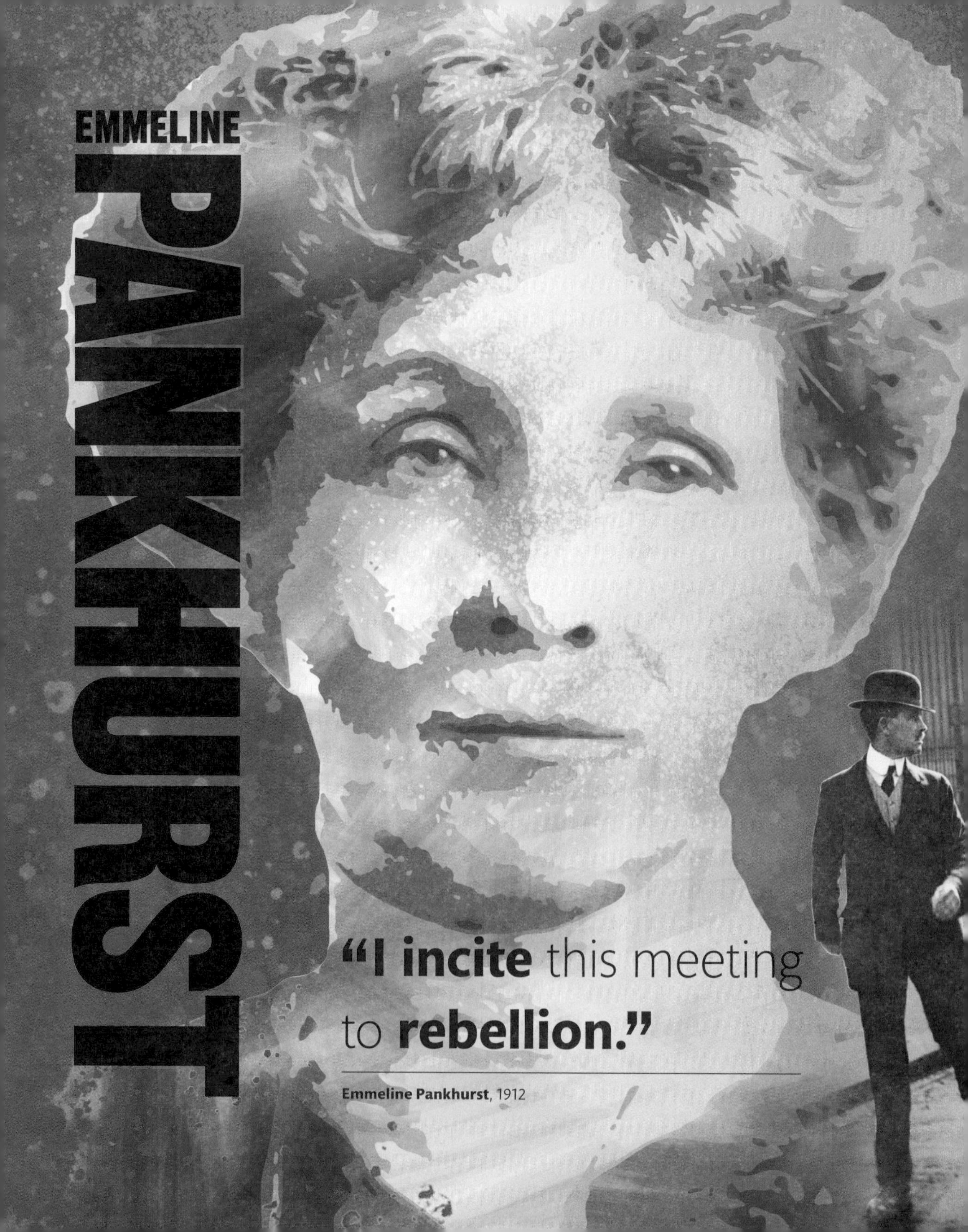

EMMELINE PANKHURST

"I incite this meeting to rebellion."

Emmeline Pankhurst, 1912

At a time when women were expected to lead quiet lives, Emmeline Pankhurst was a social and political agitator who fought tirelessly for equal rights. Today her name is synonymous with women's suffrage – the fight for women to gain the vote.

Born in Manchester, UK, on 15 July 1858, from an early age Emmeline Goulden was deeply interested in politics and women's rights. She first attended a women's suffrage meeting at the age of 14 with her mother, who came from the Isle of Man, which went on to become the first parliamentary body in the UK to grant women the right to vote in a general election. In 1879, Emmeline married barrister Richard Pankhurst. A supporter of women's rights, he had authored a bill that was passed into law as the Married Women's Property Act of 1870, granting married women control over their property and earnings.

In 1889, Emmeline Pankhurst founded the Women's Franchise League, which fought for women to be allowed to vote in local elections. Then in 1903, she set up the Women's Social and Political Union (WSPU) with her daughter Christabel to gain the vote for women in national elections.

Pankhurst was arrested during a march outside Buckingham Palace in May 1914 for trying to present a petition to King George V.

The growth of the WSPU

At first the WSPU, which was based in London, held meetings and rallies, and gave out pamphlets in the street. Over time, however, many of its members became disillusioned at the lack of results yielded by a peaceful approach to women's equality. Pankhurst began to advocate more aggressive strategies, which her children also adopted. In 1905, Christabel was imprisoned for assaulting a policeman who had tried to remove her

---

MILESTONES

FIGHTS FOR VOTE	SUFFRAGETTE	WINS THE VOTE
Founds the Women's Social and Political Union, 1903. Soon adopts aggressive approach to protest.	Adopts the term "suffragette" for her own cause after its derisory use in a *Daily Mail* article, 1906.	Goes on hunger strikes with other suffragettes, 1912–13. Within five years, women in the UK are given voting rights.

> **"We women suffragists** have a **great mission**... to **free half the human race."**
>
> **Emmeline Pankhurst**, 1912

from an election meeting. The incident appeared in the press and boosted the WSPU's profile. The following year, the Daily Mail newspaper coined "suffragette" as a derogatory term for women taking militant action, only for Pankhurst to adopt the name for WSPU members.

Radical disobedience
In 1908, still lacking government support, suffragettes turned to radical acts of civil disobedience, such as setting fire to

British women, at the beginning of the 20th century, were often restricted to domestic roles and had no political power. Many aspects of society kept them locked in this position.

BASIC EDUCATION

PATRIARCHAL SOCIETY

MALE-DOMINATED JOB MARKET

UNEQUAL VOTING RIGHTS

FALTERING START
Corsican Republic granted female suffrage, 1755.
Revoked, 1769, following invasion by the French.

FEMALE PIONEER
Lydia Taft cast first legal vote by a woman in colonial America, 1756.

buildings and smashing windows. From 1912–13, Pankhurst was arrested repeatedly for acts of protest, and sent to Holloway prison. While there in 1912 she, as other suffragettes had done since 1909, went on hunger strike to draw attention to the cause, and to force the police to release her before she starved. Between stints in prison, Pankhurst also incited rebellion, giving rousing speeches in public places and large venues such as the Royal Albert Hall, London.

Not everyone supported the WSPU's methods. Criticism of its militancy came from the media, politicians, and even within its own ranks. When Pankhurst's daughter Adela left the group in protest of its methods, Pankhurst paid for her to move to Australia, they never met again.

A shift in focus

After World War I broke out in 1914, Pankhurst called for British women to take jobs in factories, on farms, on public transport, and in coal mines to enable men to fight on the front line. This forced the government to recognize the changing role of women in society.

In 1918, property-owning women over 30 finally won the right to vote in the UK, with the Representation of the People Act. Ten years later the law was changed, giving all women over 21 the right to vote, bringing them in line with men. That year, Pankhurst died, aged 69.

EMILY DAVISON

Born 11 October 1872, Oxford graduate Davison joined the WSPU in 1906. She became known for her daring actions, including stone-throwing and arson. She was arrested nine times.

Davison is best known for her final protest, on 4 June 1913. Stepping on to the racecourse during the Epsom Derby, she was struck by a horse belonging to King George V. It is thought she may have been trying to tie a suffragette flag to it. She died of her injuries, and thousands attended her funeral in London. Many hailed Davison as a martyr of the movement.

ISLE OF HOPE
Women of the Isle of Man permitted to vote, 1881 – including Pankhurst's mother.

LEADING NATIONS
New Zealand women gained the vote, 1893.
South Australia followed one year later.

WOMEN IN POWER
World's first female members of parliament elected in Finland, 1907.

AGE COUNTS
UK women aged over 30 allowed to vote, 1918.
Over 21s, 1928.

COLOUR MATTERS
1920, white US women could vote.
All women, 1965.

One of the world's most influential industrialists, Henry Ford is credited with revolutionizing personal transportation and with the development of the moving assembly line. His vision of building a practical, affordable vehicle for all Americans resulted in his Model T car, which not only helped create a nation of drivers, but was sold around the world.

MILESTONES

BUILDS CAREER
Works as an apprentice machinist in Detroit, aged 16, and later for Edison Illuminating Company.

FAILED BUSINESS
Establishes the Detroit Automobile Company, 1899, which closes just two years later.

AFFORDABLE CAR
Founds Ford Motor Company, 1903. Produces first affordable car, the Model T, five years later.

VAST NEW FACTORY
Builds Ford Motors' River Rouge Plant, the largest integrated factory in the world, in Detroit, 1928.

TAKES CONTROL
Resumes presidency at Ford aged 79, following death of son, Edsel, 1943. Dies four years later.

Henry Ford was born near Dearborn, Michigan into a farming family on 30 July 1863 – to this day, Dearborn is still the site of the headquarters of the company he founded. His Irish-born father, William, had emigrated to the US with his family to escape the 19th-century potato famine. Henry was the eldest of six children, and was expected to take over his father's farm. Educated locally in a one-room school, he worked on the land every evening, but from an early age his affinity for mechanics and fascination with steam engines was clear. At the age of 13, he took a watch apart and reassembled it – the beginning of a lifelong passion for machinery.

Leaving home aged 16, he worked as an apprentice machinist in nearby Detroit. After a series of jobs, and a period in Dearborn working on steam engines, he returned to Detroit to work for Edison Illuminating Company. During this time Ford experimented with

Ford's car plants built millions of Model T's by 1925. He famously remarked: "A customer can have any colour as long as it is black."

HENRY FORD

"**Failure** is simply the **opportunity** to **begin again**... more intelligently."

Henry Ford, 1927

building engines. In 1896, he developed a petrol-fuelled car, and in 1899, with a group of friends, founded the Detroit Automobile Company. However, unable to build vehicles quickly enough, the company closed two years later.

Successful business

Ford had a passion for building racing cars, and soon attracted backers for a new business. Only the rich could afford cars, but he wanted to sell them to the masses.

In 1903, he established the Ford Motor Company, and launched his first successful car, the Model T, in 1908. Two years later, production moved to the newly built Highland Park Plant, which by 1913 incorporated the world's first moving assembly line - production time was cut from 12½ hours per car to 2 hours 38 minutes, and later just 1 hour 33 minutes.

For workers in the US, eight-hour-day laws passed in 1867 and 1868 remained poorly enforced at the start of the 20th century. Workers often either faced 12-hour days, or could not work long enough hours to make ends meet. Determined to acquire and keep

the best staff for the job, in 1914 Ford unilaterally provided his workers with an 8-hour day and a 5-day week, and doubled their pay to $5 per day.

Five years later, Ford bought out his original investors for $93 million. He built new plants in the US and around the world; Ford's River Rouge Plant, Detroit, completed in 1928, became the largest integrated factory in the world.

The sheer scale of Ford's motor manufacturing business changed the economic and social landscape of the US forever, and paved the way for an industrial America. In September 1945, his health failing, Ford handed control of the company to his grandson, Henry Ford II. In April 1947, following a cerebral hemorrhage, Henry Ford died, aged 83.

PEAK NET WORTH IS EQUIVALENT TO $340 BILLION TODAY

WATCHED THE 15 MILLIONTH MODEL T ROLL OFF THE ASSEMBLY LINE IN 1927

BUILT 2,718 TANKS, 277,896 JEEPS AND 8,685 B24 LIBERATOR BOMBER AIRCRAFT DURING WORLD WAR II

The Ford Motor Company expanded quickly. Plants were built across Europe, and from Japan to Argentina, 1917–25. The Model T accounted for half the world's cars.

EDSEL **FORD**

Henry's only son, Edsel Bryant Ford (1893–1943), served as Ford Motor Company's president from 1919 until he died.

Edsel was an innovator: he introduced hydraulic brakes and expanded the brand's product lines to include the updated Model A and other models. He was also instrumental in directing the company to build military vehicles and aircraft in World War II. His father resumed presidency of Ford after Edsel's death from cancer; then, on Henry's death, Edsel's son Henry II took over in 1945.

From modest beginnings as a seamstress, Coco Chanel rose to become the founder and namesake of the quintessential Chanel brand. Her designs set trends that changed the way people dressed forever.

Gabrielle Bonheur "Coco" Chanel was born in Saumur, France, in August 1883, although she often claimed that her birth year was 1893. When her mother died, her father left Chanel in an orphanage, where she learned to sew. As a young adult, these skills enabled her to find work as a seamstress in a small shop. At night, she sang cabaret in bars; her nickname "Coco" came from her two most popular numbers – "Ko Ko Ri Ko", and "Qui q'ua vu Coco".

Chanel became a milliner in 1910 and, with the help of one of her rich lovers, Captain Arthur Capel, she opened Chanel Modes, a hat boutique, in Deauville (Normandy) three years later. She soon began to design clothing and accessories too – seminal pieces include her Little Black Dress, her tweed skirt suit, and a quilted handbag with chain strap. She also launched Chanel No. 5 in 1921 – one of the most iconic perfumes of all time. By the mid-1930s Chanel Industries employed more than 4,000 people and had clients all over the world.

At the start of World War II, Chanel closed her fashion house. She became the mistress of a Nazi intelligence officer, Baron Hans Gunther von Dincklage, in occupied Paris, and was questioned about her involvement at the end of the war, but never charged. In 1954, she decided to revive Chanel and continued working right up to her death at the age of 87. The label continues to define trends in both couture and high street fashion.

Chanel became known for her classic two-piece tweed skirt suits. Introduced in the mid-1920s, they combined elegance with comfort and practicality.

"Fashion is architecture. It is a matter of proportions."

Coco Chanel, 1971

MILESTONES

OPENS BOUTIQUE
Establishes her own hat boutique in Deauville, France, 1913, and starts designing clothing and accessories.

ICONIC DESIGNS
Creates defining pieces, such as the Little Black Dress, quilted handbags, and Chanel No. 5 perfume, launched in 1921.

REVIVES BRAND
Reopens shops, 1954, closed during World War II, and cements reputation as a world-class designer.

COCO
CHANEL

DIRECTORY

The late 19th century brought expansion and rebellion. European imperialists dominated much of the world as their economies boomed. Although colonial and racial tensions peaked, progressive leaders abolished slavery in the US and instigated women's rights movements.

JOHN ALEXANDER MACDONALD
1815–91

Born in Scotland, John MacDonald emigrated to Canada as a child and was elected the Dominion of Canada's first prime minister in 1867. During his 19 years in office MacDonald contributed greatly to the development of the country; his greatest achievements included the expansion of the Dominion to include British Columbia, Prince Edward Island, and Manitoba, and the completion of the Canadian Pacific Railway. He received a knighthood for services to the British Empire.

QUEEN VICTORIA
1819–1901

The longest-reigning monarch of her time, Queen Victoria ruled the United Kingdom during one of the most expansive, prosperous, and progressive periods in its history. Her 64-year reign saw major developments in industry, science, and the arts, as well liberal political and social reform. Her name also became synonymous with the British Empire. Under her leadership the role of monarch became more ceremonial, boosting the power of royalty in a more democratic era. A much-loved figure, Victoria was mourned nationwide on her death.

FLORENCE NIGHTINGALE
1820–1910

Known as "The Lady with the Lamp", Florence Nightingale transformed the nursing profession, and dispelled prejudiced assumptions about women's role women in medicine. Her work nursing soldiers in the Crimean War led to improvements in care and sanitation. In her writing on health care, she was also a pioneer in the use of graphics to present statistical data. Nightingale set up the first training school for nurses, in London, and became the first woman awarded an Order of Merit, in 1907. Her work helped standardize nursing practices across the world, and she is widely recognized as the founder of modern nursing.

ULYSSES S. GRANT
1822–85

The 18th president of the United States, Ulysses S. Grant had also commanded the Union armies during the last years of the American Civil War. Grant's eventual victory over the Confederates, turned him into a national hero, and in 1868 he was elected as president. Although his terms in office was tarnished by corruption and nepotism, Grant remains widely celebrated for his military prowess.

ALFRED THAYER MAHAN
1840–1914

As a US naval officer, Alfred Thayer Mahan served almost 40 years of active duty. In addition, he was a historian and author, becoming one of the most influential voices in naval strategy of his time. He was a lecturer and president of the Naval War College. Later, he became president of the American Historical Association. Two of his many books became seminal works that brought him international acclaim; these emphasized the navy's essential role in any great nation, and had a significant impact on naval strategists across the world.

LUDWIG II OF BAVARIA
1845–86

The eccentric king of Bavaria, "Mad King Ludwig" or "Swan King", was famed for funding dazzling artistic projects that left him deeply in debt. From the fairy-tale castle of Neuschwanstein to a winter roof garden and grand palaces, Ludwig's architectural projects were opulent and varied. He passionately promoted the arts, and his ongoing patronage of the composer Wagner enabled the musician to complete several operas. Although his extravagance eventually led him to be deposed, Ludwig's lavish legacy remains a source of wonder, attracting millions of tourists annually.

TŌGŌ HEIHACHIRŌ
1848–1934

A fervent admirer of Horatio Nelson (p.122), Admiral Tōgō Heihachirō led the Imperial Japanese Navy during the Russo-Japanese War. Having blockaded the Russian fleet in Port Arthur, Heihachirō delivered a crushing defeat to a breakaway contingent of Russian ships, bringing an end to the war and establishing Japan as a significant power. His innovative tactics and unprecedented manoeuvres in securing victory were later adopted by European navies, ensuring Heihachirō's reputation as one of the greatest naval commanders in military history. In recognition of his victories, Edward VII admitted Heihachirō membership to the distinguished Order of Merit in 1906.

TAYTU BETUL
c.1851–1918

Empress consort of the Ethiopian Empire, Taytu Betul was the founder of Addis Ababa, the empire's capital. Exerting considerable political influence over her husband, Emperor Menelek II, she also took an active role in resisting Italian colonization. A brave military strategist, she led her own army into battle, where she commanded and fought on the frontline, securing victory over the Italians at the historic Battle of Adwa. The Italians' defeat deterred other European powers from attempting to colonize Ethiopia and protected Ethiopia's independence, which it retained until the Second Italo-Ethiopian War.

EMPEROR MEIJI
1852–1912

The 122nd emperor of Japan oversaw a period of rapid and unprecedented progress, during which he transformed Japan from an isolated feudal nation into a modern state. In 1868, in an event known as the Meiji Restoration, Meiji abolished the feudal system. His government also promoted growth in transport, trade, communications, and industry, boosted military power, created a formal constitution, and reformed the education system. Meiji became the symbol of a new Japan, which he had recrafted to be one of the most dynamic powers in the world.

BOOKER T. WASHINGTON
c.1856–1915

Born into slavery, the African-American educator Booker T. Washington went on to be the most prominent leader of the African-American community after slavery's abolition in 1865. A proponent of industrial and farming education for black people, he presided over the Tuskegee Institute in Alabama, which became a respected teaching institute. Although he was criticized for his failure to promote academic pursuits and racial equality for black Americans, he was recognized as a spokesman for his community and regularly advised the White House on racial matters.

JOHN JELLICOE
1859–1935

British Admiral of the Fleet John Jellicoe served with distinction during several conflicts, and commanded the Royal Navy during one of the most crucial maritime battles of World War I – the Battle of Jutland. Although the battle did not end in a decisive victory and Jellicoe was much criticized at the time, it was later recognized as a strategic victory as his tactics preserved the British fleet to fight again. In recognition of his wartime service and achievements, Jellicoe was made a viscount and later an earl.

JANE ADDAMS
1860–1935

A social reformer and peace activist in the late 19th and early 20th centuries, Jane Addams was the first American woman to be awarded the Nobel Peace Prize. She campaigned for women's rights and in 1889 founded North America's first social settlement, which provided care and amenities to poor communities, in particular women and children. Her settlements became a model for the social work profession in the US. Addams held several key roles during her career, including first female president of the National Conference of Social Work and chairman of the International Congress of Women.

GIULIO DOUHET
1869–1930

Italian military aviation strategist General Giulio Douhet was an early and influential advocate of aerial campaigns, in a farsighted vision of modern warfare. He commanded Italy's first aviation unit and later became head of aviation. In his famous 1921 work *Il dominio dell'aria* (The command of the air) he advocated the strategic use of air power and in particular aerial bombings. Although some of his predictions proved false and were considered optimistic by his peers, many of his theories and tactics became accepted military techniques, employed across the world.

4

CONFLICT AND HOPE

1920–1950

A Russian communist, revolutionary, and political theorist heavily influenced by Marxist principles, Vladimir Lenin orchestrated the Bolshevik revolution that overthrew the Russian tsarist regime and established the world's first single-party communist state.

Vladimir Ilyich Ulyanov (he adopted the name Lenin in 1901) was born on 22 April 1870 in the town of Simbirsk (now Ulyanovsk), east of Moscow. His family were educated, conservative monarchists. Lenin studied law at Kazan University, but was drawn into student protests, arrested, expelled, and exiled to the family estate. (He later completed his studies as an external student at the University of St Petersburg.) Lenin's mother persuaded the authorities to let him return to Kazan. There, he read Karl Marx's *Das Kapital* (see pp.130–35) for the first time, sparking his long-term interest in Marxism and his career as a revolutionary activist. His consequent political activities led to him being exiled to Siberia for three years, but he still corresponded with Russian revolutionaries.

Sparking a revolution

Lenin prepared for a people's revolution in Russia that would oust the tsarist regime. Early in 1900 he joined the Russian Social Democratic Labour Party (RSDLP), then in July he left for Europe, where he continued to study Marx and Friedrich Engels (see p.133), and met Leon Trotsky (see p.182). He became head of the RSDLP, but at a conference in London in 1903 the party split – Lenin's section were the Majoritarians (*bol-shevki* in Russian, hence Bolshevik).

In response to a wave of uprisings after Russia's defeat in the Russo-Japanese War (1904–05), Tsar Nicholas II promised the people a series of reforms. Returning to Russia, where workers were striking, and people were starving, Lenin advocated armed insurrection and revolution, before leaving for Europe to canvas support.

Lenin demanded total support. Trotsky was stood next to him when this photograph was taken in 1920, but was airbrushed out after falling from grace.

1870–1924

VLADIMIR LENIN

ABSOLUTE POWER

All land in 17th century Russia was owned by the tsar and landowners, who controlled all peasants (serfs) who worked for them.

CHOKEHOLD

Tsar Alexander II abolished serfdom in 1861. This made it difficult for the freed serfs to buy land, which led to civil unrest.

DISSENT RISES

Strikes and riots spread. In early 1905, "Bloody Sunday", Imperial guards fired on the crowds demanding radical reforms.

POWER SHIFT

High inflation and food shortages led to further riots. The tsar abdicated, 15 March 1917; by October, Lenin was in power.

"We shall **not achieve socialism** without a **struggle.** But we are **ready to fight.** We have **started it** and we shall **finish it...**"

Vladimir Lenin, 1918

By February 1917, Russia was severely weakened by its military involvement in World War I, and riots broke out in Petrograd (St Petersburg had been renamed in 1914). Widespread unrest followed, and in March, the tsar, afraid for his life, abdicated, and a Provisional Government took his place. However, Lenin and the Petrograd Soviet of Worker's and Soldier's Deputies – a growing city council with Bolshevik members – regarded the Provisional Government as incompetent, and not truly representative of the people.

In April, Russia's enemy, Germany, facilitated Lenin's return to Russia, where he encouraged demonstrations. As a result, many Bolshevik leaders were arrested, and Lenin fled to Finland. In August 1917, the pro-tsarist General Lavr Kornilov led a revolt against the Provisional Government, who turned to the popular Bolsheviks for support.

Final push for change

Lenin returned to Russia in October, renewing calls for a revolution, and led the Bolshevik army – the Red Guard – to storm the Winter Palace and remove the Provisional Government. Reinforcing his hold on Russia, Lenin dissolved the elected government and implemented a ban on all political opposition.

From 1918–21, the Bolshevik Red and the Tsarist White armies fought in a bloody civil war. In 1922, when Lenin emerged victorious from the conflict, he took control of a vast single-party communist state, stretching from Europe to the Pacific. Two years later, he died of a brain haemorrhage.

TSAR NICHOLAS II

The last emperor of Russia, Nikolai Aleksandrovich Romanov (1868–1918), was also known as St Nicholas by the Russian Orthodox church.

Nineteenth-century Russia was one of the world's most powerful empires. The tsars (emperors) had absolute authority over land, wealth, laws, and the church. Tsar Nicholas II reigned from 1894, but costly wars and class divisions led to widespread unrest. The tsar lived in luxury while his people starved. The economy and the Imperial army collapsed, and he was forced to abdicate in 1917. The entire royal family was executed in 1918.

A revolutionary, soldier, and politician, Michael Collins was a leading figure in Ireland's struggle for independence from the British and, ultimately, the creation of the Irish Free State in 1921.

Collins was born in County Cork, southern Ireland, on 16 October 1890. He left school at 15 and moved to London, where he joined the Irish Republican Brotherhood (IRB) and the republican political party Sinn Féin. Collins returned to Ireland in 1916 and took part in an armed attempt by republicans to end British rule – the Easter Rising – and was briefly imprisoned. During the UK's general election of December 1918, he won a seat in Parliament to represent Sinn Féin, but did not take it. Collins was a key strategist in the resistance to British rule known as the Irish War of Independence (1919–21). When he signed an Anglo-Irish treaty in December 1921, civil war broke out in Ireland, but Collins would not live long enough to see it resolved. He was shot by anti-treaty forces on 22 August 1922 in an ambush.

Collins attended the funeral of Sinn Féin's founder, Arthur Griffith, on 16 August 1922.

"We **have to learn** that **freedom imposes responsibilities.**"

Michael Collins, 1922

MICHAEL COLLINS

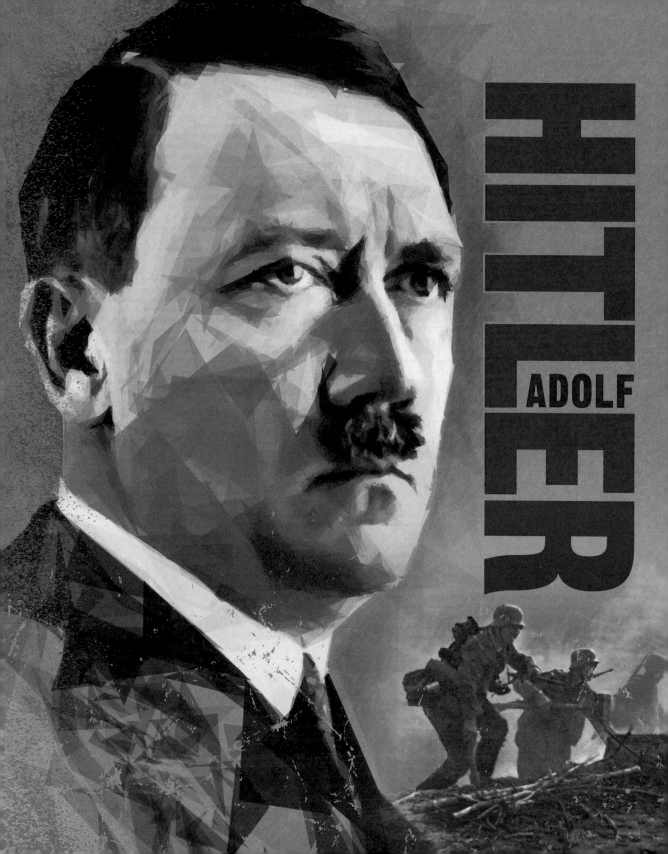

ADOLF HITLER

Responsible for the bloodiest war of all time, Adolf Hitler was a charismatic and rousing dictator who pursued his goals with fervent self-belief and ruthless devotion to his cause. The Holocaust, the genocide he spearheaded, remains the largest mass killing of its kind in history.

Hitler was born in Branau am Inn, a small town in Austria-Hungary, on 20 April 1889. Drawn to German nationalism, he moved to Munich in 1913, and fought in the German army during World War I, for which he was decorated for bravery. After the country surrendered in 1918, and signed the Treaty of Versailles, ending the war, Hitler, like many Germans, grew bitter about the sanctions imposed by the treaty, which forced Germany to disarm, pay costly reparations, and concede territory.

The National Socialist German Workers' Party
In 1919, Hitler developed an interest in the anti-Semitic and anti-Marxist ideology of Anton Drexler, founder of the German Workers' Party. After joining, Hitler's fervour saw him rise quickly through the ranks, becoming leader of the party in 1921, which he renamed *Nationalsozialistische Deutsche Arbeiterpartei* (NSDAP, or Nazi Party).

Two years later, Hitler led a 2,000-strong group of Nazis to the centre of Munich in an attempt to forcibly seize power from the government.

Hitler's unified armed forces, the Wehrmacht, lost over five and a half million men during World War II.

MILESTONES
HEADS REBELLION Leads coup d'état to seize power from the German government in Munich, November 1923.
ASSUMES LEADERSHIP Rises to position of Führer of Germany, 1934, following death of President Hindenburg.
INCITES GLOBAL WAR Rejects peace offers from the UK and France; invades Poland, 1939, and triggers World War II.
COMMITS SUICIDE Anticipating defeat, kills himself alongside Eva Braun in his bunker, 30 April 1945.

"**Germany** will either be a **world power** or will **not be at all.**"

Adolf Hitler, 1926

The Nazis were arrested, but the incident demonstrated Hitler's ability to rouse people into action. During his subsequent incarceration, which lasted nine months, Hitler wrote *Mein Kampf* (My Struggle), a manifesto outlining his ideology, blaming the Jews for Germany's woes, and urging the need to expand the country and exact revenge on France for the Treaty of Versailles.

The Great Depression of 1929 brought hardship to Germany – unemployment trebled, and the Communist and Nazi parties, promising easy solutions to the country's economic woes, flourished.

By 1933, the Nazis had gained such popularity that President Hindenburg appointed Hitler chancellor. When a fire broke out in the Reichstag (the main parliamentary building), Hitler stoked public fear by blaming communist agitators and, obtaining emergency powers, immediately banned all political parties other than the Nazis. When Hindenburg died in August 1934, Hitler became *Führer* (leader) of Germany.

Hitler established a totalitarian state based on his belief in German racial superiority. He instituted a series of civil works, as well as a rearmament programme, reducing unemployment and winning the people's admiration. At huge propaganda events, such as the Nuremberg rallies, Hitler's oratorical skills captivated the German people, promising them an empire that would endure for a thousand years. At the same time, the Nazi party increasingly persecuted Jews, and other minority groups, and

ANTI-COMMUNISM

THREAT OF CIVIL WAR

FEARMONGERING

Hitler blamed communist rebels for the Reichstag fire on 27 February 1933. Stoking public fear, he helped pass the Reichstag Fire Decree, resulting in the immediate suspension of civil liberties that were not restored until the end of WW II, some 12 years later.

introduced the concept of *Lebensraum* (living space) in Germany, as justification for invading neighbouring countries.

The world stage

Many European powers, afraid of being drawn into war once again, attempted to appease Hitler's territorial demands. However, Germany annexed Austria in 1938, doing likewise to Czechoslovakia a year later, before invading Poland, triggering World War II. In 1940, the Nazis then invaded France, Luxembourg, Holland, and Belgium. Meanwhile, across Nazi Germany, Hitler's attacks on the Jews and other minorities escalated from expulsion to genocide.

By 1945, this Holocaust had claimed the lives of 6 million Jews and 5 million other individuals, including Romani gypsies, homosexuals, and those with disabilities.

As Germany faced defeat, Hitler refused to surrender, withdrawing to a bunker in Berlin. In the early hours of 29 April 1945, he married Eva Braun, before they both committed suicide two days later.

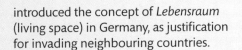

FREEDOM OF ASSOCIATION

PRESS FREEDOM

RIGHT TO LAWFUL DETENTION

FREEDOM OF ASSEMBLY

SECRECY OF ASSEMBLY

CORRESPONDENCE

"THE ART OF LEADERSHIP... CONSISTS IN CONSOLIDATING THE ATTENTION OF THE PEOPLE AGAINST A SINGLE ADVERSARY AND TAKING CARE THAT NOTHING WILL SPLIT UP THAT ATTENTION."

Adolf Hitler
Excerpt from *Mein Kampf*, 1925

◀ *Hitler's impassioned* speeches at rallies, such as in Buckeberg, Germany, 1934, drew crowds in their thousands.

Leader of the Soviet Union for almost three decades, Joseph Stalin was a ruthless dictator who ruled by terror and brutality. He successfully transformed his country into a major world power but at a cost of millions of his own peoples' lives.

MILESTONES

SEIZES POWER
Appointed secretary general, 1922. Assumes party leadership after Lenin's death, 1924.

MILLIONS STARVE
Imposes Five-Year Plans to industrialize Russia, 1928–33, causing famines that kill millions.

BETRAYS PARTY
Arrests and kills many party members and officials during the Great Purge, 1936–38.

FIGHTS NAZIS
Aligns with Britain and the US against Nazi Germany during World War II, 1939–45.

Joseph Stalin was born Iosif Vissarionovich Dzhugashvili, in the town of Gori, Georgia (then a part of the Russian Empire), on 18 December 1878. He became involved in radical politics while studying to become a priest. Adopting the name of Stalin, meaning "man of steel", he worked in secret for the early Bolsheviks (an extremist wing of the Marxist Russian Social Democratic Labour Party) and, by the time of the Russian Revolution in 1917, he had become a leading figure in the party.

Rise to power
When the Treaty on the Creation of the USSR was signed in December 1922, establishing the Soviet Union as the world's first communist state, Vladimir Lenin (see pp.170–72) appointed Stalin as secretary general of what was now the Communist Party. Ruling by oppression,

"As we know, the goal of every struggle is victory."

Joseph Stalin, 1904

Stalin's commanders defended Stalingrad against Germany and its allies in 1942–43. They were victorious after five months of fighting.

JOSEPH
STALIN

Stalin expelled or demoted anyone who spoke against him. Lenin objected to Stalin's methods and politics, and called for him to be removed from his post, but when Lenin died in 1924, Stalin had this order suppressed and assumed leadership of the Soviet Union.

Between 1928–33, Stalin enacted the first of his immense Five Year Plans to turn the country into a major economic power. He enforced rapid industrialization and ordered peasants to surrender their farms and join large collectives. Millions of people were killed for opposing Stalin's policies or used as slave labour in *gulags* (prison camps), and many died in famines that were a direct result of the reckless industrialization. Stalin achieved his political and economic aims but at a huge human cost.

Between 1936–38, Stalin's secret police, the NKVD (later becoming the KGB), arrested thousands of Communist Party members and officials. Many were imprisoned, forced to make false confessions of political crimes in "show trials", and executed or exiled. Stalin even destroyed his enemies' historical records.

War and after
In 1941, Germany invaded Russia. The Soviets' Red Army played a vital role in defeating

> **"Everyone imposes his own system as far as his army can reach. It cannot be otherwise."**
>
> **Joseph Stalin**, 1945

Stalin removed Lenin's successors (Alexei Rykov, Lev Kamenev, and Grigory Zinoviev), all of whom he regarded as potential rivals, from power and had them executed, 1936–38.

the Nazis, but millions of soldiers died unnecessarily due to Stalin's policy of "no retreat, no surrender".

After the war, Stalin used his military advantage to extend communism to East Germany, Eastern Europe, and the Baltic States. He had succeeded in turning the Soviet Union into a world superpower. However, a deep division, which would soon be known as the "Cold War", grew between East and West.

Stalin died on 5 March 1953. Nikita Khrushchev, who eventually succeeded him, denounced his campaigns of terror.

MORE THAN **75,000** PEOPLE WERE EXECUTED IN THE **GREAT PURGE**

MORE THAN **1.1 MILLION** SOLDIERS DIED AT THE **BATTLE OF STALINGRAD**

OVERSAW THE **DETONATION** OF THE SOVIET UNION'S **FIRST NUCLEAR WEAPON,** RDS-1, IN 1949

KIM KOO

The last president of an undivided Korea, Kim Koo began his nationalist struggle against government corruption when he was still in his teens. He went on to play a key role in Korea's fight for independence from the Japanese.

MILESTONES

JOINS FIGHT
As a member of Donghak, launches failed attack on Japanese-held Gang-gye fort, aged 20.

AVENGES QUEEN
Kills Japanese lieutenant he suspects of the murder of Queen Min, 1896. Imprisoned for two years.

MAKES A STAND
1919, calls for Korean independence and joins March 1st Movement against Japanese rule.

LEADER IN WAITING
Exiled in China, joins Korean Provisional Government, becoming president in 1926.

DREAM SHATTERED
Strives for Korean unity following liberation, 1945. Unsuccessful, he is assassinated, 1948.

Kim Chang-am was born near the town of Haeju, South Hwanghae Province, in what is now North Korea, on 29 August 1876. This was during a turbulent period in Korea's history that gave rise to the Donghak Peasant Movement (1894–95), triggered in 1892 when corrupt government officials manipulated the peasant farmers, forcing them to pay more tax. The farmers responded by attacking government officers, wealthy landowners, and foreigners.

Kim joined Donghak aged 16, and caught the attention of its leader Cho Si-hyeong. A year later he was in charge of the Palbong district regiment, leading attacks on government forces. In 1893, he changed his given name to Changsoo in order to confuse Japanese records (then to Koo, while in prison in 1913). He is often known by his pen name Baekbeom, meaning "ordinary person".

The last empress of Korea

On 8 October 1895, Japanese assassins broke into Korea's royal palace and murdered Empress Myeongseong (known as Queen Min). Queen Min had fostered strong ties with Imperial Russia and administered a pro-Russia policy in response to Japan's growing aggression in the region. The rest of the royal family

Thousands of mourners, seen below, queued to view the coffin of national hero Kim after his murder. Yet more lined the streets for his state funeral on 5 July 1949.

were given refuge in the Russian legation in Seoul, while Russian forces retook the palace from the Japanese.

The murder outraged the Korean public and prompted Kim to act. In 1896, he killed Josuke Tsuchida, a Japanese lieutenant, who he believed was involved in the murder. Admitting his crime, Kim was arrested, imprisoned, tortured, and sentenced to death, but Queen Min's husband, King Gojong, suspended the penalty.

Kim escaped from prison two years later and went into hiding, first entering a Buddhist monastery, before returning to his home province, where he taught in a school under an assumed name. In 1903, he converted to Christianity and the following year married Choi Junrye.

Under Japanese rule

In 1905, when Korea became a protectorate of Japan, Kim resumed his political activism and attended a mass protest against Japanese rule. Five years later, he joined *Sinminhoe*, a secret Korean independence organization. His association with *Sinminhoe* led him to being wrongly suspected of involvement in an attack on a Japanese general, and in 1912 he was imprisoned and tortured by the Japanese colonial government. When no evidence was found against him, Kim was released a year later.

In 1919, Kim and several activists declared a Proclamation of Independence and initiated non-violent countrywide protests against the Japanese – the March 1st Movement. The protests were ruthlessly suppressed by Japanese forces, and Kim went into exile to Shanghai, China. There, he joined the Korean Provisional Government, which lobbied for Korean independence.

Elected president in 1926, Kim established the Korean Patriotic Corps (KPC) in 1931. The KPC aimed to assassinate leading Japanese figures and made a failed attempt on Emperor Hirohito.

In 1940, the KPC became the Korean Liberation Army, supported by China. Following the outbreak of the Pacific War in 1941, it fought with the Allies against Japan.

Divided Korea

After Japan's surrender at the end of World War II, Korea was divided into the Soviet-run North, and US-administered South. Kim opposed this division, and in 1947 he unsuccessfully attempted to negotiate unification with the North. He then refused involvement in a general election held in the South the following year in an attempt to prevent the formation of separate governments. On 26 June 1949, Kim was assassinated at his home by a South Korean army officer, An Du-hui, who mistakenly believed Kim to be a communist allied with Russia.

Kim led a unified Korea as the 6th and last premier of the Korean Provisional Government. Despite his attempts to keep the country together after World War II, Korea was partitioned in 1948.

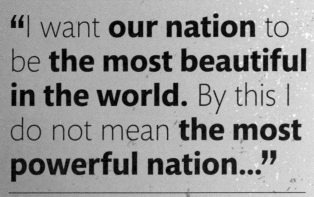

"I want **our nation** to be **the most beautiful in the world.** By this I do not mean **the most powerful nation...**"

Kim Koo, 1947

LED A **GUERILLA ARMY** AT THE AGE OF **17**

TAUGHT OVER **100 PRISONERS** HOW TO **READ**

WHILE IMPRISONED

KOREAN WAR (1950–53)

After the Japanese surrender in 1945, Korea was temporarily divided into the Soviet North and the US-administered South, but a permanent solution could not be agreed.

Kim Koo devoted himself to the cause of reunification. Negotiations between the US and the Soviets collapsed in 1947. The United Nations stepped in and a summit was held in the North's capital Pyongyang in 1948. Most of the South's leaders refused to go. Kim attended and was alarmed at the North's military strength. He returned predicting that North Korea would invade the South which they did on 25 June 1950.

"**I regard myself** as a **soldier,**
though a **soldier of peace.**"

Mohandas Gandhi, 1931

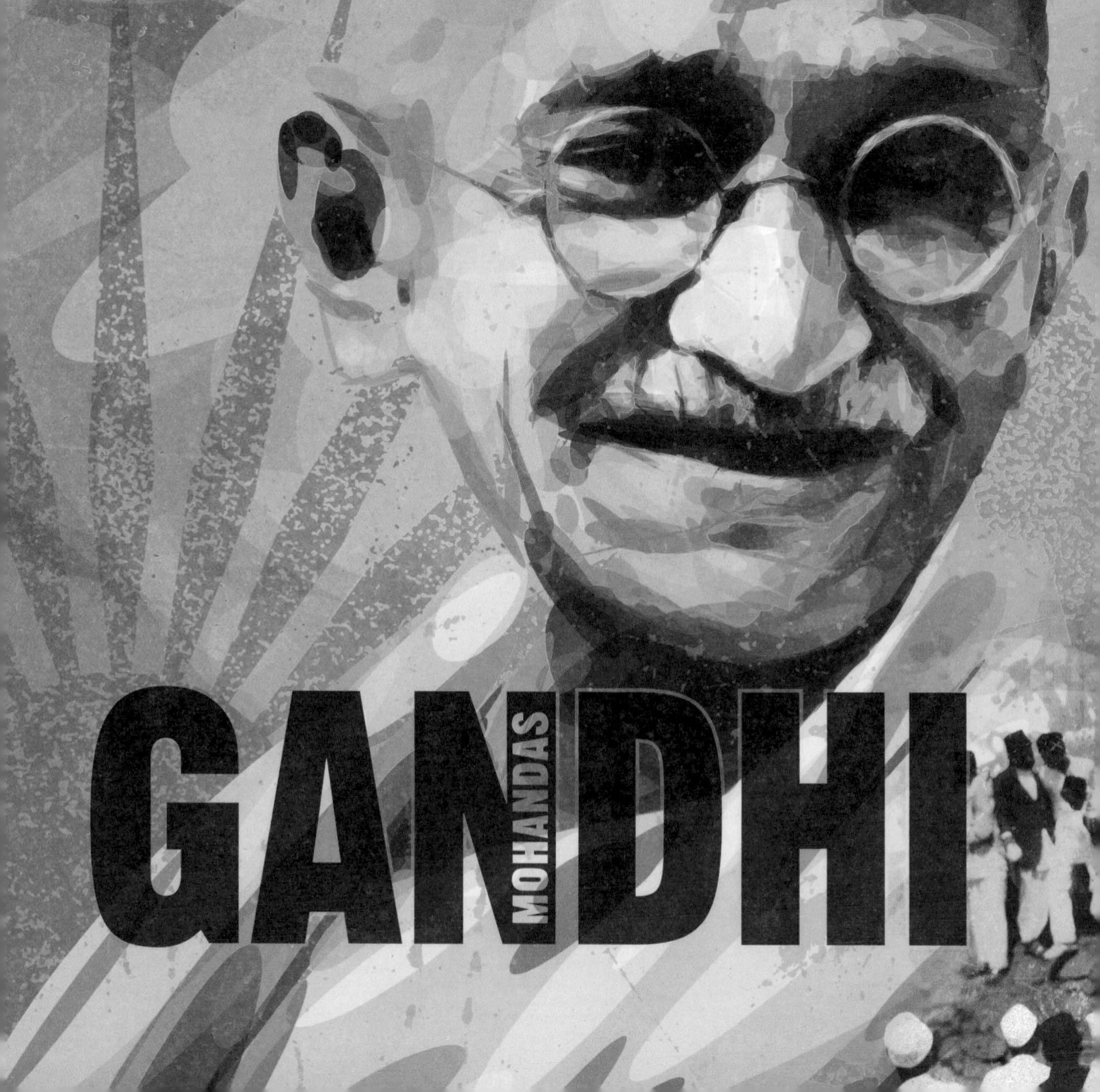

MOHANDAS **GANDHI**

Through self-discipline and determination, Mohandas Gandhi rose from humble beginnings to lead India to independence from the British Empire via non-violent protest. He remains one of the most iconic revolutionary leaders of the 20th century.

Mohandas Karamchand Gandhi was born on 2 October 1869 to a Hindu family of the middle-ranking Vaisya caste in Porbandar, India. When Gandhi was a young boy his father, Karamchand, became a *diwan* (chief minister) in nearby Rajkot. Gandhi's mother, Putlibai, was a devout Hindu and prayed daily at the local ashram (Hindu holy place). Gandhi's family hoped he would follow his father into politics.

When Gandhi was 12, he met 14-year-old Kasturba, and within a year he married her in an arranged marriage but continued his schooling. Their first son was born three years later, but died in early infancy. (They went on to have four more sons.) In the same year Gandhi's father became very sick and, despite efforts to nurse him daily, he passed away. The two deaths affected Gandhi deeply and because Gandhi was with his wife the night that his father passed away, he believed his father's death was a punishment for intimacy with her. The experience influenced his later decision to take a vow of *brahmacharya* – abstinence from all material and physical pleasures.

At the age of 18 he graduated from high school, and attended a local college, but dropped out. Advised to study law in Britain, he left his wife and their second son and, on 4 September 1888, sailed for London from Bombay (Mumbai).

MILESTONES

STUDIES LAW
Moves to London to study law, 1888. Promises to stay true to the Hindu faith and his family.

SUFFERS PREJUDICE
Starts to work in South Africa, 1893. Experiences consistent racial discrimination.

ESTABLISHES PARTY
Founds the Natal Indian Congress party, 1894. Implements its constitution in August of the same year.

FASTS FOR FREEDOM
Returns to India, 1915. Supports movement working to gain independence from the British Empire.

SECURES INDEPENDENCE
After more than 30 years of peaceful protests led by Gandhi, India gains independence, 1947.

A British-Indian soldier beat marchers who protested against salt prices imposed by the British in the 1930 Salt Marsh riot. Organized by Gandhi, 1,000 people walked 250 miles (400 km) to the coast to illegally collect salt to sell at fairer prices.

"**Strength** does not come from **physical capacity.** It comes from an **indomitable will.**"

Mohandas Gandhi, 1920

In 1891, after qualifying as a lawyer, Gandhi returned to India to establish his own legal practice, but he struggled due to his lack of knowledge of Hindu and Muslim law.

A life in South Africa

Offered a job in a law firm in South Africa, Gandhi set sail from Bombay once more, heading to the British colony of Natal. Once there he was shocked by colonial discrimination towards non-whites, experiencing it first-hand when he was thrown off a first-class train, despite having a ticket. Acts like this made him begin to question his people's standing within the British Empire.

Gandhi remained in South Africa for the next 21 years and developed his political views while involving himself in activism, opposing new legislation restricting Indian voting rights in Natal. Merchants agreed to provide legal cases for Gandhi so that he could establish a legal practice and support his campaigning. In 1894 he

CHEAPER COTTON MADE IN INDIA

Gandhi called on workers to spin and sell their own cheaper cotton to help the Indian economy.

India's subservience to Britain was lifted when it gained independence on 15 August 1947.

founded the Natal Indian Congress – the first political party in South Africa to represent the interests of its oppressed Indian population.

Gandhi pledged himself to non-violence, or *ahimsa*. His devotion to a just cause led to the practice of non-violent civil disobedience, or *satyagraha*, by him and his followers. In 1906, when the British introduced laws proposing further discrimination against the Indians, Gandhi led protestors in his first *satyagraha*. Although he and many followers were jailed for the protests, part of the law was repealed in 1914.

Road to Indian independence

The Indian National Congress (INC) had been launched in Bombay in 1885 with the aim of winning political rights for Indians. In 1915 Gandhi returned to India to help the cause, at the request of the Indian social reformer Gopal Krishna Gokhale. It was in this year that he was first named Mahatma, or "Great Soul", by his followers.

EXPENSIVE BRITISH-MILLED COTTON EXPORTED TO INDIA

The British Empire imposed unfair trading terms on India, forcing it to buy British-milled cotton.

SAROJINI **NAIDU**

Naidu (1879–1949) was another leading activist in the movement for Indian independence.

Educated in India and at Cambridge University, Naidu joined the Indian National Congress in 1905, and in 1925 became its first female president. She urged women to support national independence. In 1930 she joined Gandhi on the Salt March, a 25-day protest over Britain's taxes on salt production. She became India's first female governor when she was appointed Governor of the United Provinces, now Uttar Pradesh, in 1947.

"**Victory** attained by **violence** is... **defeat.**"

Mohandas Gandhi, 1919

Gandhi involved himself in domestic politics and took on legal cases supporting peasants and urban workers subjected to unfair legislation, land taxation, and price control by the British Empire. He was increasingly unpopular with the British, and jailed more than 20 times for political activism, but his national popularity grew. Gandhi used fasting as a form of non-violent protest. His fasts were widely reported by the press all over the world. The British, afraid of causing his death, accepted his demands.

One nationwide movement, inspired by *satyagraha*, opposed the Empire's Rowlatt Acts of March 1919 (laws that threatened the human rights of all who took part in revolutionary activities). This movement, however, eventually descended into violent riots, at which point Gandhi withdrew his support. He started two newspapers to educate the Indian people in non-violent protest. In 1921, he was appointed the head of the INC. Under his leadership, the number of members of the INC and participants in the independence movement ballooned.

Lasting legacy

On 15 August 1947 India gained its full independence, and British India was partitioned into present-day Pakistan and India along religious borders – Muslim, and Hindu and Sikh. Half a year later, on 30 January, 1948, Gandhi was shot and killed on his way to evening prayer by Nathuram Godse, a Hindu extremist who believed that Gandhi favoured the interests of India's Muslims above those of its Hindu population.

ROAD TO **REVOLUTION**

EXPLOITATION BEGINS
The British East India Trading Company founded in Surat in 1612, taking control of large parts of India.

BRITISH RULE
The Government of India Act was passed in 1858. It stated that India was ruled by the British Crown through the British Raj.

NEW PARTY
The Indian National Congress party formed in 1885. A forum for nationalism, it aimed to establish fairer laws for the Indian people.

FALSE PROMISE
Britain promised India independence if it fought for them in WWI. Over a million Indians went to war, many on the basis of this.

FULL INDEPENDENCE
In 1947, India gained independence and the country was split into two nations, India and Pakistan. Millions of refugees were displaced.

PEACEFUL CAMPAIGN
Mohandas Gandhi led a non-violent campaign for full independence from 1915; he visited London several times in the 1930s.

SHARED POWER
India still had to share its power with Britain; nationalists were frustrated and the British often violently suppressed protests.

ROAD TO FREEDOM
The UK passed the New Government of India Act in 1919, beginning a slow process towards Indian self-governance.

A militant revolutionary of the Indian independence movement, Bhagat Singh's resistance to British rule and his early death raised him to the status of national martyr.

Bhagat Singh was born in the Punjab Province of British India, now Pakistan. He left home at the age of 16 to devote himself to freeing India from British rule. A socialist and atheist, Singh was inspired by thinkers such as Karl Marx (see pp.130–35) to fight for liberation.

Singh believed that Gandhi's politics were intended to preserve the oppressive British system rather than overthrow it. To Singh, in order to effect real change, violent action was required.

In 1928 Singh shot a British policeman he mistook for the officer responsible for the death of nationalist leader Lajpat Rai. The officer's innocence led Gandhi and the wider public to condemn Singh's actions. Arrested in 1929, Singh and his followers went on hunger strike to campaign for prisoner's rights. With this, Singh's image was rehabilitated into that of a revolutionary hero. In spite of growing sympathy for his cause, Singh was eventually hanged.

Singh and his followers planted non-lethal bombs in the British Empire's political headquarters in New Delhi (below). They scattered political leaflets on the delegates, for which they were arrested.

BHAGAT SINGH

Haile Selassie was the last emperor of Ethiopia, who attempted to build a modern African nation. Born Ras Tafari Makonnen, he became the central figure of the Rastafarian movement, whose followers worshipped him as the Messiah, and believed that he would take them back to a promised land in Africa.

Selassie asserted his power by posing publicly with large animals. He had a small private zoo built at his palace, which housed cheetahs, lions, and leopards, among other animals.

Born on 23 July 1892, in the Harar province of Ethiopia, Ras Tafari took the name of Haile Selassie, meaning "Power of the Holy Trinity", when he became emperor in 1930. To the descendants of former slaves in Jamaica, the coronation fulfilled a prophecy made by Jamaican activist Marcus Garvey (see p.225) in 1924: "Look to Africa when a black king shall be crowned, for the day of deliverance is near."

Selassie created Ethiopia's first constitution and parliament, in which he approved all legislation, and reduced the powers of princes and nobles, which made it almost impossible for him to be deposed. Italian troops invaded in 1935 and Selassie fled the country the following year, living in exile for five years in the UK. He reinstated himself as emperor in 1941, after British forces liberated Ethiopia. Selassie wanted Ethiopia to be a progressive nation that prioritized education and equal rights. He founded the country's first university in 1950, and, over the next two decades, modernized the country's infrastructure.

To many Jamaicans, Selassie was a divine being, but in Ethiopia, famine and worsening unemployment led to a coup in 1974. Selassie died the following year while under house arrest. Although the new government claimed that Selassie died naturally in his sleep, Selassie's personal doctor, and millions of Africans, believed that he was assassinated.

"Leadership does not mean domination."

Haile Selassie, 1960

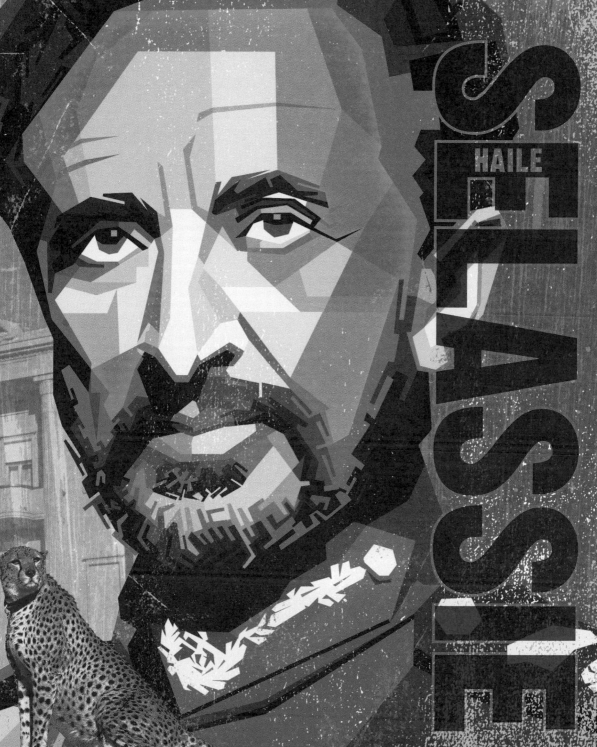

HAILE
SELASSIE

1892–1975

WINSTON CHURCHILL

Best remembered for leading the UK to victory during World War II, Sir Winston Churchill is one of the most revered leaders in British history. Despite a chequered political career, as wartime prime minister he united his country against the threat of Nazi invasion.

Winston Churchill was born into an aristocratic family in 1874, at Blenheim Palace, Oxfordshire. After graduating from Sandhurst Military Academy in Berkshire, he immediately joined the 4th Hussars cavalry regiment, travelling with them to India, Sudan, and South Africa. Although he was a serving officer, Churchill also became a well-respected war reporter, writing books about the campaigns he witnessed. However, in 1899, he decided upon a new career: politics.

A life in politics

Despite considering himself a liberal, in 1900 Churchill successfully stood for election as the Conservative member of parliament (MP) for Oldham, Lancashire. From the start, he put his principles before his party – then in government – and regularly voted against it. After just four years, Churchill defected from the Conservatives to the Liberal Party, which was voted into power during the 1906 general election.

As MP for Manchester North West, Churchill joined the Colonial Office, the first of many ministerial positions he held before being promoted to First Lord of the Admiralty – the head

Churchill lobbied the government in the 1930s to strengthen Britain's Royal Air Force. In 1940, it saved the country from invasion during the Battle of Britain.

"Never was **so much owed** by **so many** to **so few.**"

Winston Churchill, 1940

MILESTONES

ELECTED MP
Becomes politically active in 1899. Elected as Conservative member of Parliament, 1900.

GALLIPOLI CAMPAIGN
Failed Gallipoli campaign during WWI causes over 300,000 casualties, 1915. Blights reputation.

WARTIME LEADER
Prime Minister Neville Chamberlain advocates Churchill as his replacement, 1940. Leads Britain for five years during the war.

1874–1965

of the Royal Navy – in 1911. Held to account for naval failures during WWI, most notably the 300,000 Allied casualties during the Gallipoli campaign against Ottoman forces in 1915, he resigned from government later that year.

In an effort to rebuild his reputation, Churchill rejoined the army, serving on the Western Front for a number of months. He left the army and resumed his political career in 1916, and was appointed the Liberal minister for munitions in 1917. When the Liberal Party lost more than 100 seats in the 1924 general election, he joined the Conservatives, and served as chancellor of the exchequer until 1929.

World at war

Churchill raised concerns over German rearmament during the early 1930s, but the British prime minister at the time, Neville Chamberlain, adopted the policy of appeasement, conceding to Hitler's demands in an attempt to avert war. After Hitler invaded Poland in 1939, Britain declared war on Germany. Chamberlain

resigned the following year and Churchill became prime minister. When France fell to the Nazis, he travelled the world, pledging support to Hitler's opponents, including Soviet leader Joseph Stalin, and urged US President Roosevelt to enter the war. In the UK, he personally directed British military operations from secret bunkers in London, and also boosted public morale with visits to bombed-out cities and impassioned radio broadcasts.

Following the Allied victory in 1945, the Conservatives were defeated by the Labour Party. Churchill returned as prime minister from 1951–55, and remained an MP until 1964, when he retired.

DWIGHT **EISENHOWER**

Dwight Eisenhower (1890–1969) served as Supreme Allied Commander in Europe during WWII.

Eisenhower oversaw key initiatives during WWII, including the D-Day landings and the Allied advance on Paris. Although he clashed regularly with Churchill over military strategy, the two were firm friends. After the war he was appointed Supreme Commander of NATO, and became US president in 1952. His presidency saw the end of the Korean War (1950–53) and prosperity in the US.

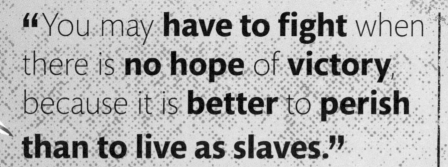

"You may **have to fight** when there is **no hope** of **victory,** because it is **better** to **perish than to live as slaves.**"

Winston Churchill, 1948

Victory in Europe Day, 8 March 1945, saw more than one million people take to the streets in the UK in celebration. Churchill became a national hero for leading his country in its "darkest hour".

CROSSED INTO **NO MAN'S LAND**

OVER 30 TIMES DURING WWI

SERVED IN THE **BRITISH PARLIAMENT** FOR **55** YEARS

350 MILLION PEOPLE WATCHED HIS **FUNERAL** ON TELEVISION

"WE SHALL FIGHT ON THE BEACHES, WE SHALL FIGHT ON THE LANDING-GROUNDS, WE SHALL FIGHT IN THE FIELDS AND IN THE STREETS, WE SHALL FIGHT IN THE HILLS. WE SHALL NEVER SURRENDER!"

Winston Churchill

Excerpt from a speech delivered following the evacuation of Dunkirk, 4 June 1940

◄ *Churchill flashes his familiar victory sign* to signify his support for Conservative party candidate, Anthony Fell, in 1949.

General Douglas MacArthur was one of the most senior officers in the US military. He led the US forces in the Pacific during WWII.

DOUGLAS MACARTHUR

Born into a military family, MacArthur first served during WWI, where he quickly distinguished himself, and was promoted from major to colonel. It was during WWII, however, as commander of the US forces in the Pacific, that he became renowned. He led the liberation of the Philippines from Japanese occupation, and officially accepted Japan's surrender in 1945. This marked the end of Japan's military culture, and the birth of its democracy. Returning home a hero, MacArthur's final command was to lead the UN forces in the Korean War (1950–53). However, he was relieved of his command for insubordination in 1951, when he retired from the army.

"**As you pointed out, we must win.** There is **no substitute** for **victory.**"

Douglas MacArthur, 1951

MILESTONES

EARLY PROMOTION	**DEFEATS JAPAN**	**FALLS FROM GRACE**
Appointed chief of staff of the US Army in 1930. Youngest person to ever hold that position at the time.	Returns to the Philippines, 1944. Liberates the islands from the Japanese Imperial Army.	Relieved of his command by President Truman for insubordination, 1951. Public approval of MacArthur wanes.

The only US president to serve four consecutive terms, Franklin Roosevelt created the New Deal programmes that helped bring the country out the Great Depression and back to prosperity.

MILESTONES

STRUCK BY POLIO
Permanently paralyzed from the waist down, 1921, but illness is hidden from the public.

BECOMES PRESIDENT
Elected as presidential candidate for Democratic Party, 1932. Elected as president later that year.

THE NEW DEAL
Pledges to lead the US out of the Great Depression with a set of economic reforms, 1933.

DECLARES WAR
In the wake of the surprise Japanese attack on Pearl Harbor, 1941, goes to war with Germany.

Outside the Capitol Building, crowds cheered for President Roosevelt in 1935.

Franklin Delano Roosevelt was born in Hyde Park, New York, in 1882. Fifty years later, in 1932, he was elected President during the height of the Great Depression. On his second day in office, Roosevelt passed the Emergency Banking Act, which helped to stabilize the nation's banking system. Later, he implemented the New Deal – a set of economic reforms designed to help the US recover. It was hugely successful, reducing the unemployment level, and giving businesses, farmers, bankers, and workers financial aid.

Throughout his entire presidency, Roosevelt spoke directly to the US public via radio broadcasts, fondly nicknamed his "fireside chats." In 1939, he persuaded a reluctant Congress to provide military support for Britain during WWII. He then proved instrumental in shaping post-war Europe and in planning what would become the United Nations. However, he did not live to see either become a reality – a month before the end of WWII, he suffered a haemorrhage and died on 12 April 1945 at his cottage in Warm Springs, Georgia. He was 63 years old.

FRANKLIN ROOSEVELT

A distinguished soldier and statesman, General Charles de Gaulle led the Free French movement, fighting the German occupation of France during World War II, while exhiled to London. In peacetime, he founded the Fifth Republic in France, and set out its new constitution. His fervent nationalism has given rise to "Gaullism", a conservative and patriotic political ideology.

Charles de Gaulle was born in Lille, France on 2 November 1890. His father taught history, literature, and philosophy, and later ran a school in Paris; the young de Gaulle developed a keen interest in these subjects and a particular fondness for military history.

Distinguished military career
In 1909, de Gaulle won a place at France's foremost military academy, Saint-Cyr, in Brittany. After graduating, he served as second lieutenant under Colonel Philippe Pétain, who later, as Marshal Pétain, was head of state of France during it's German occupation in World War II.

De Gaulle fought with distinction during World War I. Captured at Verdun in 1916, he spent 32 months as a prisoner of war, during which time he perfected his German. In the 1920s, he lectured and wrote several books and articles on politics and military strategy.

Following the outbreak of World War II in 1939, Germany invaded France in 1940. In response, de Gaulle headed an armoured division in counterattack, which although unsuccessful, led to his appointment as undersecretary of state for national defence. Despite his fierce opposition, the government then signed an armistice with Germany, Marshal Pétain became prime minister, and de Gaulle fled to London, for which Pétain branded him a traitor.

De Gaulle led French Resistance fighters and fought alongside the Allies to liberate Paris on 25 August 1944.

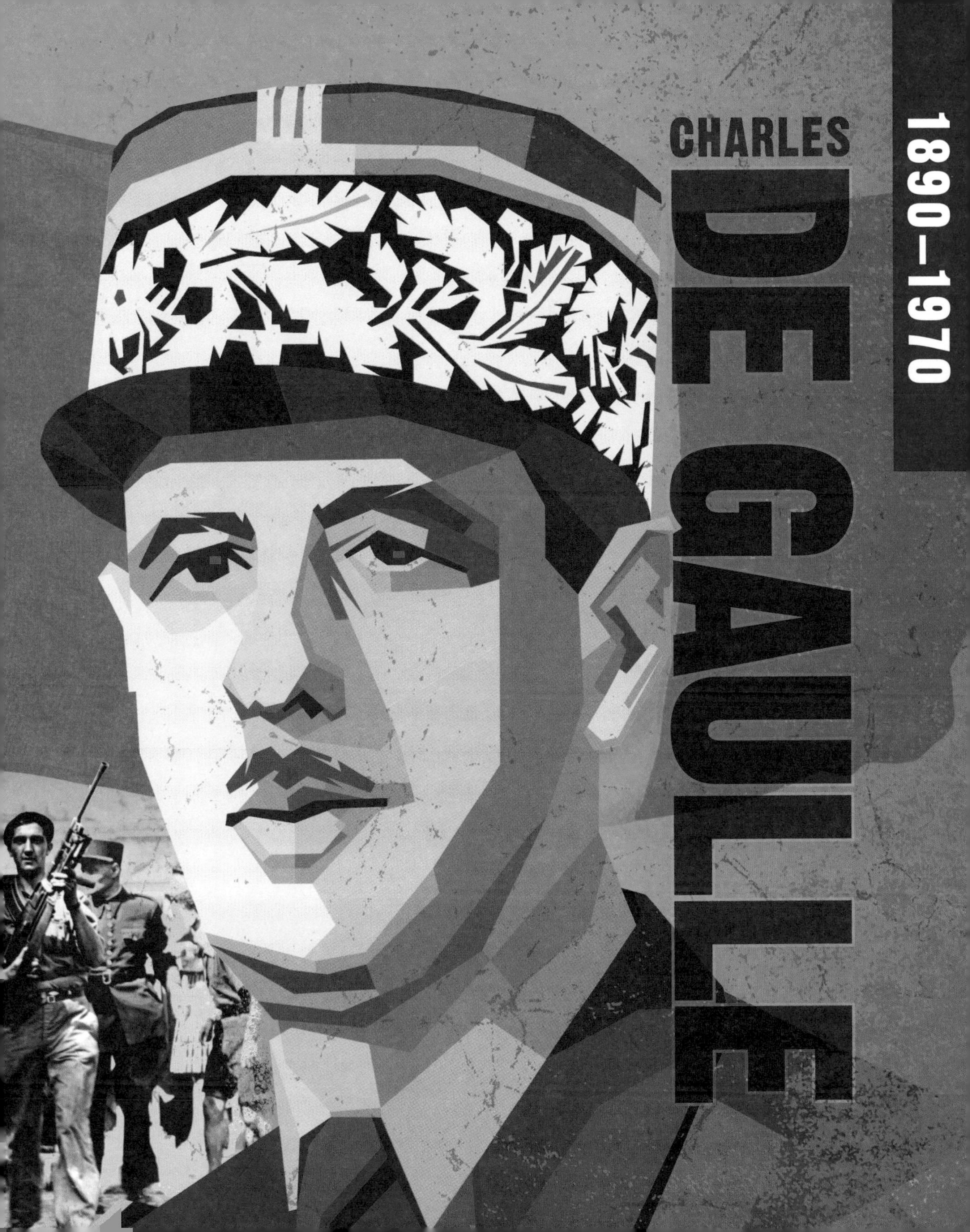

CHARLES **DE GAULLE**

1890–1970

From his London base, de Gaulle led the Free France movement, consisting of forces that had escaped German occupation and fighters from French colonies. By 1941, de Gaulle's men were fighting alongside the Allies in North Africa and the Middle East, while an underground resistance movement was active in France. In August 1944, de Gaulle, with the French 2nd Armoured Division and the US Army, liberated Paris, where he was welcomed as a hero.

Post-war politics and retirement

From 1944, de Gaulle led the Fourth Republic, the first government of the newly-liberated France, but resigned after two years, frustrated by its weak constitution. By the early 1950s, he retired altogether from politics and wrote about his war experiences: his *The Complete War Memoirs of Charles de Gaulle* became a staple of modern French literature.

In 1954, war broke out in Algeria, led by the Algerian National Front, who fought for independence from

"**France** has **lost a battle,** but she has **not lost the war.**"

Charles de Gaulle, 1940

French rule, destabilizing the Fourth Republic. Called upon to restore peace, de Gaulle was returned to government as prime minister in 1958. That same year, a referendum showed public support for the creation of a Fifth Republic, with a new constitution set out by de Gaulle, who was elected president in 1959.

During his presidency, de Gaulle granted independence to Algeria in 1962, and went on to establish France as a nuclear power, masterminded political stability and economic reforms, and ensured France's prominent position on the international stage. He retired in 1969 and died 18 months later, aged 80.

SERVED FOR 32 YEARS IN THE FRENCH MILITARY

MADE **5 ATTEMPTS** TO ESCAPE FROM **POW CAMP** DURING **WWI**

PRESIDENT OF **FRANCE FOR 10 YEARS**

GRANTED INDEPENDENCE TO 15 FRENCH COLONIES

NON! (((

In his "Appeal of 18 June" 1940, broadcast by the BBC in London, de Gaulle encouraged his countrymen to resist the Nazis and continue fighting for their freedom.

"MUST HOPE DISAPPEAR? IS DEFEAT FINAL?"

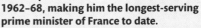

NON! (((

))) NON!

NON! (((

))) NON!

))) NON!

))) NON!

"I kept praying that **I might be able to prevent** a **repetition** of the **stupidity called war.**"

Eleanor Roosevelt, 1961

ELEANOR
ROOSEVELT

One of the most influential American women of the 20th century, Eleanor Roosevelt was the first wife of a US president to become involved in political issues. An early advocate of African-American rights, her commitment to social justice and humanitarian work earned her the respect of millions across the world.

MILESTONES

COMMUNITY WORK
Joins New York's Junior League, 1902. Teaches dance and gymnastic exercises to children.

POLITICAL EDITOR
Becomes editor of *Woman's Democratic News*, 1925. Writes monthly articles on political subjects.

FIRST LADY
Husband elected president, 1932. Her proactive approach as First Lady sets a precedent for the role.

NATIONAL DELEGATE
Becomes US representative on UN General Assembly, 1945. Franklin, her husband, dies the same year.

SAFEGUARDS RIGHTS
Chairs UN drafting committee. Co-creates the Universal Declaration of Human Rights, 1946–48.

A nna Eleanor Roosevelt was born in New York City on 11 October 1884. Her mother, a celebrated socialite, considered her daughter serious and plain, and nicknamed her "granny". Eleanor was close to her father, but he struggled with mental health issues and alcoholism, and was often away seeking treatment.

Following her mother's death, Eleanor, aged 8, went to live with her grandmother, and her father died two years later. In 1899, aged 15, she was sent to Allenwood Academy, a school in London, where she became a favourite pupil of headmistress Marie Souvestre. Eleanor later said of Souvestre: "Whatever I have become since had its seed in those three years of contact with a liberal mind and strong personality".

Returning to New York in 1902, Eleanor committed herself to public service. At 18, she worked on New York's Lower East Side with the Junior League, a local women's group, where she taught dance and gymnastics to underprivileged children. In 1905 she married her distant cousin, Franklin Delano Roosevelt,

Roosevelt headed the UN Human Rights Commission when the Universal Declaration of Human Rights was signed in 1948.

who became a New York senator in 1911. Eleanor worked with the Red Cross during World War I, serving food from its canteen in Washington to departing soldiers.

A life of politics

Devoted to women's rights in the workplace and civil rights for African-Americans, she started to write monthly articles for *Women's Democratic News*. In 1928 Franklin was elected governor of New York, and in the early 1930s he and Eleanor worked together on his presidential bid. Once Franklin was inaugurated president in 1933, Eleanor held weekly press conferences to discuss her social programmes, gave radio broadcasts outlining her personal and political views, and continued to write.

Eleanor was a key figure in the creation of the United Nations (UN). After Franklin's death, President Truman appointed Eleanor a member of the US delegation to the UN. The following year, as chair of the UN Human Rights Commission, she played a major role in the drafting of the Universal Declaration of Human Rights – the first

document to outline universal freedoms from slavery and discrimination among other rights. As the UN's most noted ambassador, Eleanor also travelled the world, investigating living conditions and urging increases in UN diplomatic aid.

Eleanor remained active in politics until her death in 1962, and her work enabled the passing of the Equal Pay Act of 1963. In a memorial address for Eleanor, US politician Adlai Stevenson read that "she would rather light candles than curse the darkness, and her glow warmed the world".

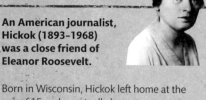

LORENA **HICKOK**

An American journalist, Hickok (1893–1968) was a close friend of Eleanor Roosevelt.

Born in Wisconsin, Hickok left home at the age of 15 and eventually became a reporter for *Associated Press* (AP). When she was assigned to cover Franklin D. Roosevelt's first presidential campaign, she formed a close bond with Eleanor. Over many years, Eleanor and Hickok shared their deep affection for each other in thousands of daily letters but the exact nature of their relationship remains unclear. Hickock inspired many of Eleanor's writing projects.

> "Surely, in the **light of history**, it is **more intelligent** to **hope rather than to fear**, to **try rather than not to try**."

Eleanor Roosevelt, 1960

Roosevelt enshrined human rights into international law, and was posthumously awarded the United Nations Prize in the Field of Human Rights in 1968 for her efforts.

SECURED **BETTER WAGES** FOR WOMEN IN **THE US**

HELPED TO CREATE THE **UNITED NATIONS** IN **1945**

WROTE OVER **8,000 ARTICLES** AND **27 BOOKS**

NOMINATED FOR THE **NOBEL** PEACE PRIZE THREE TIMES

"TOO OFTEN THE GREAT DECISIONS ARE ORIGINATED AND GIVEN FORM IN BODIES MADE UP WHOLLY OF MEN, OR SO COMPLETELY DOMINATED BY THEM THAT WHATEVER OF SPECIAL VALUE WOMEN HAVE TO OFFER IS SHUNTED ASIDE WITHOUT EXPRESSION."

Eleanor Roosevelt
Excerpt from *UN Deliberations on Draft Convention on the Political Rights of Women*, 1931

Eleanor Roosevelt addresses a group of supporters, 1948. ▶

DAVID

BEN-GURION

Widely regarded as the "Father of Israel", David Ben-Gurion had been involved in the campaign for a homeland for the Jews of Europe since he was a teenager. As Israel's first-ever prime minister, he was instrumental in developing the Jewish settlements in Palestine into a modern, prosperous nation.

David Gruen was born in Płońsk, Poland, then part of the Russian Empire, on 16 October 1886. His mother died when he was 11, and he was raised by his father, Avigdor Gruen, a lawyer and a leader in the *Hibbat Zion* (Lovers of Zion) movement that arose as a reaction to attacks on Jews in Russia during the 1880s. *Hibbat Zion* laid the foundations for modern Zionism, which sought to find a way for the Jewish people to return to Palestine, a region in the Middle East they regarded as their homeland.

The move towards Palestine

In 1903, Jewish residents of the Russian city of Kishinev were attacked by fellow citizens following a rumour that they had murdered a Christian child for sacrificial purposes. The *pogrom* (government-sanctioned violence) that followed added to the Jews' sense of urgency in creating a true, safe Jewish homeland. Convinced that the future of Judaism lay in Palestine, Gruen emigrated there in 1906, joining the 60,000 Jews who had already settled there. While working on farms, he immersed himself in the Marxist ideology of the Jewish Social Democratic Party. He also changed his name to "Ben-Gurion", after Yosef ben Gurion, a 1st century Jewish leader.

MILESTONES

ZIONIST ACTIVIST
Founds Labor Zionism group in New York, 1915, and seeks volunteers to fight in Palestine.

SUPPORTS THE ALLIES
Joins Jewish Legion, five battalions of Jewish volunteers who help fight the Ottomans, 1918.

JEWISH LEADER
Becomes chairman of Jewish Agency for Israel, 1935; leader of the Jews now living in Palestine.

LEADER OF ISRAEL
Israel founded, 14 May 1948, becomes its first prime minister. Resigns, 1953; re-elected, 1955.

ISRAEL FIGHTS BACK
Sends troops to fight in Egypt after its president, Gamal Nasser, nationalizes Suez Canal, 1956.

As Israel's new prime minister, Ben-Gurion, and his wife (centre left), were at the Haifa docks on 7 April 1948 to see the last British troops leave the Holy Land.

When World War I broke out, Ben-Gurion was deported by the German-backed Ottoman Empire that controlled Palestine. He travelled to New York, where he built an American chapter of the left-wing Labor Zionism movement, and met and married Paula Munweis.

Early signs of a divided Palestine

In 1917, the British government issued the Balfour Declaration, stating its support for the creation of a Jewish state in Palestine, which inspired Ben-Gurion to return and fight alongside the British forces. Three years later, Britain took responsibility for Palestine under a post-war mandate issued by the League of Nations, assisting in the immigration (aliyah) of 40,000 Jews. However, the local Arabs rioted at the influx, prompting the Jews, led by Ben-Gurion, to form their own militia – later becoming the basis of Israel Defense Forces (IDF).

As leader of Labor Zionism, and chairman of the Zionist and Jewish Agency for Israel, Ben-Gurion entered discussions with Britain over a proposed division of Palestine, where by 1939, there were some 450,000 Jewish settlers; about a third of the population. Britain then decided to limit immigration to Palestine for fear of antagonizing Egypt and the oil-rich Arab states.

In 1942, Ben-Gurion called on Jews to rise up in an armed struggle against the British, instigating a period of violence between British forces and the Jews in Palestine. The United Nations (UN) intervened in 1947, recommending

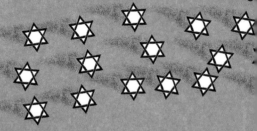

FEW POPULATIONS OF JEWS FRO

a partition of Palestine into Arab and Jewish states. Welcomed by the Jews, this was flatly rejected by the Arabs.

The birth of a homeland

Israel was established in 1948 with the support of the UN, the US, and the USSR. The British withdrew and the Arab–Israeli War erupted within months. Ben-Gurion formed the IDF, which quelled the conflict, and an uneasy truce prevailed.

In 1949, Ben-Gurion's *Mapai* (Labour) party won Israel's first general election, and he became both prime minister and minister of defence. Serving until 1963, he oversaw the construction of the new country, and its transformation from simple farming settlements into today's nation of 9 million people.

GOLDA **MEIR**

Born in Russia, Golda Meir survived a *pogrom* in Kiev in 1905 and became a leading figure the creation of Israel.

At school Meir became involved in the Zionist youth movement, and after graduating, went on to obtain a teaching qualification. In 1917, she married Morris Meyerson, a painter, and moved to Palestine in 1921 to live on a *kibbutz* (farming community). During and after World War II, she helped Jewish refugees and lobbied the British government to lift the restrictions on immigration to Palestine. She co-signed Israel's declaration of independence and held several government roles under Ben-Gurion. In 1969, she was elected prime minister and served for five years.

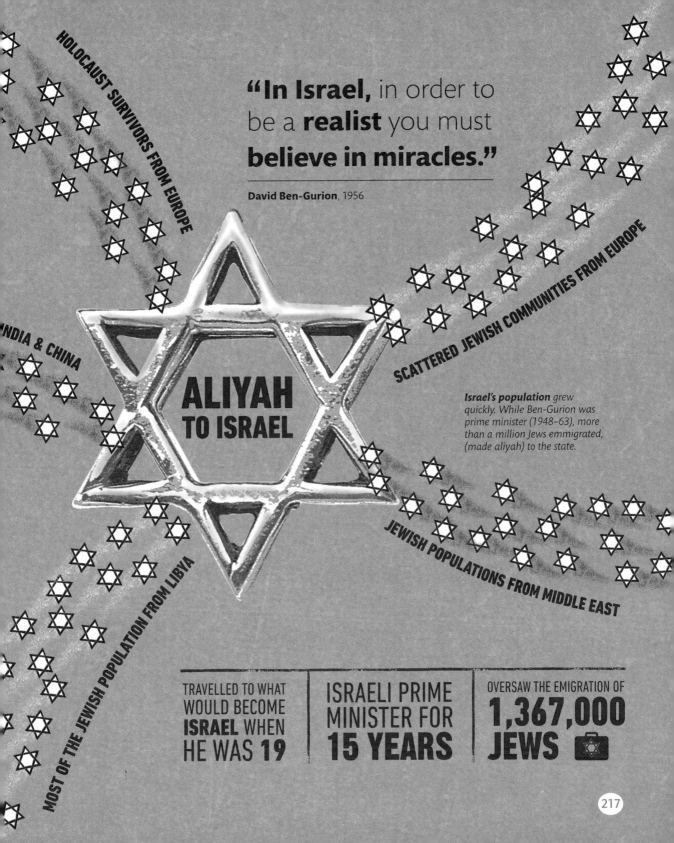

"In Israel, in order to be a **realist** you must **believe in miracles."**

David Ben-Gurion, 1956

HOLOCAUST SURVIVORS FROM EUROPE

INDIA & CHINA

SCATTERED JEWISH COMMUNITIES FROM EUROPE

ALIYAH TO ISRAEL

Israel's population grew quickly. While Ben-Gurion was prime minister (1948–63), more than a million Jews emmigrated, (made aliyah) to the state.

JEWISH POPULATIONS FROM MIDDLE EAST

MOST OF THE JEWISH POPULATION FROM LIBYA

TRAVELLED TO WHAT WOULD BECOME **ISRAEL** WHEN HE WAS **19**

ISRAELI PRIME MINISTER FOR **15 YEARS**

OVERSAW THE EMIGRATION OF **1,367,000 JEWS**

Mao Zedong forged a path to power through guerrilla warfare and, as Chairman of the Communist Party, made radical changes, transforming China into a communist state – but his economic reforms cost millions of lives.

Born in Shaoshan, Hunan province, central China, Mao Zedong was the son of a prosperous farmer. As a young man, he was rebellious – as a teenager he cut off his queue (pigtail), which was a symbol of subservience to the emperor – and abandoned an arranged marriage. However, Mao was also studious; he became a schoolteacher and also studied politics.

Communist revolution
In 1921, Mao joined the Chinese Communist Party (CCP), aiming to encourage the rural poor to become the power behind social change, in order to free the country from foreign oppression. After a failed attempt to incite a revolution in Hunan, Mao fled and became a fugitive leader of an armed group of bandits (which later became the Red Army) in Jingganshan in the mountains of Jiangxi, southeastern China. Uniting five villages as a self-governing state, Mao and his soldiers confiscated land from wealthy landowners, who were often massacred. Mao led his army under strict rules, creating an efficient and disciplined force.

Civil war in 1934 between the Chinese Nationalist Party – the Kuomintang (KMT) – and the CCP worsened, forcing Mao and his guerrilla forces to flee to Yan'an, in the province of Shaanxi. During this year-long, 5,600 mile (9,000 km) retreat,

Mao rose from the commander of a band of hunted guerrillas to the commander-in-chief of the world's largest army.

"**Politics** is **war without bloodshed** while **war** is **politics with bloodshed.**"

Mao Zedong, 1938

MAO ZEDONG

known as the "Long March", Mao established himself as the leader of the CCP and the Red Army.

Kickstarting revolution

In 1949, Mao led the Red Army to victory over the KMT, which finally ended the Chinese civil war, and declared the creation of the People's Republic of China, which he ruled as Chairman of the CCP. Mao believed that the rural poor should lead the revolution, and he sought to abolish the class system. Ruthless in imposing communist views, Mao monopolized political power and his army persecuted millions as traitors for opposing his rule. He also ensured that the economy was controlled by a powerful state bureaucracy, and elicited a mass-killing of wealthy landlords in order to redistribute land to the working class.

In 1958, Mao launched the Great Leap Forward, a campaign to mobilize the Chinese people towards industrialization. Peasants were forced into communes and to work in factories, for which they lacked the skills or equipment. The campaign resulted in mass starvation, and around 20 million people are thought to have died.

Mao made great use of propaganda to champion his beliefs, including rallies, and published his thoughts in the *Little Red Book* in 1964.

The doctrine of Maoism, *a belief system held by many at the height of Mao's rule, included a range of political and social ideas.*

SOCIAL HARMONY

EQUALITY FOR ALL

MASS MOBILIZATION

UTOPIAN SOCIETY

DESTRUCTION BEFORE CONSTRUCTION

PEASANT PROLETARIAT

REVOLUTION AFTER REVOLUTION

He believed in the need for constant revolution to prevent the accumulation of power by others. This culminated in 1966 when he launched the Cultural Revolution, designed to preserve pure communist ideology and purge the country of capitalist elements. China's youth were mobilized into forming Red Guard groups and, in just three years, cultural and religious sites were sacked, thousands of the educated elite were sent to work in the fields or factories, and millions were tortured and executed.

Mao's revolution led to a national crisis and his authority in government soon sharply declined. He remained Chairman of the CCP until his death in 1976.

ANTI-IMPERIALISM, ANTI-CAPITALISM

SUN **YAT-SEN**

Sun Yat-sen (1866–1925) played a leading role in the overthrow of the Qing dynasty and in the creation of the Republic of China in 1912.

Born near Canton, Guangdong province in China, Sun was educated in Hawaii and Hong Kong. A writer, philosopher, and revolutionary, he campaigned tirelessly for an end to imperial rule and for government based on nationalism, democracy, and socialism. After the formation of the Republic of China in 1912, Sun was elected President. In an effort to unite China, in 1912, he founded Kuomintang (KMT), the Nationalist Party of China, and served as its leader. However, the new republic was still weak and he could not stop warring factions fighting for control.

ROAD TO **REVOLUTION**

WESTERN INFLUENCE
Eager for international trade, the West flooded China with opium in the 18th century, in turn precipitating China's economic decline.

RISE OF SOCIALISM
Karl Marx wrote the *Communist Manifesto* in 1848. His ideas spread throughout the West and would go on to inspire Mao.

REPUBLIC OF CHINA
The Chinese Revolution, 1911, led to fall of the Qing dynasty. Republic of China founded by KMT, 1912, but was weakened by conflict.

EXTERNAL CONFLICTS
China was repeatedly attacked by the West and Japan during the 19th century. The Qing Emperor faced growing resentment in China.

CHALLENGE TO QING
Nationalism spread in China during the late 19th century, fuelled by famine, poverty, and concessions made to the West.

INTERNAL DISSENT
China erupted into civil war (1850–64) between Qing forces and Chinese Christians. The emperor triumphed but 20 million lives were lost.

"CLASSES STRUGGLE, SOME CLASSES TRIUMPH, OTHERS ARE ELIMINATED. SUCH IS HISTORY; SUCH IS THE HISTORY OF CIVILIZATION FOR THOUSANDS OF YEARS."

Mao Zedong

Cast Away Illusions, Prepare for Struggle, 14 August 1949.

◄ **Chinese propaganda** picturing Mao leading cheerful peasants during the Cultural Revolution, 1966.

DIRECTORY

As the 20th century dawned, the technological innovations of previous decades gave way to a series of global conflicts, fought by powerful military leaders. In many countries seeking freedom from colonial rule, nationalist voices demanded equality, recognition, and civil rights.

ROSA LUXEMBURG
1871–1919

A Polish-born writer and revolutionary, Rosa Luxemburg became a citizen of Germany aged 28. She believed deeply in Socialism acquired by revolution, although she was critical of Bolshevik dictatorship in Russia. When Germany went to war in 1914 she co-founded the Spartacus League, a radical anti-war group, and in 1919 she co-founded the German Communist Party. However, just after this, during the Spartacist Uprising – an anti-government general strike – she was arrested and executed without trial. After her death, she became a heroine of the communist cause.

SRI AUROBINDO
1872–1950

Born in West Bengal and educated at Cambridge University, Aurobindo Ghose (later Sri Aurobindo) became an influential nationalist leader in Bengal in the struggle for Indian independence from British rule. After being sent to prison for his political activities, he moved to southeast India to develop the spiritual practice of Integral Yoga, his vision for creating a divine life on Earth. He was a teacher, philosopher, poet, and prolific writer, nominated for both the Nobel Prize for Literature and the Nobel Peace Prize. The spiritual community that he founded, the Sri Aurobindo Ashram, remains a key destination for spiritual seekers.

ARTHUR CURRIE
1875–1933

General Sir Arthur Currie rose through the ranks of the army to become the first Canadian commander of Canada's forces abroad during WWI, and was awarded a knighthood in 1917 for his exemplary services. His reputation as one of Canada's leading military figures was established at several key battles, including Ypres, and in the victories he won during the final Allied offensive. Currie remains widely recognized as one of the most successful commanders on the Western Front.

MARY MCLEOD BETHUNE
1875–1955

An educator and civil rights activist, African-American Mary McLeod Bethune campaigned for social support and voting rights, and founded a school for African-American girls; this grew into a co-educational college for African-Americans. Eventually, she became president of the National Association of Colored Women. She gained national acclaim for her community works and was appointed special advisor to President Roosevelt, becoming the first African-American woman to hold a high position in US government.

MOHAMMED ALI JINNAH
1876–1948

Often referred to as "Great Leader", Mohammed Ali Jinnah was an Indian Muslim politician. Although initially a supporter of Hindu-Muslim unity, as relations between the two communities deteriorated in the early 20th century, Jinnah led the Muslim League in a battle to establish a Muslim state independent from India. With skilful negotiation Jinnah secured the creation of Pakistan in 1947, and became the first leader of the new state. He is revered as the father of the nation.

EMILIANO ZAPATA
1879–1919

The Mexican guerrilla leader Emiliano Zapata spearheaded the peasant revolt in the state of Morelos during the Mexican Revolution. He worked to bring about reforms that would restore land to the peasants and protect their rights. In 1913, along with four other revolutionaries, Zapata engaged in guerrilla warfare against former army general President Victoriano Huerta, whose unpopular military rule in Mexico was deemed a dictatorship by the public. Zapata was betrayed and killed during the conflict before his reforms were enacted, but he is revered as a visionary who battled for the rights of the ordinary people, and his ideals continue to inspire southern Mexican indigenous populations.

JOSEPH LYONS
1879–1939

One of Australia's longest-serving prime ministers, Joseph Lyons was premier of Tasmania before entering federal politics, co-founding and becoming leader of the United Australia Party, which was elected into government in 1932. As prime minister, Lyons enjoyed great public popularity, and helped to revive Australia's economy, which had suffered in the Great Depression. His government also oversaw a decline in unemployment, expansion of the military, a boost to industry, and the provision of welfare benefits. He died while still in office and was mourned across the nation.

MONA RUDAO
1880–1930

A Taiwanese aboriginal, Mona Rudao was an influential leader of the Atayal tribe, in the Wushe region of Japanese Taiwan. He led the Wushe Rebellion, the last major armed rebellion against Japanese colonial authorities, in which the Atayal killed 134 Japanese people. In response, the Japanese bombed and gassed the Atayal, killing hundreds. Mona Rudao committed suicide to evade capture and was hailed a hero of the revolution. As a result of the uprising he instigated, aboriginals were finally granted equal rights to other ethnic groups in Taiwan.

MUSTAFA KEMAL ATATÜRK
1881–1938

Mustafa Kemal, known as Atatürk ("Father of the Turks"), first came to prominence through his victory over the Western Allies in the Battle of Gallipoli in World War I. Fighting continued after the war; Atatürk led the Turkish Nationalist movement to protect Turkey against acquisition by Allied forces. The signing of the Treaty of Lausanne ended the conflict and dissolved the Ottoman Empire. Atatürk then declared Turkey an independent republic with himself as president. He implemented a series of revolutionary political and social reforms, to establish Turkey as a modern, secular state.

BENITO MUSSOLINI
1883–1945

Mussolini founded the National Fascist Party, which promoted an extreme form of nationalism in Italy. A skilled propagandist and powerful speaker, he gained political support at a time of instability and used his militia to suppress opposition. He seized power in 1922 and established a dictatorship, naming himself *Il Duce* (the Leader) of Europe's first centralized fascist state. During his 20-year rule he launched initiatives to cut unemployment and boost the economy, winning admirers worldwide. However, his alliance with Nazi Germany committed Italy to a war for which it was ill prepared, and he was eventually deposed and killed.

GEORGE S. PATTON
1885–1945

A controversial but highly-acclaimed US army officer, General George Patton is best known for his fierce, determined leadership of the US Army during World War II as they took Sicily, then liberated France and advanced into Germany. He was a brilliant tactician and practitioner of tank warfare, and a key figure in the development of this discipline before the war. An inspiring leader, his fiery temper and colourful language earning him the nickname "Old Blood-and-Guts", Patton led from the front in often aggressive and rapid offensive manoeuvres, and is remembered as one of the greatest combat commanders in US history.

RAYMOND SPRUANCE
1886–1969

Admiral Spruance commanded US naval forces in some of the most significant sea battles of World War II. Despite having little experience of naval aviation, Spruance took command of Task Force 16 in the Pacific, leading them in the Battle of Midway – the first major US victory over Japan. Despite his reserved and cautious approach, his victories in the Pacific earned him renown as one of the greatest admirals in American naval history. Following the war he was named president of the Naval War College and later American ambassador to the Philippines.

MARCUS GARVEY
1887–1940

Jamaican activist and nationalist leader Marcus Garvey aimed to unite African people around the world and free Africa from racial oppression. His mass movement, known as Pan-Africanism, attracted a huge following of people in the US who believed in his vision of social, political, and economic freedom for all black people. Garvey founded the Universal Negro Improvement Association in 1914, and established a series of African-American businesses. A charismatic, persuasive leader and a passionate speaker, Garvey reached the peak of his powers in the 1920s. Yet he was criticized by other black leaders for his advocacy of racial purity, and also convicted, for which he was imprisoned for fraud and deported back to Jamaica.

BERNARD MONTGOMERY
1887–1976

Field Marshall Bernard Montgomery served with distinction in World War I, and went on to be one of the most successful British generals of World War II. He was made commander of the British forces in North Africa, where he boosted his troops' morale and led them to victory over the Germans and Italians at El Alamein; an event considered to be the turning point of the war. Montgomery led further Allied victories in Sicily and Italy, and commanded all of the Allied troops following the D-Day landings. After the war he was made a knight of the Garter and Viscount Montgomery of Alamein.

HEINZ GUDERIAN
1888–1954

A German officer in World War I and then a general in World War II, Heinz Guderian was a pioneer in tank warfare. During the interwar years he advocated the use of independent *panzer* (armour) tank divisions backed by air and infantry forces, as well as the use of radio communications between vehicles. Actively supported by Hitler, Guderian commanded units invading Poland, France, and Russia, during which he demonstrated Germany's tactical superiority over their enemy. He was made Hitler's chief of staff of the army, but resigned as Hitler was largely performing this role himself.

JAWAHARLAL NEHRU
1889–1964

A protégé of Mahatma Gandhi, the activist and nationalist political leader Jawaharlal Nehru became the first prime minister of an independent India in 1947. He was elected president of Gandhi's Indian National Congress party in 1929, which aimed to secure independence from British rule. Once president, Nehru helped shape India as a modern democratic nation, implementing political, economic, and social change, such as promoting innovations in science and technology and outlawing caste discrimination. He was known for his neutral foreign policy and helped other nations remain neutral at a time when the US and USSR were at odds with one another.

ERWIN ROMMEL
1891–1944

Erwin Rommel was one of Hitler's most successful generals of World War II, known for his exemplary leadership of the German and Italian armed forces, notably in North Africa. His aggressive style of mobile warfare won crucial victories, particularly through the use of surprise attacks, which earned him the nickname "Desert Fox". Widely respected, even by the Allies, Rommel was promoted to field marshal in 1942. However, he started to doubt that Germany could win the war. He was falsely implicated in a plot to kill Hitler; he committed suicide to avoid trial.

FRANCISCO FRANCO
1892–1975

The Spanish dictator General Francisco Franco was a monarchist who led his nationalist army to victory during the Spanish Civil War. Aided by Germany and Italy, Franco's forces overthrew the Spanish Democratic Republic in 1939. As head of government he suppressed political opposition through the use of labour and concentration camps, as well as thousands of executions. Franco maintained Spanish neutrality during World War II, but in the Cold War emerged as a leading anti-Communist figure. He later presided over a period of economic recovery and industrial growth in Spain. He died in 1975 having restored King Juan Carlos I to the throne.

NIKITA KHRUSHCHEV
1894–1971

Nikita Khrushchev became leader of the Soviet Union in 1955 following Stalin's death. He swiftly implemented a policy of "de-Stalinization", denouncing the previous, brutal regime. The policy sent a shock through the communist world; it prompted the release of millions of political prisoners, as well as a series of uprisings in European communist states, and gave rise to a period of widespread liberalization. Khrushchev advocated greater cultural and intellectual freedom in Russia, and sought to improve living standards. His investment in the Soviet space programme saw the launch of Sputnik, the world's first space satellite.

MATTHEW B. RIDGWAY
1895–1993

US General Matthew Bunker Ridgway led the 82nd Airborne Division of the US Army in successful campaigns into Sicily, Normandy, and Germany in World War II. During the Korean War he was dispatched to command the United Nations forces against the Chinese. Ridgway's ability to rally troops helped to boost morale, and he led a counterattack that drove the Chinese out of South Korea, marking a turning point in the war. He was later appointed chief of staff of the US arm for two years.

LESTER B. PEARSON
1897–1972

The 14th prime minister of Canada, Lester Pearson was a scholar, World War I veteran, and diplomat. Involved in establishing the United Nations and the North Atlantic Treaty Organization, he also managed to secure a diplomatic end to the Suez Canal Crisis of 1956, for which he was awarded the Nobel Peace Prize. Elected prime minister in 1963, Pearson abolished capital punishment, set up a national pension plan and universal healthcare, and introduced the current Canadian flag and national anthem. He is considered one of Canada's most popular and influential figures of the 20th century.

JOMO KENYATTA
c.1894–1978

A Kenyan political activist from the Kikuyu people, Jomo Kenyatta led the movement to free Kenya from British colonial rule, and became its first president. Kenyatta joined the first African political protest in 1922; he went abroad to study in London and Moscow, before returning to carry on his battle for gradual change rather than revolution. He spent decades petitioning the British government for independence, becoming leader of the Kenya African National Union in 1961, and eventually securing independence in 1963. As the first president of Kenya, Kenyatta established a strong centralized government and oversaw economic growth and a period of political stability.

SUKARNO
1901–70

Indonesian nationalist leader Sukarno campaigned for independence from Dutch colonial rule. A brilliant speaker, he gained huge public support and unified the country's nationalist groups. When Japan occupied Indonesia during WWII, their commander, aware of his popularity, appointed Sukarno the country's leader. After Japan's surrender to the Allies in 1945, Sukarno declared independence and himself president; the Dutch relinquished power in 1949. As president, he dismantled all political parties to prevent political dissent, but Indonesia's economy soon declined, and Sukarno was deposed in 1965.

RUHOLLAH KHOMEINI
1902–89

Heading the 1979 Iranian revolution to overthrow the last shah of Iran, Mohammad Reza Pahlavi, Ruhollah Khomeini gained huge support for his rejection of Western democracy and call for an Islamic Republic. He incited riots, strikes, and the collapse of the shah's government. Once the shah had been deposed, Khomeini took power and founded an Iranian Republic that reinstated Islamic law, banned music and alcohol, ordered women to wear the veil, and adopted an aggressive anti-West and anti-USSR foreign policy. The religious government that Khomeini established continues to underpin Iranian politics and society.

EMPRESS KŌJUN
1903–2000

Japanese Empress Kōjun was the wife of Emperor Shōwa, better known as Hirohito, ruler of Japan during World War II. She was a gifted painter, calligrapher, and poet. After the war, she and her husband adopted a more public role to demystify the monarchy. Empress Kōjun witnessed a period of rapid modernization in Japan, but she still remained loyal to the traditions of the Japanese monarchy.

RALPH BUNCHE
1904–71

An African-American civil rights activist, diplomat, and leading member of the UN, Ralph Bunche is best-known for successfully brokering a ceasefire between Israel and four Arab states, following the creation of the state of Israel in 1948. In recognition of his diplomacy Bunche was awarded the Nobel Peace Prize in 1950 – the first African-American to receive the award. Other defining moments of his career were his supervision of the deployment of 6,000 peace-keeping UN troops during the Suez Canal Crisis, and mediating other conflicts in the Congo, Kashmir region, and Yemen.

DENG XIAOPING
1904–97

De facto successor to Chairman Mao as head of the People's Republic of China, Deng Xiaoping rose from a peasant background to become the most powerful figure in China from 1978 until his death in 1997. Although he never held office as leader of the Communist Party, he initiated a wide series of political, social, and economic reforms that encouraged foreign investment in China, restored cultural stability, and improved the standard of living for many millions of Chinese. As a result of Deng's reforms China became one of the fastest-growing economies in the world.

5

RIGHTS AND REVOLUTIONS

1950–1980

KWAME NKRUMAH

"We prefer **self-government with danger** to **servitude in tranquillity.**"

Kwame Nkrumah, 1957

Leading Ghana to independence from British colonial rule, Kwame Nkrumah was the nation's first prime minister and later its first president. He triggered the African independence movement, encouraging black activists across the continent to build a united Africa, free from imperial control.

MILESTONES

MOVES INTO POLITICS

Joins newly formed United Gold Coast Convention party – as general secretary, 1947.

ESTABLISHES PARTY

Founds Convention People's Party (CPP), 1949. As chairman, he campaigns for independence.

TAKES OFFICE

CPP wins 1951 general election. As prime minister, establishes all-African cabinet.

CREATES NEW NATION

Demands independence from Britain, granted 1957. Gold Coast is renamed Ghana same year.

FOUNDS REPUBLIC

Declares Ghana a republic and becomes its first president, 1960, until overthrown, 1966.

F rancis Kwame Ngolomah was born in the village of Nkroful in the Gold Coast into a poor, illiterate family in 1909. Raised by his mother and extended family, he was baptized Roman Catholic, and sent to a school run by a Catholic mission in nearby Half Assini.

Nkrumah's academic prowess caught the attention of Reverend A.G. Fraser, principal of Prince of Wales College, a government training school, in the capital, Accra. Aged 21, Nkrumah graduated in 1930 as a qualified teacher. His first job was in a Catholic primary school, and within a year he was the headmaster of a school in Axim.

Pan-African activist

Inspired by Nigerian journalist and freedom fighter Nnamdi Azikiwe, who later became president of Nigeria, Nkrumah was determined to further his education. He won a scholarship to Lincoln College, Pennsylvania, US, where he studied theology, sociology, and economics, before earning masters degrees at the University of Pennsylvania. As a student, Nkrumah

President Nkrumah greeted Queen Elizabeth II, head of the British Commonwealth, on her first state visit to the newly independent Ghana in November 1961.

SURVIVED 7 ASSASSINATION ATTEMPTS

SPENT 14 MONTHS IN PRISON

UNITED 32 NATIONS IN THE ORGANIZATION OF AFRICAN UNITY

SET UP OVER 40 STATE-RUN ENTERPRISES

Nkrumah advocated passionately for Pan-Africanism and became a symbol of what was possible for later African independence movements. He believed that Ghana's independence would prove meaningless unless it was the first step in the liberation of the entire African continent from European rule.

became engrossed in the Pan-African movement, which sought to create solidarity between all African people, and in socialist ideology. He relocated to the UK to study, and was instrumental in organizing the Fifth Pan-African Congress held in Manchester, 1945.

Nkrumah became intent on leading his native Gold Coast to independence from British rule. In 1946, British governor Alan Burns, seeking fairer representation, introduced amendments to the Gold Coast constitution that gave Africans a majority on the legislative council for the first time, prompting several academics and lawyers to form a new party – the United Gold Coast Convention (UGCC).

Ghana's hero

Nkrumah returned to the Gold Coast in 1947 to become the UGCC's general secretary, until 1949, when he founded his own Convention People's Party (CPP), which was committed to a strategy of positive non-violent action that put pressure on the colonial administration.

In January 1950, when Nkrumah and the CPP encouraged union strikes, he was imprisoned for his actions, but by then he had become a popular hero. When a general election was granted in 1951, the CPP won and Nkrumah was released from prison. A year later he was sworn in as the Gold Coast's first prime minister.

Once in office, Nkrumah called for an all-African cabinet, then pressed for independence. A general election was held in July 1956, the CPP won, and the Gold Coast gained independence from the UK on 6 March 1957. The new nation was renamed Ghana, after the Ghana Empire of West Africa (c. 700–1240), and in 1960, it became a republic, with Nkrumah as its first president.

However, Nkrumah's Ghana was a one-party state, subject to rigged elections, economic woes, and an increasing lack of press freedom. In 1966, while Nkrumah was on a state visit to Beijing, Ghana's armed forces overthrew him. Finding asylum in Guinea, he lived there until he died of cancer in 1972.

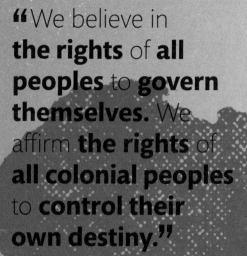

"We believe in **the rights** of **all peoples** to **govern themselves.** We affirm **the rights** of **all colonial peoples** to **control their own destiny."**

Kwame Nkrumah, 1945

ROBERT **MUGABE**

Inspired by Kwame Nkrumah's fight for Ghanaian independence, Robert Mugabe (b.1924) was at the forefront of nationalist activities to free Southern Rhodesia from British colonial rule.

Mugabe joined those calling for an independent black-led state in the 1960s, but was jailed for his activities, 1964–74. Upon his release, he began a violent campaign and the UK government eventually granted Rhodesia independence in 1980. Mugabe became its president, and ruled until 2017. Initially lauded for improving education and health for the black majority, his seizure of white-owned farms and violent oppression of political dissent led to international sanctions that resulted in economic decline and social instability.

Having overthrown a capitalist government, survived over 600 assassination attempts, and brought the world to the brink of nuclear war, Fidel Castro faced constant controversy during his 50-year term as Cuban leader, but his supporters greatly admired him. Castro made Cuba a one-party state, nationalized industry, and improved education and healthcare for the masses.

MILESTONES

PLANS FOR CHANGE
Founds "The Movement", 1952, a group dedicated to removing Fulgencio Batista from power.

IMPRISONED REBEL
Attacks Moncada Barracks, Santiago de Cuba, 1953. Serves two years in prison.

LEADS REVOLUTION
Oversees successful two-year guerrilla campaign that topples Batista, December 1958.

DEFEATS US PLAN
Becomes prime minister, 1959. Crushes US forces in Bay of Pigs invasion two years later.

THE BRINK OF WWIII
Permits Soviet building of nuclear missile bases in Cuba, leading to Cuban Missile Crisis, 1962.

Fidel Castro was born to Ángel Castro, a Spanish-born sugar plantation owner, and Lina Ruz González – Ángel's maid who later became his second wife – on 13 August 1926. While studying law at the University of Havana, in 1947, Castro joined the Party of the Cuban People, led by the charismatic Eduardo Chibàs, whose call for social justice, anti-corruption, and political freedom struck a chord with him. Meanwhile, Castro became increasingly influenced by Marxism (see pp.130–35), and started to believe that political change could only be brought about by revolution led by the working class.

Seeds of revolution

In 1952, right-wing military general Fulgencio Batista seized power in Cuba during a military coup. Castro viewed him as a dictator, and began planning ways to depose him, forming a revolutionary organization, "The Movement", with his brother Raúl. On 26 July 1953, the Castro brothers and around 150 rebels stormed Moncada Barracks in Santiago de Cuba. The operation failed, and Fidel was sentenced to 15 years in prison. Many of the other rebels, including Raúl, received shorter sentences.

Castro's success at deposing the right-wing Fulgencio Batista led to Cubans celebrating in Havana's streets in 1958.

FIDEL CASTRO

1926–2016

"Condemn me, it does not matter: history will absolve me."

Fidel Castro, 1953

After Fidel's supporters appealed for amnesty, the rebels were released early, having served almost two years. To evade being arrested again, after violent protests led to a crackdown on dissent in 1955, Fidel went into self-imposed exile in Mexico, where he joined forces with Ernesto "Che" Guevara (see box).

On 2 December 1956, Fidel, Raúl, Che, and their supporters returned to Cuba. For the next two years they waged a guerrilla campaign against Batista, finally defeating him on 31 December 1958.

Socialist Cuba

In 1959, Castro became prime minister, introduced free healthcare, and set up a nationwide literacy programme. He nationalized US-owned banks and sugar mills, reformed land ownership, and heavily taxed American products.

These policies led the US to suspend relations with Cuba in 1961. Meanwhile, in Miami, Florida, anti-revolutionary exiles, supported by the US Central Intelligence Agency (CIA), plotted to

Castro survived 638 CIA-backed assassination plots, including the use of a poisoned pen syringe, an exploding cigar, a booby-trapped seashell, and an infected diving suit.

land at the Bay of Pigs, from where they would invade Cuba and overthrow Castro. However, Castro's forces crushed them in just three days, and the US's involvement in the attack was exposed. Castro's victory boosted his popularity in Cuba. Wary of further US attacks, he formed closer ties with the USSR and allowed the Soviets to build several nuclear missile bases in Cuba. This almost triggered a nuclear world war in 1962 but eventually, after negotiations with the US, Soviet leader Nikita Khrushchev (see p.226) backed down.

Throughout his time in office, Castro was a symbol for revolution around the world, and inspired revolutionary movements in Nicaragua, Venezuela, Brazil, and Uruguay. He also sent troops to support communist activities in Angola, Ethiopia, and Yemen. Aged 81, Fidel handed over power to Raúl. He died on 25 November 2016, aged 90.

ERNESTO "CHE" GUEVARA

Born 14 June 1928 in Argentina, Ernesto "Che" Guevara studied medicine and became interested in radical politics. By the time he met Fidel Castro in 1955, he was a committed Marxist.

Eager to explore the world, Che made several long journeys around Latin America while he was still a student. He was infuriated by the poverty and social inequality he witnessed, and grew convinced that they could be ended with revolution. In 1965, having played key roles in Castro's government, Che set out to spread his theory of guerrilla warfare – going first to Congo in Africa, then to Bolivia. He was captured in Bolivia by CIA-backed troops on 8 October 1967 and executed the following day.

ROAD TO **REVOLUTION**

FOREIGN CONTROL
Following the US liberation of Cuba from Spain, Congress passed the Platt Amendment, 1901, legally justifying US intervention in Cuba.

DEADLY ASSISTANCE
In 1912, Cuban former slaves revolted against US-backed government. The US invaded Cuba to quell uprising. 6,000 Afro-Cubans were killed.

CORRUPT STATE
Batista re-took power in a military coup in 1952. Crime, corruption, and inequality arose. Castro led a resistance against him, 1952–58.

MILITARY COUP
Sergeant Batista ousted the Cuban government in 1933. Conspired with the US to become Cuba's *de facto* leader. Elected president in 1940.

MORAL LAPSE
Bribery tainted Grau's government. Organized crime infiltrated Cuban society via a US–Sicilian mafia summit (Havana Conference) in 1946.

PEOPLE'S CHOICE
Former President Ramón Grau re-elected in 1944. Sugar prices rose, which fuelled an economic boom. Domestic spending was increased.

Elected at the age of 43, John F. Kennedy, popularly known as "JFK", became the youngest US president in history. A Democrat and a staunch supporter of civil rights, he symbolized a new generation of optimistic idealists.

John Fitzgerald Kennedy was born in Brookline, Massachusetts into a wealthy Roman Catholic Irish-American family on 29 May 1917. Graduating from Harvard University in 1940, he joined the US Navy Reserve and served in World War II. After the war he entered politics and was elected to Congress in 1946, and to the Senate in 1952.

Kennedy was elected the 35th US president in 1960, at the height of the Cold War (1947–91) – a period of amplified tensions between the Soviet Union and the US. Determined to stop the Soviet-backed spread of communism in Asia, he sent US forces to train South Vietnamese troops to fight the Communist north. In August 1962, the Soviet Union, in agreement with Fidel Castro, positioned nuclear missiles in Cuba, bringing the US within firing range of Soviet weapons. The ensuing 13-day standoff became known as the Cuban Missile Crisis, but Kennedy's diplomatic talks with the Soviets and the Cubans led to the Soviet Union, the US, and the UK signing the Partial Nuclear Test Ban Treaty in 1963. Peacefully resolving this crisis is widely regarded as Kennedy's greatest political achievement.

In June 1963, Kennedy proposed the most sweeping civil rights legislation in American history, but never lived to see it enacted. He was assassinated on 22 November 1963 by Lee Harvey Oswald. The next year, President Lyndon B. Johnson finished what Kennedy had started, signing the Civil Rights Act of 1964, which outlawed discrimination based on race, religion, gender, or national origin.

Kennedy considered a US space landing vital to the country's international standing. On 5 May 1961, astronaut Alan B. Shepard, Jr. became the first American in space, and was awarded the NASA Distinguished Service Award three days later by Kennedy.

KENNEDY

MARTIN **LUTHER KING** JR.

Martin Luther King Jr. united many African-American groups, and was one of the leading voices of the US civil rights movement in the 1950s and 60s. King's courage and conviction led to the repeal of segregation laws and changed the lives of millions in the US, but ultimately cost his own.

MILESTONES

ORDAINED AS PASTOR
Follows in his father's footsteps and is ordained, 1948, aged just 19 years old.

BUS BOYCOTT
Organizes an African-American boycott of all buses to oppose segregation laws, 1955.

UNFAIRLY JAILED
Imprisoned for peaceful protest, 1963. Writes his famous "Letter from a Birmingham Jail".

"I HAVE A DREAM"
Delivers his most famous speech, 28 August 1963. Civil Rights Act signed, 1964.

FINAL HOURS
Delivers his "I've been to the mountain top" speech, 3 April 1968. Murdered the next day.

Martin Luther King Jr. was born in Atlanta, Georgia to a devout Christian family. His father was a pastor. As a boy, King used to play with a white friend. However, when they were separated by segregated schools, the boy refused to see King again, leaving him devastated. King's parents explained to a six-year-old King the complicated story of race in the US (see p.243).

As a teenager, King was intelligent and gifted with a deep, rich voice that lent itself to rousing speeches and sermons later in life. At college, King met white people who opposed African-American discrimination, and he understood that co-operation among races could solve racial inequality in the US.

Leading the civil rights movement
King became active in the civil rights movement in 1954, when he moved to Montgomery, Alabama. There, King and fellow African-American leaders collaborated to form the Montgomery Improvement Association (MIA), which was devoted to improving the quality of life for African-Americans.

As a brilliant and powerful speaker, he was the obvious spokesperson

King, his wife, and other activists marched from Selma to Montgomery in Alabama in 1965 to protest against unequal voting rights in the US.

King led over 250,000 followers during the March on Washington protest in 1963, campaigning against the discrimination they experienced.

for the MIA, and was unanimously elected as its president. In 1955, the MIA organized a year-long boycott of segregated buses in Montgomery, resulting in the US Supreme Court eventually repealing segregation laws covering buses the following year.

The civil rights movement was an incendiary issue in the US at the time. King and his family's lives were threatened many times, and King's telephone was tapped by the FBI. In 1961, a segregationist mob trapped King inside a church and he had to call Attorney-General Robert Kennedy to

POLICE BRUTALITY

UNFAIR HIRING PRACTICE

UNEQUAL VOTING

SEGREGATED BUSES & SCHOOLS

send the National Guard to subdue the crowd. Undeterred, King co-ordinated protests throughout the southern states during the 1960s.

Civil Rights Act
On 28 August 1963, during the March on Washington protest, King gave his most famous speech, "I Have A Dream", in front of 250,000 supporters, calling for a racially equal US. A year later, president Lyndon B. Johnson signed the Civil Rights Act, which banned racial segregation and discrimination in the US. Then, in 1965, King participated in the marches in Selma, Alabama, calling for the right to vote. There, violent images of police brutality shocked the public, and increased the average white American's awareness of the plight of African-Americans.

Support for King had never been greater. With increased visibility, however, came increased risk. On 4 April 1968, King was assassinated by James Earl Ray, a white supremacist who claimed to be part of a conspiracy plot.

"A **genuine leader...** is a **molder of consensus.**"

Martin Luther King Jr., 1963

15,000 PEOPLE ATTENDED HIS **FIRST** MEETING

STABBED WITH A **18 CM (7 IN)** LETTER **OPENER**

AT BOOKSIGNING IN **1958**

JAILED 29 TIMES

DISCRIMINATORY HOUSING PRACTICE

WHITE-ONLY BUSINESSES

THE **CIVIL RIGHTS MOVEMENT**

The Jim Crow laws – regulations that discriminated against African-Americans and segregated them from whites – were introduced in 1877, just twelve years after the abolition of slavery. The civil rights movement of the 1950s and 1960s aimed to abolish these laws.

State police brutally enforced segregation laws. African-Americans were prevented from sharing schools, restaurants, toilets, and public transport with white people. African-Americans were also unable to vote or live in predominantly white neighbourhoods, and were discriminated against when they were seeking work. Martin Luther King Jr. and other leaders in the civil rights movement arranged marches and protests across the country to oppose these laws. Over the course of the 1950s and 1960s, in response to these protests, the US government repealed many laws of segregation in several states. In 1964, President Johnson signed the Civil Rights Act, which outlawed racial discrimination and segregation.

"I HAVE A DREAM THAT MY FOUR LITTLE CHILDREN WILL ONE DAY LIVE IN A NATION WHERE THEY WILL NOT BE JUDGED BY THE COLOR OF THEIR SKIN, BUT BY THE CONTENT OF THEIR CHARACTER."

Martin Luther King Jr.
Excerpt from "I Have a Dream" speech, Washington D.C., 28 August 1963

◀ *Martin Luther King Jr.'s funeral,* Atlanta, Georgia, 9 April 1968.

PARTNERS MEET
Drafted into Japanese
navy, 1944, meets Masaru
Ibuka; they become
business partners, 1946.

A NEW COMPANY
Founds radio repair
company with Ibuka,
1946. Sells Japan's first
tape recorder, 1950.

SONY NAME BORN
Company name changed
to Sony, 1958 – from
Latin *sonus* (sound) and
American term "sonny"
(slang for young man).

REVOLUTIONIZES MUSIC
Launches first portable
personal stereo system,
the Walkman, 1979. Over
400 million Walkmans
sold in total by 2014.

BUYS FILM STUDIO
Acquires Columbia Pictures,
1989, and enters the
film and television
production market.

A Japanese businessman who used his knowledge of physics to enhance product design, Akio Morita helped establish the world of personal entertainment. He created iconic products and co-founded Sony, which became the leading name in visual media.

Morita was born in Nagoya, Japan, into a family of sake, miso, and soy brewers, on January 26, 1921. Although he was expected to take over the family business, his interest in electronics and sound reproduction led him to study physics at Osaka University. After graduating in 1944, Morita was drafted into the Japanese navy, where he served on the Wartime Research Committee, and met his future business partner Masaru Ibuka.

In 1946, Ibuka and Morita founded a radio repair company – Tokyo Telecommunications Engineering Corporation – and gradually branched into product design and sales. They developed Japan's first tape recorder in 1950, but their breakthrough came with a pocket-sized radio, the TR-SS, in 1955. As demand for their goods grew in the US, the company – renamed Sony – went on to create many game-changing products, from the revolutionary Trinitron colour television set in 1968, to the compact disc player (alongside Phillips) in 1982, and the PlayStation games consul in 1995.

Sony branched out from electronics in 1989, when it purchased motion picture studio Columbia Pictures. In 1994, Morita resigned as chairman of Sony – ranked as the most recognizable brand in the US by market research company Harris in 1997. The following year, *Time* magazine named Morita as one of the most influential business leaders of the century – he died in 1999.

Morita pioneered
*personal stereo equipment,
such as the Sony Walkman,
that allowed people to listen
to their own choice of music
wherever they were.*

1921–1999

AKIO
MORITA

Jailed for 27 years for fighting against white minority rule and the apartheid system in South Africa, Nelson Mandela eventually became the country's first black president in 1994. He changed South Africa's constitution in 1996 to include equal rights for all people living there.

MILESTONES

JOINS ANC
To oppose apartheid, joins the African National Congress (ANC) party, 1943.

ARMED RESISTANCE
Creates an armed wing of the ANC, 1961. Visits other African countries and sources weapons.

SENT TO PRISON
Arrested and is (falsely) charged for trying to install a communist government, 1962.

ELECTED PRESIDENT
Inaugurated president of South Africa, 1994. Became the country's first black president.

Nelson Mandela was born on 18 July 1918 and was originally named Rolihlahla, meaning "troublemaker" in the Xhosa language. He was part of the ruling family of Thembu people, a Xhosa-speaking tribe based in South Africa's Cape Province. On his first day at school, a teacher gave him the English name "Nelson". After leaving school, Mandela studied law at the University of Fort Hare, South Africa, but was expelled after taking part in a student protest against the quality of food there. Abandoning his studies, Mandela moved to Johannesburg in 1941 and became politically active, specifically in the campaign for black rights.

The African National Congress (ANC) party was one of the leading political voices of resistance to apartheid in South Africa (see p.251) after its introduction in 1948. Nelson Mandela became Deputy President in 1952 and transformed it into a focused, mass political movement, demanding full equal rights, freedom of movement and

Many of South Africa's indigenous people shared Mandela's views and expressed their anger during protests, such as this one in Johannesburg, 1952, often experiencing police brutality.

WE DEMAND FREEDOM

AW 300 YRS OF WHITE PAS OPPRESION

AFRICA BACK

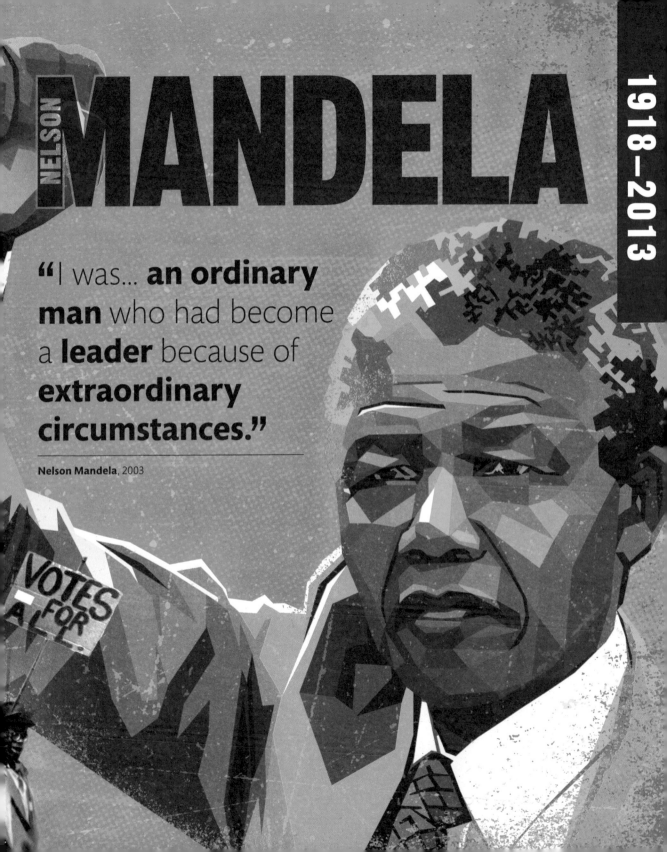

NELSON **MANDELA**

1918–2013

"I was... **an ordinary man** who had become a **leader** because of **extraordinary circumstances.**"

Nelson Mandela, 2003

VOTES FOR ALL

ENFORCED POVERTY

GHETTOS

POLICE BRUTALITY

RURAL LAND SOLD TO WHITES

APAR

speech, and democracy for indigenous Africans. The party's initial strategy of non-violent protest consisted of civil disobedience, strikes, and public protests. As tensions between the ANC and the South African government grew, the government responded to these non-violent protests by imposing sanctions and imprisoning protestors. As a result, Mandela started to doubt whether non-violence was an effective strategy to secure equal rights.

Mandela opened South Africa's first black law firm in 1952, but the government's vendetta against him was growing: he was sued for activism and banned from public speaking, from leaving Johannesburg, and from the ANC. During this time, he fell in love with a young woman named Nomzamo Winifred Madikizela ("Winnie"). Her family opposed the match because of Mandela's activism, but the couple married in 1958 and had two children together. Winnie became as fervent an activist as Mandela.

During his imprisonment, *Mandela was forced to spend hours in the sun breaking rocks by hand. Throughout his life, he fought against many injustices.*

Striking back
The South African government's response to protests became increasingly violent. In 1960 police opened fire on unarmed protestors in Sharpeville, killing 69 and leaving 180 wounded. This convinced Mandela that non-violence

could never implement change in South Africa, so in 1961 he established an armed wing of the ANC, known as Umkhonto we Sizwe ("Spear of the Nation"). Mandela became a fugitive and travelled secretly, seeking finance, support, weapons, and military training, while evading capture – earning himself the nickname "the Black Pimpernel" in

> " To be **free** is not merely to **cast off one's chains,** but to live in a way that **enhances** and **respects the freedom of others.**"

Nelson Mandela, 1994

APARTHEID

Introduced by the Afrikaner Nationalist Party in 1948, apartheid was legislation that enforced racial segregation.

Apartheid was a brutal regime of laws and policies that forced whites and non-whites to use separate facilities (such as restaurants and bathrooms) and restrict interracial contact. Non-whites were forced into designated reserves according to their race. Additionally, by separating black South African communities from each other, the minority white government could claim there was no black majority in South Africa and therefore legitimize their monopoly on political power.

POLITICAL MOBILIZATION
The South African Native National Congress (SANNC) formed in 1912 to fight social injustice for black Africans. It was renamed the African National Congress (ANC) in 1923.

APARTHEID
The Afrikaner Nationalist Party (ANP) in South Africa introduced apartheid legislation in 1948, separating the white minority from the non-white majority in order to monopolize power.

GOVERNMENT SUPPRESSION
During the 1960s, the white minority in South African government became increasingly violent towards peaceful protests against apartheid by non-whites.

REPEALING APARTHEID
In 1989, the ruling National Party elected a new leader, F.W. de Klerk, who released Mandela from prison the following year. De Klerk repealed most of the apartheid legislation in 1991.

INTERNATIONAL OPPOSITION
During the 1980s, movements outside South Africa opposing apartheid gained traction, and South Africa received economic sanctions from the US, the UK, and Japan.

LANDMARK SPEECH
In 1964, during his trial, Mandela gave his famous "I Am Prepared to Die" speech, in which he argued that all non-violent means of achieving equality in South Africa had been exhausted.

newspapers. However, in August 1962, he was arrested and, in 1964, convicted of four charges related to overthrowing the government. Mandela was sentenced to life imprisonment and would remain in jail for 27 years.

Incarceration and freedom
Mandela spent the first 18 years of his sentence doing hard labour on Robben Island, a prison off the coast of South Africa. During this time, he secretly wrote his autobiography *Long Walk to Freedom*, which was eventually published in 1994.

Mandela earned the respect of his fellow inmates, and he used his natural charisma and diplomacy to create a sense of community – even some guards came to treat him with dignity. Global opposition to apartheid was intensifying, and South Africa was facing economic sanctions as a result. Mandela became an

international symbol of hope in the global struggle for racial equality. The South African government secretly reached out to Mandela and engaged in peaceful, diplomatic talks; Mandela's vision for South Africa was inclusive and tolerant, and his target was racial injustice and white supremacy, not the white minority itself. Eventually, in 1990, the ban on the ANC was lifted and that same year the government released Mandela from prison unconditionally.

Election and legacy
In 1994, South Africa held its first democratic elections, and Mandela was elected president. He led a successful administration that tackled domestic poverty, prevented economic collapse, and changed South Africa's constitution to improve civil rights for all. Mandela retired as president in 1999 and devoted the rest of his life to philanthropy. In 2013 he died, aged 95.

"WE HAVE WAITED TOO LONG FOR OUR FREEDOM. WE CAN NO LONGER WAIT. NOW IS THE TIME TO INTENSIFY THE STRUGGLE ON ALL FRONTS. TO RELAX OUR EFFORTS NOW WOULD BE A MISTAKE WHICH GENERATIONS TO COME WILL NOT BE ABLE TO FORGIVE. "

Nelson Mandela
Speech upon his release from prison, 11 February 1990

MALCOLM X

A black nationalist, activist, and Muslim minister, Malcolm X opposed the mainstream ideals of the US civil rights movement in the 1960s, advocating a more militant approach to the fight for racial equality. His firebrand speeches on issues of racism have made him a lasting icon for black youth around the world.

Malcolm X was born Malcolm Little in Omaha, Nebraska. His mother and Baptist preacher father openly supported the black nationalist leader Marcus Garvey, and as a result the Ku Klux Klan threatened them repeatedly. In 1931, Malcolm's father died in what was officially ruled to be a streetcar accident; his mother believed that the Klan splinter group, the Black Legion, were in fact responsible. She was institutionalized after a nervous breakdown in 1939, and Malcolm went into foster care.

Malcolm excelled at school, but a teacher discouraged him from studying law, saying this was "no realistic goal" for a black person, and advising him to learn carpentry instead. His ambitions crushed, Malcolm dropped out of school, got involved in petty crime, and was imprisoned for theft in 1946.

Conversion to Islam
In prison, Malcolm studied English and Latin. Several of his ten siblings had converted to Islam and urged him to do the same, hinting that it might lead to his early release. Following their advice, Malcolm immersed himself in the teachings of the Qu'ran. In 1948, his half-sister Ella secured his transfer to

MILESTONES

LIFE OF CRIME
Goes to prison for a series of elaborate burglaries targeting wealthy white families in Boston, 1945.

FINDS RELIGION
Converts to Nation of Islam while in prison. After six years incarcerated, he gains his freedom, 1952.

POWERFUL ORATOR
Delivers "The Ballot or the Bullet" speech, 1964, urging violent protest if voting did not produce real change.

DIES FOR BELIEFS
Renounces Nation of Islam, 1964. Three of its members assassinate him the following year.

Malcolm X attended a press conference at the National Memorial African Book Store in New York, 1964. Outside, African-American citizens waited behind police barriers to catch a glimpse of him.

> "There can **be no black-white unity** until there is **first some black unity.**"

Malcolm X, 1964

CROSS

SLAVERY ABOLISHED

For over 200 years, colonists in North America practised slavery, contributing to beliefs that African-Americans were inferior. After the US civil war, President Lincoln pronounced slaves free in 1865.

DISCRIMINATION CONTINUES

African-Americans still experienced discrimination from racist whites. State governments created segregation laws in 1877 that enforced white superiority and oppressed African-Americans.

NEW IDEOLOGY SPREADS

Some African-Americans felt a lack of identity due to being separated from their homeland several generations ago. Marcus Garvey's (see p.225) ideology of black unity gained traction in the 1920s.

DIFFERING VIEWS ON RACISM

In contrast to the integrationist view of the mainstream civil rights movement (1954–68), Malcolm X argued for the separation of black people from the dominant white society.

TAKING CONTROL

After Malcolm X's death, his ideas sparked the Black Power movement (1965–85) in the US, which pushed not just for civil rights but for racial pride, political power, and economic security.

the Norfolk prison colony, which focused on rehabilitation. There, he read classic literature and works by black authors.

When Malcolm was released in 1952, he became actively involved in the Nation of Islam (see box). He changed his

Malcolm X warned the US that African-Americans should, and would be prepared to, resort to violence if they were not given equal rights to vote during his famous "The Ballot or the Bullet" speech in Cleveland, Ohio, in 1964.

surname from Little (the name given to his ancestors by their slave-master) to the letter X to signify that he denounced white suppression. In Chicago, he met Elijah Muhammad, leader of the Nation of Islam, and began to help expand Elijah's network of mosques across the US.

Charismatic teacher

Malcolm's charisma and passionate speeches on black identity found a receptive audience both inside and outside the Muslim community. He urged for the terms "negro" and "coloured" to be replaced by "black" and "Afro-American", and countered the non-violent approach of Martin Luther King (see pp.240–45) by fervently asserting that African-Americans must defend against discrimination by "any means necessary". Eventually, Malcolm left the Nation of Islam in 1964, renouncing its separatist beliefs, and became a Sunni Muslim. He also broadened the scope of his ideas, speaking at many international forums on human rights about the parallels between civil rights in the US and the rights of the oppressed in the developing world. Meanwhile, however, hostility grew between Malcolm and the Nation of Islam. He was assassinated on 21 February 1965 by three Nation of Islam members, during a lecture he was giving in Harlem, New York.

Despite the hardships of his childhood, and his early criminal activity, Malcolm X successfully reinvented himself as a campaigner for a world order without racism or injustice. His words have inspired many people, including film director Spike Lee and former US president Barack Obama (see p.302).

NATION OF **ISLAM**

A political and religious movement fusing elements of Islam and black nationalism, the Nation of Islam was founded in Detroit, Michigan in 1930 by Wallace Fard Muhammad.

By the time Malcolm X joined the National of Islam in 1952, Elijah Muhammad had emerged as its new leader, after Fard had disappeared in unexplained circumstances in 1934. Malcolm X regarded Elijah as a teacher, mentor, and close friend. Under Elijah's leadership, and with Malcolm X as a leading minister, the Nation of Islam attracted thousands of followers in the 1960s. Malcolm also inspired world-famous US boxer Muhammad Ali to drop his "slave" name Cassius Clay and join in 1964. The organization has been led by Louis Farrakhan since 1978.

"Ballot or the bullet... liberty or death."

Malcolm X, 1964

For more than half a century, Yasser Arafat was the face of the national movement of the Palestinian people for self-determination. Using military tactics and diplomacy, Arafat fought for the global recognition of Palestine as a political state for the first time and for a homeland for about 3.7 million stateless Palestinians around the world.

Born in Egypt to Palestinian parents, Arafat became part of a community of exiles displaced from Palestine by the increasing numbers of Jewish immigrants seeking to establish a homeland. He soon turned to Palestinian nationalism and counted among his friends Abd al-Qadir al-Husseini, leader of the supressed Arab Revolt (1936–1939), against British rule and Jewish immigration.

The struggle for liberation

When Israel declared itself an independent state in Palestine in 1948, Arafat fought in the Arab-Israeli War (1948–49) that immediately followed. The war saw Israel take a further 50 per cent of Palestinian territory, while a Palestinian state was not created. Dismayed at the infighting between various Arab groups, Arafat resolved to create a force answerable only to Palestinians.

At university in Cairo, where he studied engineering, Arafat became the chairman of the General Union of Palestinian Students in 1952. After graduating in 1956 he served in the Egyptian army and took work as an engineer until, in 1959, he co-founded the political party Fatah (meaning "conquest" in Arabic) with fellow activists. Fatah's driving goal was to take back control of Palestine, and in 1967 it was invited to become a major group within the Palestine Liberation Organization (PLO), a political body

Arafat fought in the Arab-Israeli War (1948–49), in which 700,000 Palestinians were displaced.

YASSER ARAFAT

1929–2004

that represented the Palestinian people. Operating from Damascus, Jordan, and Lebanon, Arafat led Fatah in launching non-lethal guerrilla action against Israel in 1964. Palestinians continued to be displaced – the Six-Day War in 1967 between Israel and Egypt, Syria, Jordan, and Iraq, led to 300,000 Palestinians fleeing the area.

As Fatah's attacks became more disruptive, Israel retaliated, launching a strike on the Jordanian village of Karameh in which 150 Palestinian guerrillas and 29 Israelis were killed. This attack strengthened the resolve of Arafat and his comrades to fight for Palestinian rights. In response, Arafat led Fatah forces in retaliatory attacks against Israel. By the end of the 1960s, Fatah had emerged as one of the most powerful Palestinian groups within the PLO. Arafat was appointed chairman of the PLO in 1969, and moved its headquarters to Beirut in 1971. Now the undisputed leader for both local and displaced Palestinians, he continued his guerrilla war against Israel for the next decade.

From guerrilla to president

In 1979, Arafat tried to negotiate peace with Israel, but this attempt failed, the PLO continued to attack Israel, and the ensuing conflict thwarted any further peace talks. Eventually, Israeli troops forced Aarafat out of Beirut, and he relocated to Tunisia in 1982. Peace talks only began after the PLO accepted the United Nations ruling that guaranteed Israel's safety in 1988.

A breakthrough came in 1993 when Arafat and Israeli prime minister Yitzhak Rabin signed the Oslo Accords, which agreed on Palestinian autonomy in Israeli-occupied territories. The PLO accepted Israel's right to exist and rejected violence, and in return, Israel accepted the PLO as the representative of the Palestinian people. A year later, Arafat became president of Palestine's fledgling

AHMAD SA'ADAT

A Palestinian nationalist and Marxist, Ahmad Sa'adat has spent most of his life campaigning for the right of Palestinian refugees and their descendants to return to their former homes.

Sa'adat is the leader of the Popular Front for the Liberation of Palestine (PFLP), which is the second-largest group within the PLO, behind Fatah. In 2001, Sa'adat was accused of ordering the successful assassination of Israeli tourism minister Rehavam Zeevi. He took refuge with Arafat, who refused to hand him over to Israel. In January 2006, he was elected to Palestine's government. However, in March, as part of a deal with Israel, he was tried by the Palestinian Authority and sent to Jericho prison, before Israeli forces raided the prison and captured him. An Israeli military court sentenced him to 30 years in prison for heading the PFLP.

government, and provided shelter for a number of political rebels, including Ahmad Sa'adat (see box).

Arafat died in 2004 shortly after suffering a stroke, with his goal of full Palestinian statehood unfulfilled. However, in 2012, in a move contested by Israel, the United Nations recognized Palestine as a state.

Arafat brought the plight of the Palestinian people to global attention. In 1956, he attended the International Students Congress in Prague wearing the keffiyeh (head scarf), which soon became his trademark and a symbol for Palestinian solidarity.

"Do not let the olive branch fall from my hand."

Yasser Arafat, 1974

LI KA-SHING

Property, retail, utilities, and telecommunications tycoon, Li Ka-shing is one of the most influential business people in Asia, and an eminent philanthropist. His inspiring rags-to-riches story is emblematic of a generation of Chinese entrepreneurs who left the mainland and made their mark in 20th-century Hong Kong.

MILESTONES

GROWING WEALTH
Aged 22, starts building his fortune and becomes largest manufacturer of artificial flowers in Asia.

BUILDING BUSINESS
Moves into real estate during 1960s, when prices low, and makes a fortune when the market recovers.

EXPANDS OVERSEAS
1979, buys investment company, Hutchison Whampoa, followed by other overseas businesses.

WEALTH FOR WELFARE
Li Ka-Shing Foundation founded, 1980; supports educational and medical projects worldwide.

Li Ka-shing was born in Chaozhon, Guangdong Province, southeastern China in 1928. His father was the principal of a local school, until the family was forced to flee the mainland for the then British territory of Hong Kong, when Japan bombed their home town during World War II. Li's father died from tuberculosis two years later, and although Li had also been infected, his family came to depend on him. He left school to support them and, before he was 15 years old, began working up to 22 hours a day in a plastics factory. By the age of 18, he was the company's top salesman and had been promoted to factory manager.

Plastics and real estate
In 1950, aged 22, Li left his job and, with 50,000 HK$ in savings and loans, established his own plastics business – Cheung Kong Plastics. Attuned to trends, Li refitted the factory to produce artificial flowers, used in local festivals, and taught himself accountancy. The business proved a success, and from its profits, Li began to invest in Hong Kong real estate.

He bought his first property in 1960 and went on to invest in apartments and factories all over the island. Following a collapse

Self-educated Li Ka-shing (centre) with son Richard, (right) at a graduation ceremony at Shantou University, China, 2017, where Li was honorary chair of the council.

in property prices in Hong Kong during Mao Zedong's Cultural Revolution in China (see p.221), Li invested heavily. As the market recovered he made substantial profits and in 1970, set up Cheung Kong Real Estate, which was listed on the Hong Kong Stock Exchange two years later.

Ever-expanding empire

In 1979, Li purchased the investment company Hutchison Whampoa, which went on to purchase the retail chain A.S. Watson. Four years later he acquired Hong Kong Electric, which resulted in him controlling most of Hong Kong's telecommunications and electric utilities.

As a venture capitalist aware that Hong Kong would return to Chinese rule and communism, Li began to seek investment opportunities abroad. He launched the mobile phone provider Orange in 1994, which he sold in 1999 to German conglomerate Mannesmann AG for a profit of more than $15 billion. In 2017, Li completed his biggest overseas purchase, that of the Australian energy firm Duet Group. He has also invested in technology companies that make his business holdings more cutting-edge. For example, through his association with the company Horizons Ventures, he was one of the first major investors in Facebook, in 2007.

Philanthropy and retirement

Li is widely admired for his loyalty, generosity, and commitment to philanthropic causes, which he ascribes to his early, first-hand experiences of poverty. The Li Ka-Shing Foundation, which Li refers to as his "third son", was set up in 1980 as a charitable organization dedicated to aiding social progress by supporting educational reform and increasing the availability of medical services. It is the second-largest private foundation of its kind in the world. Since its inception, Li has used the foundation to urge people across Asia to disregard traditional values that mean wealth passes only through the family, instead advocating a new, broader, approach to charity.

In March 2018, Li retired, handing over to his son Victor. In total, he has amassed a fortune of over $36 billion, and has pledged to donate a third of his assets to charities around the world.

> "The **more** you **know**, the **more confidence** you **gain**."

Li Ka-shing, 2006

Nicknamed "Superman Li" for his acumen as a deal maker, when Li purchased Hutchison Whampoa in 1979, he negotiated to buy the shares at less than half their value.

HIS COMPANIES SPAN **50 COUNTRIES** AND **EMPLOY OVER 323,000**

THE LI KA-SHING FOUNDATION HAS HELPED EDUCATE OVER **120 MILLION STUDENTS** AND CARE FOR OVER **17 MILLION PATIENTS**

SOLINA **CHAU**

One of Li Ka-shing's most trusted business associates, Solina Chau (b.1961) is listed in _Forbes_ magazine as one of the 100 most powerful women in the world.

Chau is a partner in the Cheung Kong group and director of the Li Ka-Shing Foundation. She met Li in the 1990s when she was building Beijing's Oriental Plaza, which she then sold to him. They co-founded a Chinese media company, Tom.com. Li also invested in her business Horizons Ventures, which focuses on technological innovation.

DIRECTORY

The fallout of World War II left many nations devastated and divided. Colonialism crumbled, no longer compatible with prevailing liberal ideals, as many nations rose up behind revolutionary leaders. Brutal dictators also emerged to exert their power over newly independent nations.

RONALD REAGAN
1911–2004

The former Hollywood actor Ronald Reagan became president of the US in 1981. As an actor, he was president of the Screen Actors' Guild from 1947 to 1952, and fought alleged Communist infiltration in the SAG. In 1962 he joined the Republican party, was elected governor of California in 1966, and elected president in 1980. Just 69 days after taking office, he survived an assassination attempt. Reagan imposed far-reaching reforms to reduce taxes and government spending, and invested heavily in the military. He also oversaw an economic resurgence in the US, he gave financial aid to anti-Communist movements abroad, and pressured the Soviet Union into ending the Cold War.

VÕ NGUYÊN GIÁP
1911–2013

A staunch Communist, Võ Nguyên Giáp was a Vietnamese political and military leader who is widely regarded as one of the 20th century's foremost military commanders. A master of guerrilla warfare, Giáp led the Viet Minh nationalist movement to victory against the French occupation of Vietnam in 1954, thus ending French colonial rule in Southeast Asia. As military leader of North Vietnam, Giáp invaded South Vietnam; after a 20-year conflict he led his troops to victory against the South Vietnamese and US armies, successfully reuniting the country in 1976.

KIM IL-SUNG
1912–94

The first Communist leader of North Korea, Kim joined the Korean guerrilla resistance against Japanese occupation in the 1930s. After Korea was divided in 1945, he established Communist rule in the north. In 1950, he invaded South Korea, aiming to reunite the country under his authority, but was repelled by UN forces. Kim ran an isolated totalitarian state from 1948 until his death in 1994; at first North Korea thrived, but by 1990 the country faced ruin, cut off from all foreign powers except China and the USSR. His death saw a nine-day mourning period.

INDIRA GANDHI
1917–84

Daughter of Jawaharlal Nehru (p.226), Indira Gandhi became the first female prime minister of India in 1966. She set up successful agricultural programmes, boosted exports, established India as a regional and nuclear power, and backed East Pakistan in its bid for independence, leading to the formation of Bangladesh in 1971. A controversial figure, she ordered the army to attack Sikh separatists in 1984; due to her role in the attack, her Sikh guards killed her.

GAMAL ABDEL NASSER
1918–70

Egyptian army officer Gamal Abdel Nasser led a military uprising in 1952 that overthrew the Egyptian monarchy, ending the British occupation of the Sudan and Egypt. Becoming president in 1956, Nasser nationalized the Suez Canal, defeating the British, French, and Israeli forces that tried to reclaim it. He advocated pan-Arabism to unite the Arab world, but this failed. Nasser ruled Egypt as a one-party police state, he was a popular leader. He implemented land reforms, boosted industry, improved women's rights, and oversaw a cultural revolution.

VINCENT LINGIARI
1919–88

A member of the Gurindji tribe, Vincent Lingiari was an Australian-Aboriginal activist who became a national symbol for the struggle of indigenous people. In 1966 Lingiari led a strike of 200 men in protest against pay and working conditions at a cattle station. He also demanded the return of traditional tribal lands. During the nine-year strike Lingiari petitioned the government and travelled to raise public awareness, gaining national and international support, until in 1975 the government granted Lingiari's people the rights to their traditional lands.

PIERRE TRUDEAU
1919–2000

Canadian Liberal politician Pierre Trudeau became prime minister in 1968 on a wave of popularity dubbed "Trudeaumania". A firm anti-separatist, he secured national unity by overpowering a pro-independence movement in Quebec, and defeated a Quebec-led terrorist group. During his presidency Trudeau brought in a policy of official bilingualism, softened divorce laws, secured Canada's independence from Britain in 1982, and amended the Canadian Constitution to include the Charter of Rights and Freedoms which legalized homosexuality.

JULIUS NYERERE
1922–99

A leading figure in the campaign for independence from British rule, Julius Nyerere became the first prime minister of Tanganyika, and then president of the Republic of Tanzania after its union with Zanzibar in 1964. As president, he brought in agricultural reforms, free education, and promoted literacy. He also helped to found the Organization of African Unity, initiated the Uganda-Tanzania War to overthrow Ugandan dictator Idi Amin, and actively opposed white supremacy in countries such as South Africa. Although his agricultural policies failed, Nyerere created one of the most peaceful, politically stable, and socially egalitarian countries in Africa, based on socialist principles.

JIMMY CARTER
1924–

The 39th president of the United States, Jimmy Carter faced serious international and domestic challenges during his term. His greatest achievements include the negotiations that led to the 1979 Egypt–Israel Peace Treaty, and his securing of amnesty for Vietnam War draft-evaders. Following his presidency, Carter turned to promoting global human rights, supporting social and economic development, and securing diplomatic solutions for international conflicts. He was awarded the Nobel Peace Prize in 2002.

PATRICE LUMUMBA
1925–61

African nationalist leader Patrice Lumumba founded the Congolese National Movement, the first national political party in Congo, and helped the country to gain independence from Belgium in 1960, becoming Congo's prime minister. A supporter of pan-Africanism, Lumumba advocated for the liberation of every African colony from foreign empires. When he asked for help from the UN and the Soviet Union to quell a secessionist movement in the state of Katanga, however, he was arrested and executed.

ELIZABETH II
1926–

Queen of the UK and ruler of Canada, Australia, New Zealand, and other territories around the world, Elizabeth II is the longest-reigning monarch in British history. She has overseen the independence of many former British colonies, and the British Empire converted to the Commonwealth of Nations. Although devoted to her traditional ceremonial duties, the Queen has reshaped the monarchy and modernized its attitudes – enabling the institution to remain relevant, with a valid role in the 21st-century.

CESAR CHAVEZ
1927–93

Mexican-American activist and union leader Cesar Chavez is renowned for his work in promoting the rights of US farm labourers, particularly for migrant communities. In 1962 he founded the National Farm Workers Association which became United Farm Workers in 1972. Advocating non-violent protests he organized marches, strikes, and boycotts; his campaigns resulted in improvements in the pay, working conditions, and treatment of labourers, and he also raised public awareness about the dangers of pesticides. In 1994, he was posthumously awarded the Presidential Medal of Freedom in recognition of his contribution to the rights of Mexican workers.

BHUMIBOL ADULYADEJ
1927–2016

The ninth king of Thailand, Bhumibol Adulyadej was the longest-ruling Thai monarch - his reign totalling seven decades. Although his role was officially restricted to ceremonial duties, through his crucial negotiations Bhumibol was instrumental in securing the peaceful resolution of several domestic political conflicts, including a military coup and Thailand's difficult transition from absolute monarchy to democracy. Revered by the nation, and admired internationally, Bhumibol was presented with the Human Development Lifetime Achievement Award by the UN in 2006.

6

FREEDOM AND OPPORTUNITIES

1980–PRESENT

The UK's first female, and longest serving, prime minister, Margaret Thatcher was also the most divisive leader in modern British history. Dominating politics in the 1980s, her economic policies changed the country's political landscape forever.

MILESTONES

RISE TO POWER
Wins Conservative party leadership contest, 1975. Becomes prime minister of the UK four years later.

REFORMS ECONOMY
Initiates policies urging free market economics. Unemployment reaches record levels, 1983.

VICTORY FOR BRITAIN
Defeats occupying Argentinian forces in the Falklands War, 1982, after 74 days of fighting.

PUBLIC REVOLT
Introduces unpopular poll tax, 1989 – riots ensue. Resigns the following year.

Born in Grantham, Lincolnshire, on 13 October 1925, Thatcher was first elected as member of parliament (MP) in 1959, and quickly rose through the ranks of the Conservative Party. In 1975, she successfully challenged Ted Heath for leadership of the Conservatives, becoming the first-ever female party leader in UK politics. When the Conservatives won the 1979 general election, she became the UK's first female prime minister.

Thatcher rejected the "post-war consensus", which had been introduced by the Labour Party in 1945, and rested on the idea that the UK government should encourage a strong welfare state, economic equality, and full employment. By increasing interest rates and taxation, she succeeded in reducing inflation, but the country fell into recession. Unemployment climbed from 1980, reaching 3 million in 1983 – its highest level since 1939. Thatcher's popularity fell accordingly.

Re-election seemed unlikely until 1982, when Thatcher's swift victory over Argentina during the Falklands War won her a second term in office. She then initiated a series of privatizations, selling off former state-owned industries – measures that gradually improved the economy, but crushed the trade unions and eradicated mining communities across the UK. Thatcher was elected for the third time in 1987, but lack of support within her own party forced her to resign in 1990.

Known as the "Iron Lady", *Thatcher sought to live up to her reputation during her 1986 re-election campaign by posing on board a British army tank.*

MARGARET THATCHER

1925–2013

GATES

BILL

The co-founder of Microsoft, which ultimately became the world's largest software company, Bill Gates is now one of the richest men in history. Philanthropic as well as wealthy, in 2000 he and his wife set up the Bill and Melinda Gates Foundation, which aims to reduce poverty, and improve education and healthcare.

MILESTONES

MEETS CO-FOUNDER
Forms friendship with Paul Allen over shared interest in computer programming while at school, 1968.

CREATES MICROSOFT
Registers company name "Microsoft", 1976. Sales exceed $1 million in just two years.

RECORD WEALTH
Becomes youngest ever billionaire at the time, 1987, aged 31, with a net worth of $1.25 billion.

LEAVES MICROSOFT
Resigns as chairman of Microsoft to concentrate on Bill and Melinda Gates Foundation, 2014.

Known by his family as "Trey", Gates grew up in Seattle, Washington, where he was enrolled in a private school, Lakeside, in 1967, at the age of 12. The following year, at a time when few people outside universities, military research, and big businesses had access to computers, Lakeside bought computing time from the nearby Computer Center Corporation (CSC). Gates and a few fellow students, including his friend Paul Allen (see p.275), became hooked and learnt to write programs in BASIC computer language. The young programmers soon found bugs and security failings in CSC's system. Eventually, the company offered Gates and the others free computing time if they fixed these bugs, and helped to identify any further security weaknesses in their system.

Obsession to career
Gates and Allen quickly developed a talent for writing useful applications, such as payroll programs and ways to automate Lakeside's class timetable (which also enabled Gates to put himself in lessons with his preferred classmates). Although initially his schooling suffered due to his computer

Microsoft Office became staple software for most businesses globally from the 1990s onwards.

> "Your **most unhappy customers** are your **greatest source** of **learning.**"

Bill Gates, 1999

obsession, Gates still earned a place at Harvard University in 1973. However, once there, he rarely attended lectures, spending his time in the computer rooms instead.

Developments in computing in the mid-1970s saw home computers go on sale to the public for the first time. Gates and Allen envisaged computers becoming as common as typewriters in offices and televisions in homes. This prediction prompted Gates to drop out of Harvard in 1975, in order to write software for one of the first computers, the Altair 8080. He and Allen formed Microsoft that year.

Booming business

Microsoft remained a small business until 1980, when it struck a deal to supply IBM with an operating system for its new Personal Computer (PC). With no software of its own, Microsoft bought an existing system, QDOS, from Seattle Computer Products, modified it, then sold it to IBM as MS-DOS, while retaining the rights to sell the system elsewhere.

As sales of IBM's PCs soared, many companies began manufacturing their own PCs, known as "clones". With millions of computers running MS-DOS, and from 1985, Microsoft Windows, business boomed. Successive software releases bolstered Microsoft's status as the industry leader. Today, more than four out of five of the world's desktop PCs and laptops use Microsoft Windows.

Desire for a better world

In 1999, Gates wrote *Business @ the Speed of Thought*, which showed how computer technology could solve business problems. He donated all profits from book sales to charity, and resigned as CEO of Microsoft the following year. With his wife, he established the Bill and Melinda Gates Foundation in 2000, to which he devoted increasing amounts of time and personal wealth. Since 2008, he has worked full-time for the foundation and other philanthropic interests.

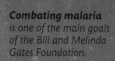

Combating malaria is one of the main goals of the Bill and Melinda Gates Foundation.

ACHIEVED HIGHER COLLEGE ADMISSION TEST SCORE

THAN 99.9995%

OF HIS US STUDENT PEER GROUP

CHARITABLE DONATIONS HAVE HELPED TO

SAVE AROUND

6 MILLION LIVES

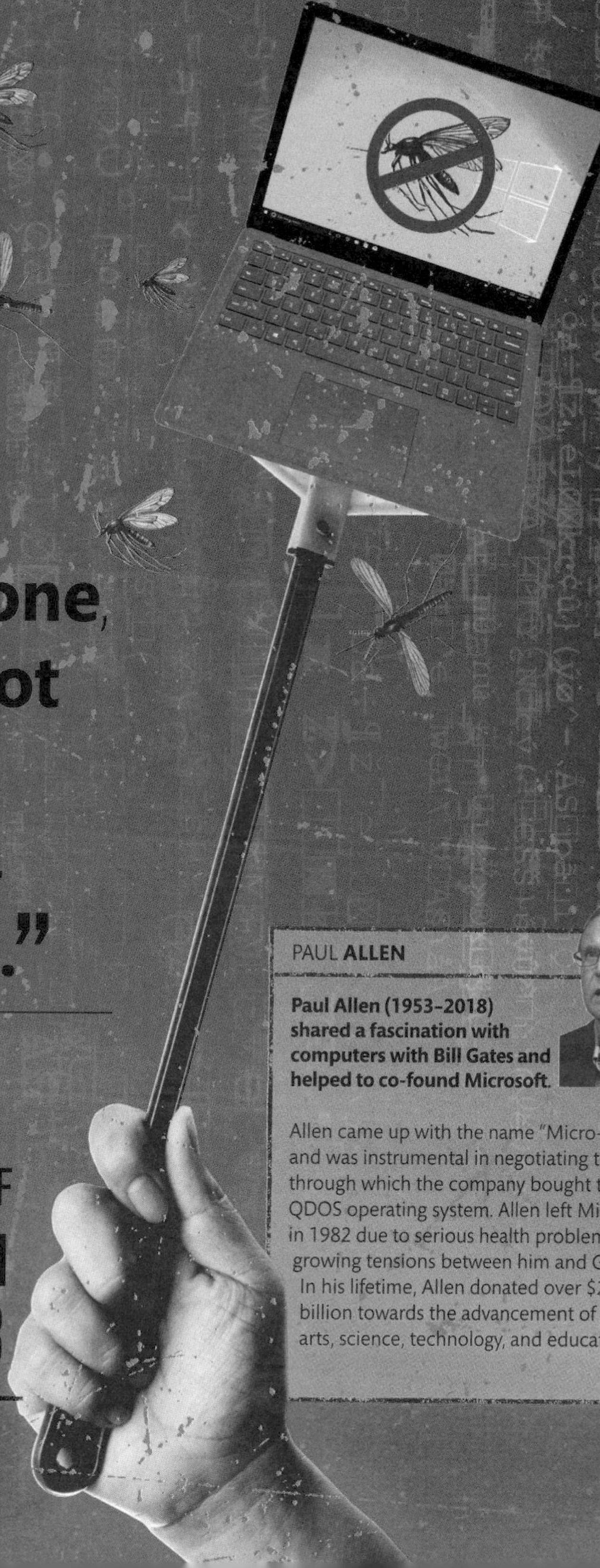

"We're **not done**, and we **will not stop** working, **until malaria is eradicated.**"

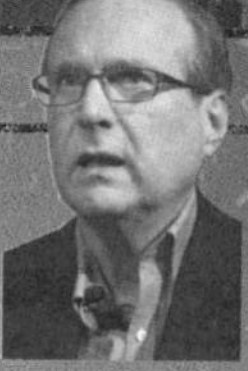

Bill Gates, 2007

ACHIEVED A NET WORTH OF **$95 BILLION** IN 2018

PAUL **ALLEN**

Paul Allen (1953–2018) shared a fascination with computers with Bill Gates and helped to co-found Microsoft.

Allen came up with the name "Micro-Soft" and was instrumental in negotiating the deal through which the company bought the QDOS operating system. Allen left Microsoft in 1982 due to serious health problems, and growing tensions between him and Gates. In his lifetime, Allen donated over $2 billion towards the advancement of the arts, science, technology, and education.

"WE CALL OURSELVES IMPATIENT OPTIMISTS. OPTIMISTIC BECAUSE WE KNOW AMBITIOUS GOALS CAN BE ACHIEVED WHEN WE ALL WORK TOGETHER. IMPATIENT BECAUSE WE'RE NOT GETTING THERE FAST ENOUGH... TO END EXTREME POVERTY, WE NEED YOU."

Bill Gates
Excerpt from a speech at the Global Citizen Festival, 2015

Gates' 2018 "Hug Me, I Save Lives" campaign honoured
Canada's charity work fighting disease worldwide. ▶

A reformer who attempted to liberalize the Soviet Union, Mikhail Gorbachev triggered sweeping changes that brought the Soviet era to an end, saw the demise of communism in Europe, and the end of the Cold War.

Born in Privolnoye, southwestern Russia, Gorbachev's climb through the ranks of the Communist Party began in his home village. In 1946, at the age of 15, he joined Komsomol, the Young Communist League, and began work on a state farm driving a combine harvester. At 17 he became one of the youngest recipients of the Soviet Union's Order of the Red Banner of Labour for helping to bring in the bumper wheat crop of 1948.

Ascent to power

After graduating from the Moscow State University in 1955, he became a provincial party official in Stavropol. At a time when food imports were highly restricted, Gorbachev succeeded in making improvements to the local economy, which saw him appointed to the agricultural central committee in Moscow in 1967.

At the start of the 1980s, the Soviet economy was in crisis, and urgent action was required to prevent national bankruptcy. The Soviet leader, Yuri Andropov, saw a potential successor in the energetic Gorbachev, and promoted him to the *Politburo* (the supreme policy-making body of the Communist Party) as one of its youngest members. By 1985, after the death of three elderly Soviet leaders in quick succession – Brezhnev,

"For a **new type** of **progress**... to become a reality, **everyone must change.**"

Mikhail Gorbachev, 1990

Gorbachev called for a reduction in the number of US and Soviet nuclear weapons in 1986, which was met with anti-war rallies across the Soviet Union, such as in Kharkov, Ukraine.

ПУСТЬ ВОСТОРЖЕСТВ
НА ПЛАНЕТЕ М
БЕЗ ОРУЖИЯ И ВО

MIKHAIL **GORBACHEV**

1931–

> **"The market is not an invention of capitalism. It is an invention of civilization."**

Mikhail Gorbachev, 1990

Andropov, and Chernenko – Gorbachev had been appointed general secretary of the Communist Party.

Reform and openness
In his speech of 1986, Gorbachev made political history by being the first senior official to criticize the state's economic policies. Over the coming months he advocated reform of the economy and to the party's structure, a policy called *perestroika*. However, his reforms had little positive effect, and were undermined by in-fighting in the Kremlin and resistance from officials across the USSR. As the Russian economy worsened, Gorbachev became deeply unpopular.

While some of his fellow party members had lost faith in him, in the West, Gorbachev was widely admired for the transparency of his government, a policy known as *glasnost*, and for taking steps towards disarmament. He forged warm relationships with US president Ronald Reagan,

PERESTROIKA

Gorbachev's domestic reforms allowed citizens of satellite states to assert their independence from the USSR. These reforms acted as catalysts for the Berlin Wall's collapse on 9th November 1989.

SELF DETERMINATION

West German chancellor Helmut Kohl (see box), and British prime minister Margaret Thatcher (see pp.270–71).

Russia's new openness under Gorbachev prompted people in the Soviet satellite states in Eastern Europe to reject communism and demand independence. It also led citizens of East and West Germany to breach the Berlin Wall in 1989 and the consequent reunification of Germany. The fall of the Berlin Wall symbolized an end to Cold War tensions between the East and West; Gorbachev was awarded the Nobel Peace Prize in 1990 for his leading role.

However, in Russia, during the turmoil, a group of hardline communists mounted a coup against Gorbachev in August 1991.

HELMUT **KOHL**

As chancellor of Germany from 1982 to 1998, Helmut Kohl (1930–2017) became the architect of German reunification.

As a middle-class boy in his home town of Ludwigshafen, Kohl, like many of his contemporaries, joined the Hitler Youth. Later, he devoted his political career to rebuilding international trust in Germany. Kohl served as leader of the Christian Democratic Union (1973–98) and became the country's longest serving chancellor. In 1992, he put together the Maastricht Treaty that created the European Union. Kohl is credited with playing a crucial role in the fall of the Berlin Wall.

The attempt failed, but it triggered the unravelling of the Soviet Union. On 25 December 1991, the USSR ceased to exist, and Gorbachev resigned.

ENDED 46-YEAR LONG COLD WAR

REFORMS LIBERATED 15 STATES

GLASNOST

FREE SPEECH

BENAZIR BHUTTO

The first woman ever to lead a Muslim nation, Pakistan's Benazir Bhutto was an active member of the Pakistan People's Party from the age of 13, and to date, its only female prime minister.

Bhutto was born in Karachi, Pakistan, into an affluent, influential, political family on 21 June 1953. Her father, Zulfikar Ali Bhutto, founded and led the Pakistan People's Party (PPP), and served as both prime minister and president. Aged just 16, Bhutto left Pakistan to study in the US at Harvard University, then the UK at Oxford. She returned to her country in 1977 to see her father ousted in a military coup and executed in 1979. That same year, she became leader of the PPP, and between 1979 and 1984 she was imprisoned and kept under house arrest multiple times.

In 1984, amid mounting international pressure, the Pakistan government released her. She flew to Switzerland, then the UK, only returning to Pakistan in 1986 when martial law was lifted.

Bhutto was elected prime minister in 1988, but found herself unable to tackle Pakistan's extensive poverty and corruption. Defeated in 1990, she served a second term 1993–96, during which she oversaw economic privatization and appointed the country's first female judges. After another coup in 1996, Bhutto went into exile to the UK and Dubai. She returned to Pakistan in 2007 to run for a third term but was assassinated. While the government named Taliban chief Baitullah Mehsud as the individual who ordered her killing, the person/group behind Bhutto's death remains disputed.

> **"**I put my **life in danger**... because I feel **this country is in danger."**

Benazir Bhutto, 2007

Bhutto's rallies, such as this one in Punjab on 16 January 1988, drew huge crowds. She became the 11th prime minister of Pakistan following a general election.

283

MILESTONES

LEADS UNREST
Helps organize protests in cities across Poland against sudden food price increases. 1970.

VOICE OF DISSENT
Enlists 10 milliun members into Solidarity by 1981, almost half of Poland's adult population.

AIDS GOVERNMENT
As leader of banned Solidarity, holds talks with the government to resolve growing unrest, 1989.

POLAND SET FREE
Becomes first elected president of Poland, 1991; negotiates retreat of Soviet troops, 1993.

Shipyard worker turned trade union leader, Lech Wałęsa guided Poland's non-violent transition from communism to democracy. In 1990, he became the county's first non-communist president in 45 years.

Lech Wałęsa began his career as an activist while working as an electrician at Gdańsk shipyard. During the 1970s, he organized strikes and protests that were illegal under Soviet rule, and was arrested several times. In 1980, during further unrest at Gdańsk shipyard, Wałęsa headed an inter-factory strike committee that demanded the right to strike and form free trade unions. The movement grew into a national federation of unions, Solidarity (*Solidarność*), led by Wałęsa, which called for an end to Soviet control of Poland. However, when the government imposed martial law in 1981, Solidarity's operations were forced underground.

By 1989, the strikes instigated by Wałęsa forced the government to work with Solidarity. Wałęsa helped to set up a new non-communist coalition government, and in 1990 he was made president of Poland.

LECH
WAŁĘSA

Striking workers under Wałęsa's leadership delivered food to their colleagues at Gdansk shipyard, 1980.

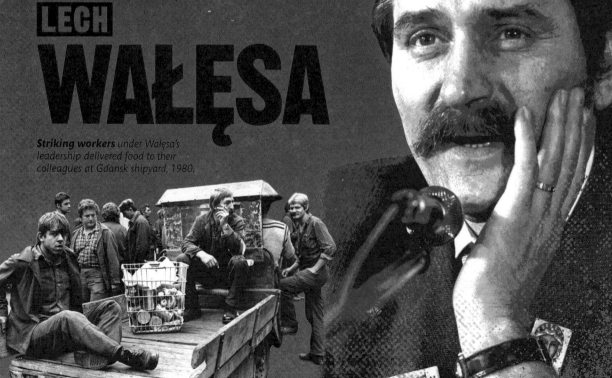

VÁCLAV HAVEL

From playwright, to prisoner, to president, Václav Havel helped to free Czechoslovakia from harsh Soviet rule.

Václav Havel began his political activism writing plays about the absurdity of life in a totalitarian state. In 1968, Havel's works were banned and he was imprisoned for "anti-state activity". His 1977 essay *The Power of the Powerless* bolstered the anti-Soviet movement, along with Charter 77, which he cofounded that year.

In 1989, the fall of the Berlin Wall prompted a mass demonstration and general strike in Prague. In response, the government stepped down after 41 years of one-party rule. The anti-communist Civic Forum, led by Havel, took power during the "Velvet Revolution" – so called because there was no violence – and Havel became president. In 1993, he was re-elected as president of the new Czech Republic a position he held until 2003.

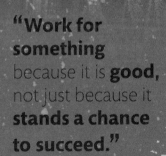

Havel's poster could be seen at the front of streetcars in Prague during the Velvet Revolution, 1989.

> "**Work for something** because it is **good,** not just because it **stands a chance to succeed.**"
>
> Václav Havel, 1986

MILESTONES

PUBLISHED SATIRE
Writes critically-acclaimed *The Memorandum*, 1965, satirizing the ruling communist government.

BECAME POLITICAL
Co-founds Charter 77, 1977: political group that forms the basis of Civic Forum he leads, 1989.

DEMOCRATIC FIRST
As leader of Civic Forum, is elected President of Czechoslovakia, 1989, after fall of communism.

POPULAR LEADER
Becomes president of Czech Republic following break up of the former Czechoslovakia, 1993.

285

OPRAH WINFREY

In a career spanning over 30 years, Oprah Winfrey has built a media empire based on cultural debate, women's issues, and spirituality. With a vast and dedicated international following, she is the greatest African-American philanthropist in US history, and one of the most influential women alive today.

Born in rural Mississippi in 1954, Oprah Winfrey rose from a low-income background to become the most powerful woman in American media. Her parents separated soon after her birth, and she was raised by her maternal grandmother. Oprah later moved between her mother and father, but it was while in her mother's care that a family friend sexually abused her. Falling pregnant at 14, she gave birth to a son, who died in infancy.

Oprah then moved back to Nashville, Tennessee, to live with her father, whom she would later credit with changing her life. Under his strict guidance, she excelled at school and won a scholarship to Tennessee State University. With a natural talent for performing, Oprah enrolled in a drama club, and later landed a job reading the news at a local radio station.

Television stardom

At 19, Oprah debuted on television as the first female African-American news reader at Nashville's WLAC TV, before moving to WJZ TV in Baltimore. However, station managers felt her informal, personal presenting style was not suited to the newsroom and they moved her to co-host a morning chat show, *People Are Talking*. In 1984, she took over as host on a different show, *A.M. Chicago*, and after just two years she was appointed the host of her own show – *The Oprah Winfrey Show*.

Meanwhile, Oprah was cast in Steven Spielberg's *The Color Purple* (1985). Her appearance in the Oscar-winning film boosted ratings for *The Oprah Winfrey Show*, and audience numbers grew higher still from

MILESTONES

TELEVISION DEBUT
Makes her broadcasting debut aged 19 as a news anchor on Nashville's WLAC TV, 1973.

STARTS TALK SHOW
The Oprah Winfrey Show premieres, 1986. Ratings soon top those of rival talk show host Phil Donahue.

FOUNDS NETWORK
Launches Oprah Winfrey Network (OWN), 2011, broadcasting talk shows, dramas, and reality TV.

PROVIDES SUPPORT
Establishes boarding school in South Africa for girls from disadvantaged backgrounds, 2007.

Oprah met with fans at the Royal Botanical Gardens, Sydney, in 2010, and the following year, she and 302 audience members taped the final episodes of the 25th and final season of her talk show at the Sydney Opera House.

> "What I **learned at a very early age** was that **I was responsible** for **my life**. You are your **possibilities**. If you know that, **you can do anything.**"

Oprah Winfrey, 2007

1994 onwards, when she decided to change the nature of the chat show in order to, in her words, "lift people up". This new focus on empowerment saw Oprah's audience hit 48 million viewers a week, and her influence expanded significantly, both as a trend-setter and as someone who highlighted social issues.

Continued success

With her newfound wealth, Oprah started the magazine *O*, and began producing films and TV content under her company Harpo Productions. She refused to sell her show and continued to serve as chairwoman and CEO of Harpo Productions, and of *The Oprah Winfrey Show* until the end of its run in 2011. She also launched a TV network, the Oprah Winfrey Network (OWN). Oprah remains best known for her talk show, which ran for 25 years, making it one of the longest-running daytime programmes in the US. Transcending the race divide there, she appealed to all demographics – including the white middle class – by focusing on universal issues and concerns, and, unlike other talk shows which emerged in her wake, by emphasizing a message of empathy and positivity. Oprah is also credited for raising the media visibility of LGBT+ people in mainstream television, and for bringing their issues to the wider attention of the US public.

Oprah's other defining legacy is her philanthropic work. She has donated over $350 million around the world for educational projects, and has established two foundations – Angel Network, funded by viewers, and Oprah Winfrey Leadership Academy for Girls in South Africa.

THE OPRAH WINFREY *SHOW* WON **16** EMMY AWARDS

 ENDORSED OBAMA, GAINING HIM **ONE MILLION** VOTES

NET WORTH OF **$4 BILLION** IN 2018

As editor-in-chief of American *Vogue* since 1988, and from 2003, artistic director at Condé Nast, Anna Wintour's influence has made her one of the most powerful women in fashion.

When appointed editor-in-chief at American *Vogue*, Wintour instantly rejuvenated the title. Her first cover featured model Michaela Bercu in jeans and smiling – a departure from the usual cover shots of models in designer clothes and formal poses.

Under Wintour, *Vogue*'s covers have continued to ignite debate. She has put Michelle Obama on the cover three times, a statement that fashion can be political. A taste-maker and trendsetter, endorsement from Wintour hugely boosts brands, and the Vogue CFDA Fashion Fund, which awards cash prizes to new talent, has launched the careers of many designers. Such is her influence that the Metropolitan Museum of Modern Art in New York named its costume centre after her.

MILESTONES

STARTING CAREER
Spurred on by her parents, works at Biba boutique, 1965, and begins training programme at Harrods.

MOVES TO PUBLISHING
Begins career as journalist on the UK magazine *Harpers & Queen*, 1970. Moves to New York, 1975.

JOINS VOGUE
Becomes chief editor of UK *Vogue*, 1985. Nicknamed "Nuclear Wintour" for her authoritative manner.

BECOMES DIRECTOR
Appointed artistic director at Condé Nast, 2013. Oversees all of the company's magazines.

"You **either know fashion**, or **you don't.**"

Anna Wintour, 1965

Anna Wintour sat in the front row of the Mulberry 2013 Spring/Summer Show during London Fashion Week 2012, reflecting her power in the fashion world.

ANNA WINTOUR

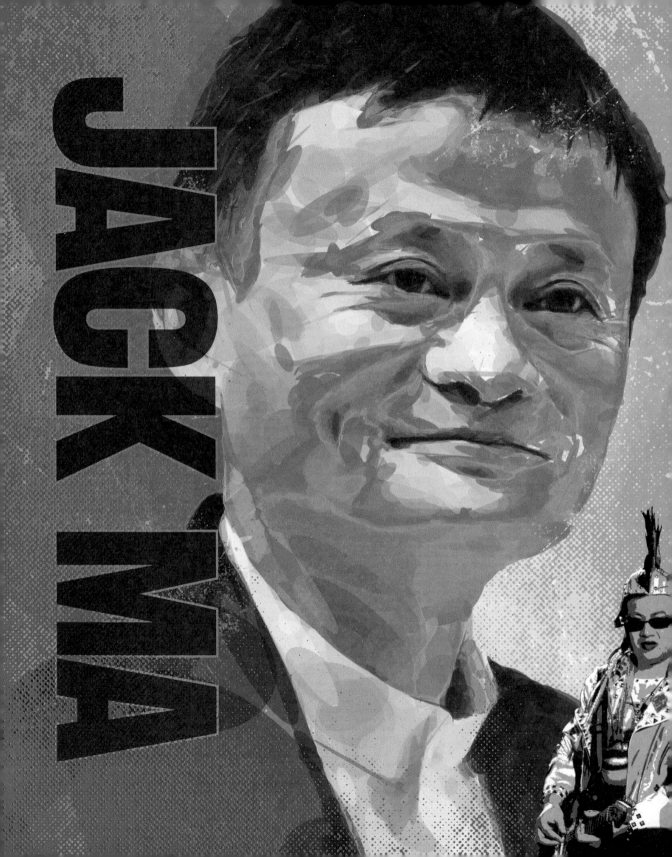

Chinese entrepreneur Jack Ma, a struggling English teacher who knew little about technology or management, rose to become an e-commerce billionaire. The founder of a multinational conglomerate, the Alibaba Group, he transformed the way China does business with the rest of the world.

Now China's richest man, Ma Yun was born into a poor family in Hangzhou, eastern China, in 1964, during the Cultural Revolution (1966–76), which saw communist ideology preserved and capitalist elements purged from Chinese society. As a boy, Ma struggled with maths but had a strong desire to learn English. Every morning for nine years, from the age of 12, he rose early to cycle to the Hangzhou International Hotel to offer his services as a tour guide, for free, to practise his English. One of the tourists nicknamed him Jack, and the name stuck.

Despite his efforts to master English, Ma failed the annual university entrance exams twice, before passing and being accepted to Hangzhou Teachers' College. Struggling to find work after he graduated, Ma began teaching English at Hangzhou Institute of Electronics and Engineering, before starting his own translation business the following year.

Embracing the internet

It was on a business trip to the US in 1995 that Ma discovered the internet, a phenomenon that was in its infancy in China at the time. Initially searching for Chinese brands of beer, he was unable to find any results, or even anything to do with China. He and a friend decided to create their own "ugly" web page about Ma's own

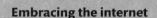

Ma performed for 16,000 employees at Alibaba's 10th anniversary ceremony in 2009. He is known for his eccentric performances.

MILESTONES

FIRST STEPS ONLINE
Establishes China Pages, one of China's first internet companies, 1995; leaves business after two years.

GLOBAL MARKETPLACE
Founds Alibaba online marketplace, 1999; attracts $25 million in investments by 2000.

FOUNDS CHARITY
Steps down as CEO of Alibaba, 2013; establishes charitable Jack Ma Foundation following year.

MARKET LEADER
Alibaba Group exceeds $430 billion in sales, 2016. Becomes world's largest online retailer.

> **"Young people** will have the **seeds you bury** in **their minds** and **when they grow up** they will **change the world."**

Jack Ma, 2014

291

translation agency. They launched it one morning, and by noon the same day, they had their first enquiries.

Back in Hangzhou, Ma founded China Pages, an online directory of Chinese companies, backed by the Ministry of Foreign Trade and Economic Cooperation. It was at their offices, in 1997, he met the founder of Yahoo, Jerry Yang, who was on his first trip to China. On an outing to the Great Wall, the two discussed their fascination with the growth and potential of the internet.

The birth of Alibaba

In 1999, Ma left his job and, with 17 friends, including his wife Zhang Ying, started an online marketplace, which Ma called Alibaba. His idea was to help small and medium-sized exporters in China find global buyers online, offering them a place to list their products for sale and avoid the usual route of attending trade fairs to gain sales.

By 2005, Alibaba was employing 2,400 people and had achieved sales of $50 million. Over the next decade Ma grew Alibaba into a conglomerate that included a consumer shopping site, Taobao, and an online payment platform, Alipay.

In January 2013, at the age of 48, Ma announced that he was stepping down as chief executive of his Alibaba Group to allow "younger, better equipped" colleagues to take control. However, he stayed on to orchestrate the company's initial public offering (IPO) on the New York Stock Exchange in 2014. The IPO raised $25 billion, setting a new record for the world's biggest public stock offering, and making Ma the richest man in China.

Philanthropic success

After passing on day-to-day control of Alibaba, Ma devoted time to pursuing charitable causes, establishing the Jack Ma Foundation to improve educational opportunities for poor and rural Chinese people, and to addressing environmental damage caused by industrial growth. Today, Ma is China's biggest philanthropist. Meanwhile, over 75 per cent of Chinese e-commerce transactions are made through Alibaba, and its sales outstrip those of eBay and Amazon combined.

SAW HIS **FIRST COMPUTER,** AGED **31**

ALIBABA HAS 550 MILLION ACTIVE **MONTHLY** **USERS**

RAISED INITIAL FUNDING FOR ALIBABA WITHIN **2 HOURS**

"With **our technology**, our innovation, our partners – **10 million small business sellers** – they can **compete** with **Microsoft** and **IBM**."

Jack Ma, 2017

CLOUD

SOCIAL MEDIA

EXPORT

FILM INDUSTRY

FOOTBALL

Ma took advantage of the internet and launched a varied portfolio of businesses, many of which are leading names in China.

PAYMENT SYSTEM

SHOPPING

SHIPPING

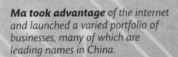

When Vladimir Putin was democratically elected president of the Russian Federation in March 2000, his country was still shaking off its communist past. Within a decade, Putin had revived Russia's economy and raised its profile on the international stage, but for many he remains a highly controversial figure.

Born in Leningrad (now St Petersburg), Vladimir Putin was raised in a working-class family. After leaving school, where he became fluent in German, Putin studied law at Leningrad State University. Graduating in 1975, he immediately joined Russia's secret police, the KGB, as an intelligence officer. After 10 years in mostly administrative roles, he moved to Dresden, in Soviet East Germany, to work undercover as a translator.

Tasting power

Returning to Russia in 1990, Putin became an assistant to Anatoly Sobchak, mayor of St Petersburg (and a former professor at Putin's university), before being promoted to first deputy chairman of the Government of St Petersburg in 1994. When Sobchak failed to be re-elected in 1996, Putin moved to Moscow and joined the office of president Boris Yeltsin (see p.297).

Yeltsin, then in ailing health, was an early supporter of Putin. In 1998, he appointed Putin director of Russia's secret service, the FSB, then as acting prime minister the following year – when he also proclaimed Putin to

Putin was blessed by the head of the Russian Orthodox Church at the Annunciation Cathedral, Moscow, following his inauguration in 2018.

1952–

"**Russia needs** a **strong state power** and must have it. But **I am not calling** for **totalitarianism.**"

Vladimir Putin, 2000

VLADIMIR PUTIN

GAINED BLACK BELT IN JUDO AT AGE 18

WORKED AS A KGB AGENT FOR 16 YEARS

ACHIEVED 9 CONSECUTIVE YEARS OF ECONOMIC GROWTH BETWEEN 1999 AND 2008

be his successor as acting president. When Yeltsin resigned in 1999, Putin used the presidential election campaign to portray himself as Russia's saviour from decline. Victorious, Putin was inaugurated as president in 2000.

Russia reborn
Putin quickly set about reorganizing the Russian economy, including cutting corporation tax and formalizing a new tax system. Industrial productivity steadily increased, oil and gas exports soared, and within 5 years, Putin was able to repay the $70 billion of debt accrued by the Soviet Union to international creditors.

As the economy improved, ordinary Russians also prospered, enjoying rising wages, greater consumer choice, and increasing standards of living. Putin was understandably popular, and when he stood for re-election in 2004, he received 71 per cent of the vote.

Putin's popularity was not universal, however, and the first of many rallies against his leadership were held in cities across Russia in 2007. Although Russia's constitution prevented him from standing for a third consecutive term as president, his grip on power continued as prime minister (2008–12), and then again as president from 2012. Accusations of electoral fraud led to further large-scale protests across the country in 2011–13.

Putin's international reputation has also fluctuated during his leadership. He has faced condemnation and sanctions from the West for his country's suspected involvement in the assassination of former spies overseas, its annexation of the Crimea region in Ukraine in 2014, and its intervention in the war in Syria. However, many Russians feel that Putin has restored their pride in their country, and when he was re-elected in 2018, it was with 77 per cent of the vote.

> " The **task of the government** is not only to **pour honey into a cup**, but sometimes to give **bitter medicine.** "

Vladimir Putin, 2011

Putin imposed tighter controls on former state-owned businesses that were funnelling money outside Russia to avoid paying taxes. This strategy helped to transform the Russian economy.

BORIS **YELTSIN**

President of the Russian Federation from 1991 to 1999, Boris Yeltsin (1931–2007) was the country's first democratically elected leader following the collapse of the Soviet Union.

Inaugurated on 10 July 1991, Yeltsin, alongside the leaders of Ukraine and Belarus, dissolved the Soviet Union five months into his tenure through the Belavezha Accords. Yeltsin was regarded as a reformist, but his style of leadership was autocratic. In an effort to boost Russia's economy, Yeltsin eradicated price controls, which led to state-wide hyperinflation. He also privatized most state-owned industries, and introduced an ill-conceived tax system, which undermined both the economy and the government's own finances. In 1999, Yeltsin made Vladimir Putin one of his three deputies, and named Putin his successor later that year.

ELLEN
JOHNSON
SIRLEAF

GOVERNMENT CAREER
Serves as assistant minister of finance, 1972–73, before becoming minister of finance, 1979–80.

SEEKING POWER
Stands for president, 1997, following first Liberian Civil War (1989–97). Loses vote to Charles Taylor.

FIGHTS CORRUPTION
As president, establishes Truth and Reconciliation Commission, 2006, to investigate corruption in her government.

RETURNS TO OFFICE
Resumes presidency for second term following re-election, 2012.

President of Liberia for more than a decade, Ellen Johnson Sirleaf was the first woman to be elected as a head of state in Africa.

Born in Monrovia, Sirleaf was the daughter of Jahmale Carney Johnson, the first indigenous member of Liberia's National Legislature. In 1961, she left Liberia to study in the US at Harvard University, before returning to Liberia in 1971 to work in president William Tolbert's cabinet as assistant finance minister. Nine years later, Master Sergeant Samuel Doe led a coup against Tolbert, executing him and many of his cabinet. Sirleaf fled to the US, then Kenya, working for Citibank and Equator Bank. In 1985, Sirleaf returned to Liberia and ran for the vice presidency. Following the election of Samuel Doe, Sirleaf was briefly imprisoned, then forced into a 12-year exile.

Sirleaf returned to Liberia in 1997 to run for president, coming second to Charles Taylor, who exiled her for alleged treason to the Ivory Coast. Finally voted into office in 2005, Sirleaf stabilized the nation after years of civil war. Popular for her free market economics, she was re-elected in 2011 and erased almost $5 billion in foreign debt. She resigned in 2017.

"The **future belongs to us**, because we have taken charge of it."

Ellen Johnson Sirleaf, 2006

Sirleaf's supporters cheered when her political party, Unity, met in 2011 in Liberia's capital Monrovia, following her re-election.

The first female chancellor of Germany, Angela Merkel has won four elections and continuously served since she was elected in 2005. As the leader of the strongest economy in Europe, she is considered by many to be the unspoken head of the European Union, and the most powerful woman in the Western world.

Born in West Germany on 17 July 1954, but raised in the East, Merkel is the daughter of a Lutheran pastor. As a student, she studied physics, graduating in 1978 with a doctorate in quantum chemistry from Karl Marx University, Leipzig. She then applied for an assistant professorship at an engineering school – asked to spy on colleagues, she declined.

After the Berlin Wall came down in 1989, Merkel was excited at the prospect of a united Germany with a free market economy, and sought a career in politics to help bring this to fruition. Standing for the Christian Democratic Union (CDU), she was first elected to the *Bundestag* (German's federal parliament) in 1990. There, as a protégé of chancellor Helmut Kohl (see p.281), she progressed her career and became party leader in 2000.

During her time as chancellor, her acute understanding of the economy has proved to be her key strength; during the 2008 global economic crisis, she stimulated Germany's economy by subsidizing workers' wages and cutting their hours. Merkel will be remembered for her commitment to making the Euro a stable currency on the global market, and for her progressive and inclusive belief on the universal human right to asylum.

Angela Merkel has hosted many G8 summits, such the one in Heiligendamm, Germany, 2007, in which state leaders from (clockwise from Merkel) US, UK, Italy, the EU Commission, Japan, Canada, France, and Russia convened.

ANGELA

MERKEL

1954–

The charismatic Barack Obama was the first African-American president of the United States, serving two terms from 2009 to 2017. His speeches inspired the public, who saw a vote for him as a rejection of the status quo, and, in the wake of Republican George W. Bush's presidency, welcomed Obama's optimistic, liberal politics.

MILESTONES

HIGH ACHIEVER
Studies at Harvard Law School, 1988. Soon becomes president of the Harvard Law Review.

TARGETS YOUTH
As director of Project Vote, 1992, greatly boosts voter registration levels in state of Illinois.

ELECTED PRESIDENT
As Democratic nominee, wins 2008 presidential election with 52.9 per cent of the vote.

HEALING A NATION
Passes the Affordable Care Act, "Obamacare", 2010, giving millions in the US access to health insurance.

Barack Hussein Obama was born in Honolulu, Hawaii, to Ann Dunham, a white American, and Barack Obama Sr., a black Kenyan on 4 August 1961. He was mostly raised by his mother, and he has credited her for bringing him up to have a strong sense of morality, recalling that she "disdained any kind of cruelty or thoughtlessness, or abuse of power". At 6 years old, he moved to Jakarta, Indonesia, with his mother to live with his stepfather Lolo, who treated him like his own. Four years later, in 1971, Obama moved back to Honolulu to live with his grandparents, where he completed his middle school and secondary school education.

Prestigious education
After high school, Obama attended Occidental College in Los Angeles. For the first time, he met other African-Americans who, he realized, had less privileged backgrounds than his. He then transferred to Columbia University, in New York City, graduating in political science in 1983.

In 1985, Obama became director of the Developing Communities project, a church-based organization in Chicago.

Obama's supporters attend a campaign rally in Fort Worth, Texas, in 2008. He was the first Democrat to win more than half of the popular vote in three decades.

"Yes we can!"

Barack Obama, 2008

1961–

BARACK OBAMA

MICHELLE **OBAMA**

The first African-American First Lady, Michelle Obama used her position and prestige to champion social issues, and remains an active voice in US politics.

A trained lawyer, Michelle met Barack in 1989, and married him three years later. She was actively involved in his presidential campaign, while also fighting obesity in children, and poverty. In 2016, she received acclaim for her public condemnation of sexual misconduct following controversial remarks made by then-presidential candidate Donald Trump.

Project Vote's campaign was a huge success, hitting its target of registering 150,000 new African-American voters.

Political career

Obama entered politics aged 34. He was elected to the Illinois senate in 1996, and the US senate eight years later. In 2008 he beat Hillary Clinton for the Democrat party nomination, winning over many young and minority voters, who responded to his promises to bring lasting social change.

Obama was sworn in as the 44th US president in 2009. Within days, he implemented an executive order banning "enhanced interrogation techniques", including waterboarding. He also successfully passed the Affordable Care Act (ACA), known as Obamacare, which divided public opinion but saw dramatic increases in the number of people with health insurance. Many of Obama's bills, however, notably those on climate change, were defeated by Republicans, who blocked them in Congress.

Obama worked hard to foster positive links with other world leaders, thawing decades of icy political tensions with Cuba by visiting it in 2016. A year later, his second term as president ended.

There, he worked to rebuild communities devastated by steel plant closures, setting up programs for job training and tutoring.

In autumn 1988, Obama entered Harvard Law School in Cambridge, Massachusetts, where he attracted media attention as the first African-American president of the Harvard Law Review, a respected scholarly journal. Four years later, he briefly became director of Project Vote, a nonprofit organization that aimed to increase the number of registered voters in under-represented social groups. Under his guidance,

"We are the change that we seek."

Barack Obama, 2008

PROMOTED ENERGY EFFICIENCY

REDUCED US TRADE DEFICIT

CREATED 11.6 MILLION JOBS

Obama revived a failing healthcare system, saw the US through the 2008 financial crisis, ended the war in Iraq, and oversaw environmental reform.

WON THE 2008 ELECTION WITH LARGEST VOTE COUNT IN US HISTORY

69.5 MILLION VOTES

1.8 MILLION ATTENDED HIS INAUGURATION

GAY MARRIAGE LEGALIZED NATIONWIDE DURING HIS PRESIDENCY

MALALA YOUSAFZAI

Aged 15, Malala Yousafzai survived an assassination attempt by the Taliban, a radical Islamic group, in retaliation for her vocal activism. Since her recovery, Malala has campaigned globally for girls to have the right to an education.

Malala was born in Mingora, in Swat, northern Pakistan, to Muslim parents on 12 July 1997. Her father, Ziauddin, an outspoken social activist, campaigned for girls to be educated, and Malala followed in his footsteps. Aged 11, she blogged for the BBC, under a pseudonym, about life in Mingora under Taliban rule, which had banned young girls from going to school. After the Taliban were pushed out of Swat by the Pakistani military in July 2009, Malala gained recognition for her activism, appearing publicly on television, and on local and international media.

On 9 October 2012, in response to her growing influence as an activist, Malala was shot in the head by a Taliban gunman on the bus going home after an exam. First airlifted to Peshawar and treated by a team of doctors who saved her life, Malala then travelled to the UK for further treatment. Now, she lives in the UK with her family, where she campaigns for girls' education, as it is too dangerous for her to return permanently to Pakistan. The Malala Fund, which she co-founded with her father in 2013, continues to support the education of young girls in countries across the world, including Brazil, Nigeria, Syria, Pakistan, and India.

MILESTONES

WORLD REPORTER
Aged 11, blogs about life under the Taliban, who leave her home city the next year. Gains international profile.

ATTACKED ON BUS
Suffers near-fatal injuries at Taliban hands, October 2012, while travelling on the bus to school.

EARNS ACCLAIM
Receives the Nobel Peace Prize, 2014, for her work on behalf of children's rights, aged just 17.

"I am those **66 million** girls who are **deprived of education."**

Malala Yousafzai, 2014

Malala's views resonated with women who held a vigil for her in Birmingham, UK, while she was recovering from her injuries in October 2012.

DIRECTORY

The last 50 years has witnessed the rise of global businesses, human rights activism, and the growth of the internet, connecting ordinary people to each other. In today's world, leaders range from heads of state and politicians to activists and tech entrepreneurs.

OMAR TORRIJOS
1929–81

Military leader of the National Guard of Panama, Omar Torrijos led the National Guard to victory in a coup against the Panamanian government to become the self-appointed dictator of Panama from 1968–78. Seen as a supporter of the poor, mixed-race majority population, he implemented social reforms, created jobs, and promoted education. In 1977 Torrijos made political history through his successful negotiations with US president Jimmy Carter to secure Panama's sovereignty over the Panama Canal and the surrounding Canal Zone. He died in a plane crash in 1981.

HARVEY MILK
1930–78

US politician and activist Harvey Milk gained legendary status in the gay community after his assassination in 1978. Milk was a leading voice for gay rights in the Castro district of San Francisco – elected to the city's Board of Supervisors in 1977, he was one of the first openly gay officials in US history. His liberal policies won huge public appeal, but earned him political enemies among conservatives, and he was assassinated by a conservative former city supervisor. Milk was posthumously awarded the Presidential Medal of Freedom in 2009.

RUPERT MURDOCH
1931–

Rupert Murdoch is the Australian-born entrepreneur who, in 1979, founded News Corporation (News Corp), which would become one of the largest mass-media companies in the world. He specialized in buying newspapers and transforming them into bestsellers by emphasizing sex, crime, scandal, and overtly conservative views. Although controversial, this formula gained huge successes in Australia, the UK, and US. Murdoch has since expanded his empire into entertainment, buying 20th Century Fox and launching Fox News. His media presence has made him one of the most powerful and influential people in the world.

CORAZON AQUINO
1933–2009

Corazon Aquino was a leading figure in the People Power Revolution that ended the dictatorship of Ferdinand Marcos in the Philippines. Supported by factions of the military, Aquino led an exceptionally peaceful revolution, overthrowing Marcos in 1986 and becoming the country's first female president. Her economic policies had mixed success, but she fostered human rights and civil liberties and tackled corruption. Aquino is still revered among the Filipino people.

NORMAN SCHWARZKOPF, JR
1934–2012

US army officer Norman Schwarzkopf directed the 1991 military action that liberated Kuwait from Iraqi occupation during the Gulf War. A Vietnam War veteran known for his fiery temper, rigid discipline, and military diplomacy, he was appointed major general in 1983 and chief of US Central Command in 1988. Schwarzkopf led Operation Desert Storm, the multinational air campaign during which 750,000 troops launched air and ground offensives that drove Iraqi forces out of Kuwait. He became a US national hero and was also knighted by Queen Elizabeth II.

JACK WELCH
1935–

US executive Jack Welch was the CEO of General Electric, a multinational conglomerate based in New York and Boston. Rising through the ranks from chemical engineer (when he blew up a factory), he became the youngest chairman and CEO of the company, aged 46. He streamlined and grew the business, reduced bureaucracy, and made brutal cuts in staffing. Within two decades he had grown revenues from $25 billion to $130 billion, and overseen a 4,000 per cent increase in the company's value. Following his retirement he launched the Jack Welch Management Institute, a highly acclaimed online business school.

EDDIE MABO
1936–92

Torres Strait Islander Eddie Mabo was an Australian-indigenous activist who fought a decade long campaign for land rights for the islanders and invalidated the 200-year-old legal doctrine of *terra nullius*. This concept, meaning "nobody's land", had been used by white settlers to build on indigenous territory. Through petition, campaign, and negotiation, Mabo led the Australian-indigenous people to be recognized as legal custodians of their land. Mabo had died five months before the victory, but his success marked a watershed in Australian history. He was posthumously awarded the Australian Human Rights Medal.

SADDAM HUSSEIN
1937–2006

Iraqi political leader Saddam Hussein participated in the coup that brought the revolutionary Ba'ath Party to power in 1968. As party leader, and later president in 1979, he nationalized Iraq's oil industry, boosting the economy, and expanded the military before launching costly invasions into Iran (1980) and Kuwait (1990). Saddam was a brutal dictator, responsible for the deaths of thousands in wars and state-sanctioned executions. In 2003 a military coalition led by the US and UK invaded Iraq,

alleging that he had weapons of mass destruction. Saddam was captured, convicted of crimes against humanity, and hanged in 2006.

MUAMMAR GADDAFI
1942–2011

Military and political leader Colonel Gaddafi deposed Libya's King Idris I in 1969 and established a new republic. He expelled Italian settlers, removed Western military bases, and promoted Arab nationalism. By nationalizing the oil industry Gaddafi made Libya the first developing country to have a majority share in its own oil production. He invested in the military, improved housing facilities and access to clean water and food, and introduced free education and healthcare. However, Gaddafi was later condemned for human rights abuses in Libya, and for funding international terrorist groups. He was overthrown during the 2011 Arab Spring and killed by militants.

HAROLD CARDINAL
1945–2005

A lawyer and leader of the Cree people, Harold Cardinal was a political activist from the age of 23, when he was elected president of the Indian Association of Alberta later helping to found the National Indian Brotherhood. His bestselling book *The Unjust Society* caused Pierre Trudeau's administration to abandon legislation that denied the legal rights of Indigenous populations. Through his dedication to enforcing radical change, as well as preserving and developing Indigenous rights and culture, Cardinal gave a voice to the First Nations of Canada. He also played a vital role in fostering a sense of understanding between Indigenous and white people.

DANIEL ORTEGA
1945–

President of Nicaragua from 1985 to 1990, and elected again in 2007, Daniel Ortega was previously the leader of the revolution that overthrew Nicaragua's former dictatorship. He became one of the heads of the Sandinista National Liberation Front (FSLN), and trained in guerrilla warfare after being exiled to Cuba in 1974. Returning to Nicaragua, he unified and strengthened the FSLN, and led them to victory in a civil war against the government in 1979. As president, Ortega won strong support from poor communities, and introduced food distribution, literacy, and unemployment programmes.

DONALD TRUMP
1946–

The 45th president of the United States, Donald Trump began his career as a high-profile businessman. Trump transformed his family's real-estate business into a conglomerate including hotel-casino complexes, golf courses, and high-rise apartments. During his presidential campaign, Trump distanced himself from the political establishment; his provocative manner, populist politics, and conservative views gained him huge appeal with working-class Americans. With no previous political experience, Trump's election as US president represents one of the greatest political upheavals in American history.

SHIRIN EBADI
1947–

An Iranian human rights activist and lawyer, Shirin Ebadi won international renown for her efforts to protect the human rights of women, children, and political dissidents in Iran. A former president of the Tehran City Court, Ebadi and her all female co-judges were dismissed following the 1979 coup by leaders of the new Islamic republic. She set up a private practice to defend dissidents, founded the Defenders of Human Rights Center, and led a campaign to end legal discrimination against women and child abuse in Iran. In 2003 Ebadi was awarded the Nobel Peace Prize for her work in human rights and diplomacy; she is the first Muslim woman to receive the award.

THOMAS SANKARA
1949–87

A Marxist revolutionary, Thomas Sankara became president of what was then Upper Volta, in West Africa, in 1983 aged 33, and launched the widest set of reforms in African history. In just four years he shook off French colonial rule, re-naming the country Burkina Faso, and instigated radical change to benefit the masses. His policies led to improvements in healthcare, education, women's rights, infrastructure, and agriculture; he planted trees to combat desertification, promoted national self-sufficiency, and redistributed lands. However, Sankara became increasingly authoritarian and was eventually assassinated by his opponents.

NARENDRA MODI
1950–

Elected prime minister of India in 2014, Narendra Modi has been a Hindu nationalist since joining the right-wing Rashtriya Swayamsevak Sanga (RSS) in the 1970s. As chief minister of Gujarat (2001–14) he was dogged by allegations of complicity in Hindu-Muslim riots in 2002 and involvement in extra-judicial killings. Yet Modi has had sustained

political success, and won a landslide election victory in 2014 as leader of the Bharatiya Janata Party (BJP), the political arm of the RSS. Modi's administration has focused on attracting foreign investment and boosting infrastructure.

TONY BLAIR
1953–

Leader of the British Labour Party from 1994 to 2007, Tony Blair shifted the party from its left-wing past to the political centre, distancing it from trade unions, and supporting integration into the European Union. He was elected prime minister in a landslide victory in 1997. His government brought about devolution in Scotland and Wales, and successfully brokered the Good Friday Agreement in Northern Ireland. He damaged his reputation by taking Britain into the Iraq War, fearing Iraq possessed weapons of mass destruction; he resigned during his third term.

HUGO CHÁVEZ
1954–2013

A military leader and revolutionary, Hugo Chávez served as president of Venezuela from 1999 to 2013 (with a brief removal from power in 2002). In 1992 Chávez and fellow military officers led an unsuccessful coup against the government, and he was imprisoned. After his release he founded the Movement of the Fifth Republic; in 1998 he was elected president. Chávez used Venezuela's oil wealth to boost healthcare, education, and housing for poor people. However, his popularity waned as his policies grew increasingly radical, alienating the middle-class. He also pursued ties with Cuba, Iran, and Iraq, and united many Latin American countries against globalization and US-led economic policies.

RECEP TAYYIP ERDOĞAN
1954–

Turkish political leader Recep Tayyip Erdoğan has been a lifelong nationalist and Muslim. After being jailed for his early Islamist politics, Erdoğan founded the Justice and Development Party (AKP) in 2001 and was elected prime minister in 2003. He oversaw economic recovery, expanded religious freedoms, and led turkey into the European Union. Gradually, he became more authoritarian, curbing freedom of the press and increasing political control of the judiciary. After three terms as prime minister, Erdoğan was elected president; he amended the constitution to abolish the post of prime minister and grant supreme powers to the presidency.

SHINZŌ ABE
1954–

Originally elected prime minister of Japan in 2006, Shinzō Abe stepped down the following year, only to stage a political comeback in 2012. Abe's administration has taken a tough stance on North Korea, backing UN sanctions against it, and has also strengthened ties with the US. In 2013 Abe launched an ambitious set of economic reforms, popularly called "Abenomics", intended to boost Japan's long-term economic-slump, which in part encouraged greater participation for women in the workforce. A number of his nationalist policies have attracted criticism both in Japan and internationally, however.

STEVE JOBS
1955–2011

The CEO of Apple Inc., Steve Jobs was a pioneer of the computer era, whose innovations dictated the evolution of modern technology. In 1976 he and Steve Wozniak launched the company Apple. Having developed the ground-breaking Macintosh computer, Jobs left first setting up NeXT, a computer development company, then Pixar Animation Studios before returning to Apple as CEO in 1997. Jobs instigated the trend for sleek, high-end computers, and pioneered a string of revolutionary technologies, including iTunes, and the iPod, iPhone, and iPad. He redefined the way humans use and relate to computers, transforming businesses and generating a new wave of technological innovations.

DONATELLA VERSACE
1955–

Donatella Versace is an Italian fashion designer and the sister of Gianni, the iconic designer and founder of the Versace label who was killed in 1997. Assuming control of the business after his death, she has successfully developed and reinvented the high-end brand. In addition to her creative skills as artistic director, Donatella's shrewd PR talents helped her to expand the company into new global markets, seek out business collaboration opportunities, and used celebrities to boost advertising campaigns. She has moulded the label in her own style, giving it a new and enhanced image for which she was awarded a Fashion Icon Award in 2017.

RIGOBERTA MENCHÚ
1959–

Guatemalan political activist Rigoberta Menchú is a member of the indigenous Quiché Maya people. In her teens she campaigned for women's rights and social reform, but when her family were murdered for their activism, Menchú fled to Mexico. From there she organized efforts to protect native peasants' rights and fight human-rights violations. She was awarded the Nobel Peace Prize in 1992 for her work in social justice and human rights; with the money she set up an aid organization for indigenous people. Her autobiography I, Rigoberta Menchú has won international acclaim.

LARRY PAGE
1973–

US computer scientist Larry Page is a co-founder of Google. In 1998 Page and his friend Sergey Brin, while PhD students at Stanford University, created an algorithm that ranked web pages' importance by the number of other pages that linked to them. By 2000 Google had become the premier internet search engine. A perfectionist and technical genius, Page had a creative, anti-bureaucratic leadership style that was not to everybody's taste. He stood down as CEO in 2001, focusing instead on initiatives such as the purchase of YouTube and Android, but returned as CEO in 2011. In 2015, Larry and Brin restructured Google, and its secondary companies, into a new conglomerate called Alphabet Inc.

EMMANUEL MACRON
1977–

The youngest president in French history, Emmanuel Macron was 39 years old when he was elected in 2017. A former investment banker and then finance minister under President François Hollande, Macron had never held elected office before founding the new centrist party "La République En Marche!" in 2016. He made political history when he was decisively voted into office, with a fledgling party with no existing formal structure. A strong but not uncritical supporter of the European Union, Macron has taken a liberal centrist political stance.

HYEON-SEO LEE
1980–

The North Korean human rights activist Hyeon-seo Lee was a teenager when she defected from her country of birth, seeking asylum in South Korea. After escaping, she returned to escort her family to safety, too. She made history when she published the global bestseller The Girl with Seven Names, a memoir of her life in North Korea that provides an unprecedented window into life under the brutal regime. Lee travels globally to raise awareness of human-rights violations in North Korea and the plight of North Korean refugees. She has gained a strong media presence and actively supports other defectors from the country.

MARK ZUCKERBERG
1984–

The US entrepreneur Mark Zuckerberg is the CEO and co-founder of Facebook, the global social-networking site. A programming prodigy, Zuckerberg, alongside two fellow students at Harvard created Facebook in 2004. It was an instant success, gaining one million users within a year, and by 2012, a billion. Facebook held its initial public offering (IPO); at $16 billion it was the largest internet IPO in history. Due to the dominance of his social media empire, business magazine, Forbes, ranked Zuckerberg as the tenth most powerful person in the world in 2016. Although Facebook has attracted controversy in relation to alleged influence on political outcomes in 2016, Zuckerberg is committed to widening internet access around the world.

ACKNOWLEDGMENTS

Dorling Kindersley would like to thank the following: Tom Morse and Joe Scott for additional design assistance, and:

Additional illustration: Agung Yuwanda (www.fiverr.com)
Jackets Editorial Coordinator: Priyanka Sharma
Jacket Designer: Priyanka Bansal
Senior DTP Designer: Harish Aggarwal
Managing Jackets Editor: Saloni Singh

PICTURE CREDITS